TEACHER'S MANUAL to GLOBAL LAWYERING SKILLS

■ ■ ■

By
Mary-Beth Moylan
Director of Global Lawyering Skills
McGeorge School of Law

Stephanie J. Thompson
Assistant Director of Global Lawyering Skills
McGeorge School of Law

Adrienne Brungess
Gretchen Franz
Kathleen Friedrich
Jennifer A. Gibson
Hether C. Macfarlane
Maureen Moran
Jeffrey E. Proske
Edward H. Telfeyan
Maureen Watkins
Global Lawyering Skills Faculty
McGeorge School of Law

AMERICAN CASEBOOK SERIES®

WEST.

Mat #41179584

This publication was created to provide you with accurate and authoritative information concerning the subject matter covered; however, this publication was not necessarily prepared by persons licensed to practice law in a particular jurisdiction. The publisher is not engaged in rendering legal or other professional advice and this publication is not a substitute for the advice of an attorney. If you require legal or other expert advice, you should seek the services of a competent attorney or other professional.

Nothing contained herein is intended or written to be used for the purpose of 1) avoiding penalties imposed under the federal Internal Revenue Code, or 2) promoting, marketing or recommending to another party any transaction or matter addressed herein.

American Casebook Series is a trademark registered in the U.S. Patent and Trademark Office.

© 2013 LEG, Inc. d/b/a West Academic Publishing

610 Opperman Drive
St. Paul, MN 55123
1-800-313-9378

West, West Academic Publishing, and West Academic are trademarks of West Publishing Corporation, used under license.

Printed in the United States of America

ISBN: 978–0–314–27748–0

TABLE OF CONTENTS

CHAPTER 1 Introduction 3
CHAPTER 2 Domestic and Foreign Legal Systems 21
CHAPTER 3 Intercultural Competence 32
CHAPTER 4 Rules: An Overview of Statutory Interpretation and Synthesis 35
CHAPTER 5 Legal Reasoning and Analysis Toolkit 40
CHAPTER 6 The Process of Legal Writing 72
CHAPTER 7 Knowing Your Audience 85
CHAPTER 8 Objective Legal Writing 89
CHAPTER 9 The Formal Memorandum 91
CHAPTER 10 The Short-Form Memorandum 121
CHAPTER 11 Interviewing the Client 144
CHAPTER 12 Counseling the Client 171
CHAPTER 13 Professional Correspondence 185
CHAPTER 14 Persuasive Legal Writing 194
CHAPTER 15 Pre-trial Motions 216
CHAPTER 16 The Appellate Process and Standard of Review 257
CHAPTER 17 The Appellate Brief 270
CHAPTER 18 Oral Argument 300
CHAPTER 19 Alternative Dispute Resolution 308
CHAPTER 20 Negotiations and Settlement 329
CHAPTER 21 Contract Drafting 338
CHAPTER 22 Research Strategies 349
CHAPTER 23 Foreign and International Legal Research 359
CHAPTER 24 The Citation Requirement 363
CHAPTER 25 The Last Critical Task: "White-Glove Inspection" . 365

CHAPTER 1

INTRODUCTION

■ ■ ■

By Mary-Beth Moylan

The purpose of this chapter is to give students some context for the skills they will be learning, and to provide some explanation for why global lawyering skills are important. Given the brevity of the introduction, this first chapter can be assigned together with Chapter 2 and Chapter 3, if the first week or class session of your course is devoted to basic framework of the legal system and the importance of learning lawyering skills.

While we have a two year integrated skills program at our school, this text book can be used in a first year only course, or in a program with three semesters of skills instruction. Below are attached the "About the Course" handouts that we use in our first and second year classes. They provide an overview of our skills program, and the number and weight of assignments we give in each year.

ABOUT THE COURSE FOR GLOBAL LAWYERING SKILLS I

Global Lawyering Skills I is a four-unit, year-long course. You will receive two units in each semester, but only one grade at the end of the year. In this course you will be taught the fundamental skills of legal research, legal writing, legal analysis, and professional communication. These are skills that all lawyers use, regardless of their area of practice or expertise. Each GLS I professor will be exposing you to these skills differently, and possibly on a different time-line over the course of the year, but every student will be taught the skills outlined on the attached list.

<u>Goals of the Course For You:</u>

1. Learn how to analyze a legal issue using both legal authorities and facts presented by a client.

2. Develop legal writing skills that will enable you to communicate your legal analysis in writing in a format that lawyers and judges expect to read and will understand.

3. Develop a sense of ethical practice and professionalism that will be foundational for your future practice of law.

4. Gain a practical understanding of the court systems in the United States and how the systems impact your client's legal problem.

5. Learn about how other legal systems differ, and gain some understanding of transnational legal practice.

6. Learn how to use both print and electronic research sources and how to develop research strategies that will enable you to address legal issues.

7. Learn how to develop legally relevant facts from interviewing a client and using other factual resources.

8. Learn how to craft citations in a format that other lawyers will be able to use to identify the sources of law and fact that you use for support in your legal analysis.

How You Can Achieve These Goals:

1. Read all assignments listed in your Syllabus or otherwise assigned by your professor.

2. Participate in class discussions, in-class exercises, and peer review opportunities.

3. Engage in research and writing assignments fully and work diligently on all assignments, including writing multiple drafts, editing and revising all work.

4. Attend mandatory conferences with your professor, and visit your professor's office hours when you do not understand the materials presented in class.

Assessment Methods To Be Used By GLS Professors Include:

1. Reviewing and commenting upon ungraded research and writing assignments.

2. Evaluating some first draft writing on a Pass/No Pass basis to give you a sense of how your skills are developing.

3. Holding mandatory conferences and mid-project conferences to provide oral feedback with respect to your performance.

4. Reviewing, commenting upon, and assigning a grade to writing assignments of varying length.

5. Reviewing, commenting upon, and/or grading research assignments and a citation test.

GRADING AND ASSIGNMENTS

During the course, you will submit several written assignments. All of these assignments are required, but some are ungraded. Your <u>final grade in the course</u> will be based on the following elements:

P/NP - First Graded Assignment – draft of formal memo

15% - Second Graded Assignment – formal memo revised

35% - Third Graded Assignment – short form memo

P/NP - Fourth Graded Assignment –letter/transactional document

30% - Fifth Graded Assignment – persuasive writing

10% - Research Assignments

P/NP - Citation Assignments

P/NP - Mid-Project Conference

P/NP - Oral Presentation

5% - Citation Test

5% - Professionalism

Preparation of the assigned reading, attendance, and participation in classes, as well as timely completion of all "pass/no pass" and ungraded assignments is mandatory. <u>Poor preparation, attendance, or participation</u>

in class will lower your Professionalism score. Failure to hand in any assignments or to participate in ungraded oral assignments may cause you to receive an incomplete in the course.

Late Penalties

The **deadlines** for turning in written assignments are indicated in your syllabus. Unless otherwise indicated for a specific assignment, the **penalties for late papers** are as follows:

1. Assignments turned in up to 30 minutes late will lose up to **5 points**.

2. Assignments turned in more than 30 minutes and up to 24 hours late will lose up to **10 points**.

3. Assignments turned in more than 24 hours late and up to 48 hours late will lose up to **20 points**.

4. If you have not turned in an assignment within 48 hours of the due date, you must contact the Dean of Students Office to make arrangements for completion of the assignment.

You may request an extension or exemption from any of the requirements of the course, but you must do so by face to face communication, telephone or email **prior to the due date and time** of the requirement (unless the reason for the extension or exemption make this communication impossible). Each professor will determine "good cause" for an extension or an exemption at his or her discretion. Any verbal arrangement must be confirmed in writing.

Formatting Requirements

Penalties will also be imposed on these written assignments for failure to observe page length and other formatting requirements, including but not limited to kerning, adjusting margins and changing font size. In typography, "kerning" refers to adjusting the space between characters, usually to place the characters closer together than normal. Using "Make It Fit" or "Shrink It" on a GLS paper is a violation of both the formatting rules and the page limit rules announced by your professor and may result in penalties for both failure to follow instructions and exceeding the page limit.

The format requirements and page limits are designed to ensure that every student has the same amount of space in which to complete the assignment; this assures fairness for each student. The page limits are intentionally stringent because courts impose very short page limits and because brevity is a necessary part of good legal writing. If your draft is longer than the page limit, the proper approach is to edit the draft until it falls within the page limit, not to resort to technology and typography.

COLLABORATION RULE FOR ALL GLS COURSES

Students may <u>discuss</u> the course materials and assignments with one another. However, <u>sharing written work</u> with another student or <u>copying</u> from another student's work is against the rules of the course and a violation of the McGeorge *Code of Student Responsibility*. A student who is found to have violated the *Code* will be subject to disciplinary action. While you are free to <u>discuss ideas</u> with your classmates, your <u>written work</u> must be your own and must <u>not</u> be shown to anyone else except under conditions stated by your professor for the purpose of peer editing or other class exercises.

You may not have any other person (whether or not enrolled in this course) read, review, comment on, or edit your written work prior to submission. All written work that you create for this course must reflect only your own drafting, critiquing, revising, and editing your individual work product. Copying any part of another person's paper, including but not limited to introductions, factual statements, rule formation, or analysis is a violation of this rule and the *Code of Student Responsibility*. You also may not enlist another person to format your final written product for you.

You must attribute any ideas or information that you borrow or copy from any other source. If you use information, ideas, or arguments that you read in another source, you must identify that source in your written work with an appropriate citation. Failure to do so constitutes plagiarism and is in violation of the *Code of Student Responsibility*.

GLS POLICIES

1. You are responsible for ***all*** reading assignments, written assignments, and any other assignments in your Syllabus and any additional assignments given in class, sent by your professor via email, or posted on TWEN for the class in which they are assigned. You must complete all assignments ***before*** class and, unless instructed otherwise, you must submit all written assignments at the ***beginning*** of class

2. You must check TWEN and your email on a ***daily basis*** to be aware of any changes, additions, substitutions, or any other information that your professor provides. You are accountable for any information posted on TWEN and for any information provided via email. If you have questions about TWEN, please contact the Westlaw representative or Brandon Abell in Media Resources at the Gordon Schaber Law Library.

3. Any written submissions may be used as good or bad samples in class and distributed to the entire class, or may be put on the screen in front of the class. All personal or identifying information will be removed from the submission.

4. GLS I is a very detail-oriented class and requires your utmost professionalism. Any written assignment can be rejected for typos, grammatical errors, failure to follow instructions, formatting problems, and/or spelling errors. If a written assignment is rejected, it will be returned to you and you will be provided a time frame in which to correct the errors and return it to your professor.

5. All writing assignments, ***graded or ungraded***, must be typed, double-spaced, using Times New Roman 12-point font.

GLS I List of Skills to be Taught by All GLS I Professors

Introduction to Lawyering

Understand what lawyers do

Court Structures

Types of Authority

Weight of Authority

Transnational Practice

Client Interviewing & Fact Investigation

Introduction to ADR

Ethics and Professionalism

Collaboration

Analysis and Writing

Objective Writing Paradigm

Rule Synthesis & Drafting Rules (Objective & Persuasive)

Explaining Rules (case illustrations and parentheticals) (Objective & Persuasive)

Legal Analysis (Objective & Persuasive)

Deductive Reasoning

Analogical Reasoning

Policy-based Reasoning

Interpreting Statutes

Outlining Statutes

Reading and Using Cases Effectively

Outlining and Organization

Umbrellas and Roadmaps (Objective & Persuasive)

Question Presented

Brief Answer

Objective Statement of Facts

Objective Conclusions

Point Headings (Objective & Persuasive)

Using Quotations

Professional Correspondence Generally (including e-mail)

Advice & Demand Letters

Introduction to the Persuasive Paradigm

Persuasive Writing Strategies & Tone

Persuasive Introductions and Conclusions

ADR Brief Writing

Effective & Grammatically Correct Writing

Research

Citation Form

Generating Search Terms

Research Strategy

Basic Legal Research Sources (Print & Online)

Secondary Sources

Statutes & Using Annotated Codes

Cases & Digests

Citators (Shepard's & KeyCite)

U.S Treaty Research

Citations

Citation Form

Frequency of Citation

Oral Advocacy

ADR Oral Presentation

Mid-Project Conference (presentation to supervising attorney)

Professionalism

Time Management

Professional Demeanor

Civility

Collaboration

Ethical considerations

ABOUT THE COURSE FOR GLOBAL LAWYERING SKILLS II

Welcome to Global Lawyering Skills II. Global Lawyering Skills II is a year-long, four-unit course that will build upon the practical research and writing skills you learned in GLS I as well as teach you new skills such as complex persuasive writing, oral argument, client counseling, and settlement negotiation.

The goals of this course are for you to:

- Gain a practical understanding of how the court systems affect the law that applies to your client's case;
- Practice using advanced print and electronic research sources and more advanced research methodologies and strategies;
- Further develop your ability to analyze the law and how it applies to your client's case in a format that lawyers recognize and expect; and
- Learn how to create citations to authorities using the Bluebook that are technically correct and allow lawyers to find the authorities you have cited.

To realize these goals of the course, your activities will include:

- Reading the assignments listed in your Syllabus;
- Participating in class discussions, in-class exercises, and peer review opportunities;
- Engaging in research assignments using print materials in the Library and various online sources;
- Engaging in independent research for a simulated client case and choosing the most appropriate authorities;

- Giving well-organized and persuasive oral presentations; and
- Writing, editing, and rewriting both short and longer memoranda and briefs.

Your progress in this course will be assessed in a number of ways throughout the year, including:

- Reviewing and commenting on ungraded research and writing assignments;
- Evaluating and commenting upon graded and ungraded oral arguments;
- Holding mandatory conferences with you to discuss writing assignments; and
- Reviewing, commenting on, and assigning a grade to various writing assignments of varying length throughout the year.

GLS POLICIES

1. You are responsible for ***all*** reading assignments, written assignments, and any other assignments in your Syllabus and any additional assignments given in class, sent by your professor via email, or posted on TWEN for the class in which they are assigned. You must complete all assignments ***before*** class and, unless instructed otherwise, you must submit all written assignments at the ***beginning*** of class.

2. You must check TWEN and your email on a ***daily basis*** to be aware of any changes, additions, substitutions, or any other information that your professor provides. You are accountable for any information posted on TWEN and for any information provided via email.

3. Any written submissions may be used as good or bad samples in class and distributed to the entire class or put on the screen in front of the class. All personal or identifying information will be removed from the submission.

4. This is a very detail-oriented class and requires your utmost professionalism. Any written assignment can be rejected for typos, grammatical errors, failure to follow instructions, formatting problems, and/or spelling errors. If a written assignment is rejected, it will be returned to you and you will be provided a time frame in which you must correct the errors and return it to your professor.

5. <u>All</u> writing assignments, ***graded or ungraded***, must be typed, double-spaced, using Times New Roman 13-point font unless otherwise indicated by your professor.

COURSE COMMUNICATIONS

All students are required to "enroll" in the ALL GLS II TWEN site <u>and</u> their own section's GLS II TWEN site. You <u>must</u> register an e-mail address where course-related communications may be received. Be sure to check your e-mail daily. You are responsible for updating your email address on TWEN if it changes during the course of the year. If you need help with TWEN, check with Brandon Abell in Media Resources at the Gordon Schaber Law Library.

COURSE RULES ON GRADING AND DEADLINES

During the fall semester, you will submit several written assignments and make a number of oral presentations. All of these assignments are required, but some are ungraded. During the spring semester, you will submit a complete appellate brief and argue an appeal before a three-judge appellate panel. All assignments will build on one another, so focus on the fall semester assignments is advisable.

Your <u>final grade in the course</u> will be based on the following required assignments:

P/NP	CRAC Assignment
5%	First Graded Written Assignment
3%	First Graded Oral Argument
10%	Revision of First Graded Written Assignment
15%	Second Graded Written Assignment
7%	Second Graded Oral Argument
P/NP	Telephone Counseling Assignment
P/NP	Mediation Group Assignment
P/NP	Settlement Drafting Group Assignment
P/NP	Transnational Research Assignment
35%	Final Appellate Brief
20%	Final Oral Argument.
5%	Professionalism

Preparation of the assigned reading, attendance, and participation in classes, as well as timely completion of all "pass/no pass" and ungraded assignments is mandatory. <u>Poor preparation, attendance, or participation in class will lower your Professionalism score. Failure to hand in any assignments or to participate in ungraded oral assignments may cause you to receive an incomplete in the course.</u>

Penalties will be applied for failure to meet assignment deadlines. Unless otherwise indicated for a specific assignment, the **penalties for late papers** are as follows:

- Papers turned in up to 30 minutes late will lose up to **<u>5 points</u>**.

- Papers turned in more than 30 minutes and less up to 24 hours late will lose up to **10 points**.

- Papers turned in more than 24 hours late and up to 48 hours late will lose up to **20 points**.

- If you have not turned in an assignment within 48 hours of the due date, you must contact the Dean of Students Office to make arrangements for completion of the assignment.

- **Total failure to complete a graded assignment before the end of the grading period may lead to a failure to pass the course.**

You may request an extension or exemption from any of the requirements of the course, but you must do so by face to face communication, telephone or email **prior to the due date and time** of the requirement (unless the reason for the extension or exemption make this communication impossible). Each professor will determine "good cause" for an extension or an exemption at his or her discretion. Any verbal arrangement must be confirmed in writing.

COURSE RULES ON COLLABORATION

Students may <u>discuss</u> the course materials and assignments with one another. However, <u>sharing written work</u> with another student or <u>copying</u> from another student's work is against the rules of the course and a violation of the McGeorge *Code of Student Responsibility*. A student who is found to have violated the *Code* will be subject to disciplinary action. While you are free to <u>discuss ideas</u> with your classmates, your <u>written</u>

work must be your own and must not be shown to anyone else except under conditions stated by your professor for the purpose of peer editing or other class exercises.

You may not have any other person (whether or not enrolled in this course) read, review, comment on, or edit your written work prior to submission. All written work that you create for this course must reflect only your own drafting, critiquing, revising, and editing your individual work product. Copying any part of another person's paper, including but not limited to introductions, factual statements, rule formation, or analysis is a violation of this rule and the *Code of Student Responsibility*. You also may not enlist another person to format your final written product for you.

You must attribute any ideas or information that you borrow or copy from any other source. If you use information, ideas, or arguments that you read in another source, you must identify that source in your written work with an appropriate citation. Failure to do so constitutes plagiarism and is in violation of the *Code of Student Responsibility*.

GLS II List of Skills to be Taught by All GLS II Professors

Analysis and Writing

Persuasive Paradigm-CRAC

Conclusion

Rule

Analysis

Conclusion

Multi-Issue Brief Writing

Components of Trial Level Briefs

Introduction

Statement of Facts

Argument

Point Headings

Conclusion

Motion Standards in Trial Courts

Components of Appellate Briefs

Jurisdiction Statements

Statement of Oral Argument

Issue Questions

Statement of the Case

Statement of Facts

Argument

Conclusion

Addendum

Standards of Review on Appeal

Organization and Outlining

Core Theory and Theme

Storytelling

Persuasive Tone

Persuasive Writing Strategies

Editing

Research

Advanced on-line in Lexis and Westlaw

International Research

Advanced Secondary Sources

Research Planning

Oral Advocacy

Oral Argument in Trial Court

Oral Argument in Appellate Court

Theme

Practice Skills

Introduction to Initial Pleadings & Discovery

Mediation

Settlement Drafting

Settlement Negotiation

Client Counseling

Cultural Barriers to Effective Advocacy

Transnational Litigation Practice

Introduction to Foreign Legal System

Citation (Introduce Bluebook)

Appellate Strategy

Professional Skills

Time Management

Professionalism

Civility

Collaboration

Ethics

Given the brevity of the introduction, this first chapter can be assigned together with Chapter 2 and Chapter 3, if the first week or class session of your course is devoted to the basic framework of the legal system and the importance of learning lawyering skills.

The Civility Exercise at the end of this introductory chapter can be used as a first day of class assignment. I like to assign this exercise to students before the first class, because the definition of civility serves as a "rule" which the first year students can then apply to something that really happened to them. The discussion can include ethics, cross-cultural experiences and responses to behavior, and the importance of perspective. Moreover, the discussion can also turn to legal analysis and a discussion of how the "rule" of civility was applied to the facts of their life to support a conclusion.

A couple of examples of completed assignments are provided below. These are student responses, written by first year students before their first day of legal skills class. I have edited them to reflect the type of structure that I expect of students a little further on. One of the benefits of this exercise is the opportunity to teach students to start with a conclusion or thesis, then provide the rule, and then explain and apply the rule to the new set of facts. Few students start out with an understanding of this basic CRAC or CREAC structure.

Civility Exercise Example #1

College campuses are generally thought of as a place of understanding, respect, compassion, and cultural exchange. My time at a distinguished public university often reflected this general assumption. However, one experience cast a shadow on my overall sense of the campus as a safe and open environment. I witnessed the shameful and appalling incident of a campus police office violently pepper-spraying a group of my innocent peers. This experience was a sad moment in the history of the university, but also displays an instance of a person lacking civility.

Professor Sparrow defines civility as "valuing the reactions, views, and cultures of others. It implies the ability to disagree without violence or insult." Sophie Sparrow, Practicing Civility in the Legal Writing Course: Helping Law Students Learn Professionalism, 13 LEGAL WRITING J. 113, 119 (2007). Under this definition, the action of the police officer at my university and the administration of the university failed in meeting the standard of civility.

The students who gathered to protest unfair and unjust treatment by a public university were peacefully occupying a quad on the campus. Instead of "valuing the reactions, views, and culture of others," campus authorities chose to punish students for voicing their protestations. They chose to ignore "the assumption that humans matter." *Id.* at 119. Rather than listen to and communicate with student protesters, the officers and campus authorities took forceful action.

Civility should govern the way that humans interact with each other. According to Professor Sparrow, this means listening, paying attention, and "speaking kindly." *Id.* at 119. None of these devices were used in the interaction I witnessed between campus police and student protesters. The campus police blatantly ignored all rules of civility pertaining to human interaction, and chose to take the road to violent confrontation. Since the protesters were demonstrating in an entirely peaceful manner, the disproportionate and uncivil reaction to them was the ultimate display of a lack of civility.

Civility Exercise Example # 2

Before I came to law school, I worked as a regional field director for a major political party. I learned a great deal at this job, and by-and-large found it very worthwhile. In my capacity as field director, I got to meet some great people, travel to new places, and attend the high profile – and high dollar – political functions that I once thought were open only to the rich and powerful. Unfortunately, I also got a first-hand lesson in what incivility means from my boss, who I will call "Jessica."

Professor Sparrow defines civility as "the assumption that humans matter, that we owe each other respect, and that treating each other well is a moral duty." Sophie Sparrow, Practicing Civility in the Legal Writing Course: Helping Law Students Learn Professionalism, 13 LEGAL WRITING J. 113, 119 (2007). I am quite sure Jessica never read Professor Sparrow's article.

Jessica seemed to subscribe to the idea that the only value anyone had was in the title under their name, and if yours was any less in stature than hers she would take it upon herself to berate, insult, and embarrass you any chance she got. In a world run by carrots and sticks, my boss Jessica had a decided affinity for the sticks. She would look for someone to demean or punish, and never look for someone to praise.

Fortunately, through a good mixture of hard work, great volunteers, and lots of pizza and ice cream, my office managed to maintain the number one ranking in the state for eight consecutive weeks. Rather than treat me with respect or pay me a compliment, Jessica chose to single out the struggling field directors. In our daily conference calls, rather than providing respect or treating others well, Jessica would threaten to replace the field directors if their performance did not improve. In direct contradiction to Professor Sparrow's definition of civility, Jessica regularly exhibited the attitude that humans do not matter by attacking people's intelligence, attire, looks, and other attributes.

In my office, I chose to take a different path. I treated my interns, volunteers, and subordinates well and respectfully. I listened to people's opinions. I tried to follow Professor Sparrow's observation that, "Civility means valuing the reactions, views, and cultures of others. It implies the ability to disagree without violence or insult." Not only do people inherently deserve this kind of respect, regardless of whether they have earned it, but also it makes for a better environment for you. Civility is not something that you do for others; it is something you do for yourself. My mom always told me, "It's not about the other guy. It's about you." When you show civility to others you are beyond reproach and can ultimately say you acted in the best manner possible in your given situation. I hope that someday Jessica will read Professor Sparrow's article or talk to my mom. She might learn something that would help not only her future co-workers but also herself.

Chapter 2

Domestic and Foreign Legal Systems

■ ■ ■

By Hether C. Macfarlane

This chapter introduces students to the major legal systems of the world. It is a place to reinforce the idea that a 21st century lawyer is likely to have to interact with lawyers and clients from other legal systems and therefore needs to understand how those systems operate. The discussion of the U.S. legal system is very similar to the discussion of the topic in almost all legal research and writing texts in terms of coverage and depth. The discussion of the other legal systems is meant as an introduction only. It should provide you with enough material to stimulate a discussion of the similarities and differences around the world.

A. THE U.S. SYSTEM

This part of the chapter is the most important for first year law students because it is the system they need to master for law school and, most likely, their legal careers. The discussion in this chapter should be familiar to all American lawyers, but students may come to law school not understanding that for the most part the federal and state legal systems are parallel, not hierarchical. The most common misunderstanding the students have is a belief that federal law is paramount in all areas of the law and that all U.S. Supreme Court decisions are binding on all federal and state courts.

The discussion of the parallel systems and mandatory versus persuasive authority can be reinforced by having the class work through one of the exercises at the end of this chapter. Both of them posit hypothetical situations involving state or federal law and ask the students to determine which named sources of law will be mandatory or persuasive authority. These exercises can be assigned as homework, but they work well as a platform for in-class discussion of the topic.

Our assumption is that most classes will supplement this text with a research text that will provide a discussion of primary and secondary sources, so that topic is not included in this chapter. You may want to assign reading from that supplemental text at the same time that you have the students read this chapter. If you do, and if that text has exercises that address primary and secondary authority along with mandatory and persuasive authority, those exercises may either supplement or substitute for the exercises here.

B. THE CIVIL LAW SYSTEM

This section of the chapter may be the most difficult to teach because civil law is very different from common law while appearing to be very similar. Civil law countries have courts that decide cases, and common law countries have statutes. In addition, a complete understanding of a civil law country's legal system and culture requires knowing the language of that country, which many U.S. students do not have.

The most important thing to emphasize to U.S. students is that civil law countries do not regard case law as establishing law or serving as precedent. Cases in civil law systems with similar facts have similar outcomes not because the courts follow the reasoning and holding of a past case but because the Code establishes a clear rule, the application of which leads to the similar, correct outcome.

It is possible to find English translations of the codes of various civil law countries if you want to have students compare a code section with a U.S. statute. Another resource for comparison purposes is the English translations of cases decided in foreign countries that have signed the U.N. Convention on the International Sale of Goods (CISG). Pace University Law School maintains a website devoted to the CISG at **http://www.cisg.law.pace.edu/cisg**. The CISG Database at the site organizes cases by CISG article; the list of cases indicates after the case name all the cases that have been translated into English. It is possible to use some of these opinions to demonstrate some of the differences between the structure of common law and civil law cases and as examples of civil law reasoning. Unfortunately, what is more difficult is comparing civil law cases that have applied a particular article of the CISG with U.S. federal court cases that have applied the same article.

C. THE EUROPEAN UNION: A DEVELOPING SYSTEM GROWING FROM CIVIL LAW

The discussion of the EU is included in this chapter because its documents are all written in or translated into English, which allows the monolingual among us to access a foreign legal system.

Access to EU law is available through the EUR-Lex website, found at **http://eur-lex.europa.eu**.

Resources available through the website include:

- The Official Journal of the EU
- EU law, including treaties, directives, regulations, and decisions
- Preparatory acts, including legislative proposals, reports, green and white papers
- EU case law (judgments, orders)
- International agreements
- Other public documents.

For information about the EU itself, consult the EU website: **http://europa.eu**. The website is very informative.

If you want or have the time to go into some depth with the EU, students could certainly be assigned to go either to the EU website to study particular parts of the EU or to EUR-Lex to look at case decisions. As with the CISG decisions at Pace Law School, students could study the EU decisions with a view to seeing how they differ in their elements and approach from U.S. cases.

D. LEGAL SYSTEMS BASED IN ISLAM

We included this section largely because the phrase "Shari'a law" has had so much play over the past several years. Americans tend to think of Islamic law solely in terms of harsh punishments for criminal offenses and what Americans tend to see as subjugation of women. The information in this section is designed at least to broaden the discussion.

The majority of the information came from the Internet. Doing a Google search brings up a large number of sites of varying reliability. Sifting through those results in class could be an early introduction to the necessity to judge the reliability of all secondary sources and particularly sources found on the Internet.

E. INTERNATIONAL LAW

International law is a subject worthy of a law school course on its own. The primary points of this section are the different sources of international law, particularly treaties, and the International Court of Justice.

The website of the ICJ contains information on the court, its history, and its current workings. It is also a source for decisions of the Court, as well as of its predecessor, the Permanent Court of International Justice. You can find the website at **http://www.icj-cij.org**.

Practice Exercise

The objects of this exercise are to introduce the students to Internet research in the area of international and foreign law and to have them look at a particular treaty or convention. A Google search in April, 2013 brought up 10 main entries plus a large number of related entries, some of which led to an English-language version of the Convention.

Article 11 of the Convention specifies the ways a state can express its consent to be bound by a treaty: "The consent of a State to be bound by a treaty may be expressed by signature, exchange of instruments constituting a treaty, ratification, acceptance, approval or accession, or by any other means if so agreed."

One of the entries from the original search is likely to be to the U.S. Department of State website, which explains that the U.S. is not a party to the Convention because the Senate has not ratified the Convention by giving its advice and consent to it. The State Department website also states, however, that "[t]he United States considers many of the provisions of the Vienna Convention on the Law of Treaties to constitute customary international law on the law of treaties." This note can form the basis for a discussion of the role of customary international law in the international legal system.

Mandatory and Persuasive Authority Exercises

Exercise 1

For each of the following factual situations, decide whether the stated authority will be mandatory or persuasive authority in the named court.

1. Your client, Karen Branigan, was seriously injured in a car accident when a car driven by John Snow forced her car off the road outside of Sacramento, California. Before the accident, Snow had been at a wine tasting and dinner party at the home of Bill and Debbie Hall. The Halls arranged a tasting of fourteen different red wines, and Snow tasted all of them. After the tasting, the Halls served dinner with more wine. They realized that Snow was somewhat drunk by the end of the wine tasting, but they continued to refill his wine glass at dinner. Indeed, by the time Snow left the Halls' house, he was visibly drunk. You believe you can sue the Halls for Branigan's injuries, so your first step is to research whether California law recognizes the liability of social hosts who provide alcohol to obviously intoxicated guests who then injure third parties. Decide whether each of the following sources will be mandatory or persuasive authority in a case brought in the trial court in Sacramento County. Sacramento is in the Third District of the California Court of Appeal. Be prepared to explain why each source is mandatory or persuasive authority.

    a. A 1975 decision of the California Supreme Court that refused to establish social host liability.

    b. A 1980 California statute that established social host liability.

    c. A 1987 decision from the Third District Court of Appeal that applied the social host liability statute.

    d. A 2004 decision from the Oregon Supreme Court that applied Oregon's social host liability statute, which is identical to California's.

    e. A 2010 U.S. Supreme Court case that applied California's social host liability statute.

2. You represent Albert Goldman, a fifty-six-year-old gay man who was recently fired by his company after working there for ten years. Albert's replacement is a thirty-year-old straight man, who Albert believes is being paid significantly less than Albert was for doing the same job. Albert believes he was fired because of both his sexual orientation and his age. You know there are federal statutes that bar employment discrimination on the basis of gender and age, so you need to research those statutes. Decide whether each of the following sources will be mandatory or persuasive authority as to application of these federal statutes in a case brought in the U.S. District Court for the Western District of New York, a federal trial court. New York is in the 2d Circuit. Be prepared to explain why each source is mandatory or persuasive authority.

   a. A 2003 decision by the highest court in New York, the Court of Appeals, holding that New York law bars employment discrimination based on sexual orientation.

   b. A 1967 federal statute, the Age Discrimination in Employment Act, that protects workers forty-years-old and older from being discharged solely because of their age.

   c. A 2000 decision from the 2d Circuit Court of Appeals holding that the inclusion of "gender" as a protected status in the federal Civil Rights Act of 1964 does not apply to sexual orientation.

   d. A 2008 decision from the First Circuit Court of Appeals holding that replacing a worker over forty with a worker younger than forty is prima facie evidence of age discrimination.

   e. A 2012 decision from the U.S. District Court for the Northern District of New York that held that a defendant company had violated the federal age discrimination statute based on facts almost identical to your client's.

3. You represent June Rose Bates, whose son Norman was killed in an industrial accident at his workplace in Tulsa, Oklahoma. June Rose is a resident of Arlington, Texas. June Rose has hired you to sue her son's employer for negligence that led to Norman's death. You have determined that you can sue under Oklahoma's wrongful death statute. Since the employer is an Oklahoma corporation and June Rose is a citizen of Texas, you decide to bring the case in federal court in Oklahoma under diversity of citizenship. The court will apply Oklahoma law. Decide whether each of the following sources will be mandatory or persuasive authority in the U.S. District Court for the Northern District of Oklahoma in Tulsa; Oklahoma is in the 10th Circuit. Be prepared to explain why each source is mandatory or persuasive authority.

   a. Okla. Stat. Ann. Tit. 12, § 1053 (West 2012), the Oklahoma wrongful death statute, as amended in 2005.

   b. A 2008 Oklahoma Supreme Court case applying the state's wrongful death statute.

   c. A 2006 decision from the Tenth Circuit Court of Appeals applying the Oklahoma wrongful death statute.

   d. A discussion of the history of wrongful death statutes in a 2000 case decided by the Texas Supreme Court.

Answers to Exercise 1

Question 1

a. Mandatory
b. Mandatory
c. Mandatory because the trial court is within the Third Appellate District
d. Persuasive because it's a decision from another state. The identical wording of the statute could make the opinion highly persuasive if the case turns on statutory construction.
e. Persuasive because it's a decision from a court not in the California court system.

Question 2

  a. Persuasive
  b. Mandatory
  c. Mandatory because the Western District of New York is in the Second Circuit
  d. Persuasive because the Western District of New York is not in the First Circuit
  e. Persuasive because authority comes from above, not laterally

Question 3

  a. Mandatory because the federal court is applying state law
  b. Mandatory because the federal court is applying state law
  c. Persuasive because a federal court cannot establish binding state law, even as to application of state law by another federal court
  d. Persuasive because the applicable law is that of Oklahoma, not Texas

EXERCISE 2

1. Your firm represents Karen Nakashima. She was seriously injured in an accident caused by a drunk driver. According to Nakashima, Susan Perry drove her Ford Explorer into the River City Café parking lot and left it with the restaurant's valet service. Perry had a number of drinks with her dinner and became very intoxicated. When Perry went to retrieve her vehicle, the valet service turned over her keys and the Explorer even though it was clear to both the valet service and restaurant personnel that she was so intoxicated as to be unfit to drive. As she exited the parking lot, Perry hit Nakashima while Nakashima was standing on the sidewalk.

    You believe that the restaurant and its valet service had a duty to withhold Perry's keys, and you plan to file suit in California Superior Court, County of Sacramento, seeking damages against the restaurant. Decide whether each of the following sources will be mandatory or persuasive authority in the case. Sacramento is in the Third District of the California Court of Appeal. Be prepared to explain why each source is mandatory or persuasive authority.

a. A decision by the California Supreme Court on whether a restaurant or valet service has a duty to withhold vehicles from intoxicated persons.

b. A California statute imposing sole and exclusive civil liability on the person who consumes, rather than on the person who furnishes, alcohol.

c. A decision by the United States Court of Appeals for the Ninth Circuit applying California law on the duty of a restaurant or valet service to withhold automobiles from intoxicated persons.

d. An unpublished opinion by the California Court of Appeal for the Third District on whether a valet service has a duty to withhold automobiles from intoxicated persons.

2. In November of 2005, Michael Newdow filed a complaint in the United States District Court for the Eastern District of California, which sits in Sacramento. Mr. Newdow sued Congress and several federal officials, alleging that by inscribing U.S. coins and currency with the national motto, "In God We Trust," the defendants were establishing a religion in violation of the First Amendment of the Constitution. Mr. Newdow also alleged that the defendants violated his rights under both the Free Exercise Clause of the First Amendment and the federal Religious Freedom Restoration Act. In June 2006, United States District Judge Frank C. Damrell, Jr. granted the defendants' motions to dismiss Mr. Newdow's complaint for failure to state a claim upon which relieve can be granted. In his order, Judge Damrell cited a number of authorities, including those identified below.

Decide whether each of the following sources was mandatory or persuasive authority for Judge Damrell's decision. Be prepared to explain why each source was mandatory or persuasive.

a. The United States Constitution, Amendment I, which reads as follows:

Congress shall make no law respecting an establishment of religion, or prohibiting the free exercise thereof; or abridging the freedom of speech, or of the press; or the right of the people peaceably to assemble, and to petition the Government for a redress of grievances.

b. A Ninth Circuit Court of Appeals decision, *Aronow v. U.S.*, 432 F.2d 242 243 (9th Cir. 1970), in which the court held as follows:

> It is quite obvious that the national motto and the slogan on coinage and currency "In God We Trust" has nothing whatsoever to do with the establishment of religion. Its use is of patriotic or ceremonial character and bears no true resemblance to a governmental sponsorship of a religious exercise.

c. 42 U.S.C. § 2000bb (2006), the Religious Freedom Restoration Act.

d. A United States Supreme Court decision, *Wooley v. Maynard*, 43 U.S. 705, 717 n. 15 (1977) in which the Court held that the State of New Hampshire could not require citizens to display the state motto, "Live Free or Die," on their vehicle license plates. While the Court recognized that the issue was not before it, the Court distinguished its analysis of New Hampshire's requirement of placing the state motto on license plates from the placement of the national motto, "In God We Trust," on currency:

> Currency, which is passed from hand to hand, differs in significant respects from an automobile, which is readily associated with its operator. Currency is generally carried in a purse or pocket and need not be displayed to the public. The bearer is thus not required to publicly advertise the national motto.

Answers to Exercise 2

Question 1

    a. Mandatory
    b. Mandatory
    c. Persuasive because the federal court cannot establish state law
    d. No authority at all. In California, unpublished opinions have no precedential value and cannot be cited to or quoted from in any court. This question provides an opportunity to discuss the precedential value of unpublished opinions in your state.

Question 2

    a. Mandatory
    b. Mandatory because the U.S. District Court is within the Ninth Circuit
    c. Mandatory
    d. Persuasive. Chapter 2 does not discuss *dicta,* so this footnote provides an opportunity to discuss the concept.

CHAPTER 3

INTERCULTURAL COMPETENCE

■ ■ ■

By Maureen Watkins

The purpose of this chapter is to introduce students to the concept of intercultural competence and the need for intercultural competence in the increasingly globalized practice of law. This chapter should be assigned very early in the first semester in order to provide a framework for the intercultural aspects of the curriculum which are integrated throughout the academic year. It is intended to provide students with an overview of the key aspects and criteria; it is certainly not exhaustive.

One of the most important steps on the path to intercultural competence is evaluating and recognizing one's own cultural background and how it affects how each person processes information and functions in society. The following exercise is intended to help start a discussion about students' own cultural context and the assumptions that flow from such constructs. It is also useful for exploring the students' base of knowledge about other peoples and the need for expanding such knowledge.

For the following exercise, give students approximately ten minutes to read and complete the quiz. When they are finished, post the answers on the whiteboard and review them as a group. Explore opportunities to discuss various answers reached by students and the role that their own cultural backgrounds and assumptions affect their thought processes.

<u>In-Class Exercise</u>

Intercultural Competency Quiz
True/False

1. The number 4 symbolizes good luck in China.

2. An Arab who gestures by joining all finger tips and thumbs together and bobbing them up and down is indicating that the other party should calm down.

3. In most Latin American cultures, a finger placed and pointing below the eye means, "Tell the truth!"

4. Hausa is the name of a people, their religion, and their language in Africa.

5. Shiite Islam is the primary religion of Egypt.

6. In Tuareg society, the tent in which a married couple lives is typically considered to be the property of the wife.

7. In Muslim countries it is best to schedule business meetings on Friday as it is the most productive day of the business week.

8. At least 50 different languages are spoken in the United States.

9. The city of Timbuktu is located in The Gambia.

10. Indonesia is predominantly Muslim, except for the island of Bali, which is predominantly Hindu.

11. In many Asian cultures it is inappropriate to touch the head of another person as it is considered to be where the person's soul lives and is therefore sacred.

12. In Poland when someone flicks his finger against his neck, he is indicating that time is up.

13. When receiving a business card from an Asian counterpart, it is both appropriate and expected for the recipient to put it away immediately and review it later in private.

14. The caste system still largely determines a person's place in Indian society.

15. Raising your right fist above your head is considered offensive in Chile.

Answers to the Intercultural Competence Quiz

1. False. The number 4 is associated with bad luck.
2. True
3. False. It means, "Be careful!"
4. False. Hausa is not a religion.
5. True
6. True.
7. False. Friday is a day of prayer in the Muslim religion.
8. True
9. False. Timbuktu is located in the country of Mali.
10. True
11. True
12. False. This gesture is intended as a warning not to test the individual's patience.
13. False. It is appropriate to take the card with both hands, to read it carefully and acknowledge the information before putting it away.
14. True
15. True

Chapter 4

Rules: An Overview of Statutory Interpretation and Synthesis

■ ■ ■

By Adrienne Brungess

The purpose of this chapter is to provide students an overview of statutory rule construction and case rule synthesis; they are separate topics but can be linked. This material is generally assigned early in a 1L legal research and writing course when students are learning to locate and apply relevant legal authority. This material can be referenced again when teaching the materials in the Legal Reasoning and Analysis Toolkit, Chapter 5.

To connect these skills in an exercise, students can initially search for statutory authority on a selected topic (or it can be provided to them). It's a good idea to choose a topic that the students are covering in other first year courses as it allows them an opportunity to practically apply knowledge they are acquiring elsewhere (e.g., Torts, Contracts, Civil Procedure).

Students should outline the statute's requirements. Students can compare findings and discuss the statutory scheme and components in small groups, creating a collective final product. Is the rule conjunctive or disjunctive? What is covered and what is excluded? Is it mandatory or permissive? (See also Chapter 5.) Students can then be tasked with locating relevant case law that applies the statutory language (or can be provided that information). They should read, extrapolate rules and reasoning, and create a synthesized rule based on all the information they've found. Small group discussions also work well when crafting synthesized rules from cases.

For an example of a problem that starts with location and interpretation of the statute, is followed by case selection and synthesis, and then ultimately analyzed in an objective memorandum and argued in a persuasive mediation brief, please see Chapter 14 in the Teacher's Manual.

Chapter 4 is certainly not exhaustive; statutory interpretation is extremely complicated and there are many ways to illustrate rule synthesis. But, it provides students a solid foundation to proceed with research and writing projects.

PRACTICE EXAMPLE – CHAPTER 4, PAGE 4

This hypothetical is based on *Muscarello v. U.S.*, 524 U.S. 125 (1998). See also: Brian G. Slocum, *Linguistics and 'Ordinary Meaning' Determinations,* STATUTE L. REV., Oxford University, pp. 11-15, available at SSRN: http://ssrn.com/abstract=1970012 (Dec. 8, 2011).

Start by having the students frame the issue precisely by using the exact statutory language, interpretation of which will decide the case one way or the other. Students can also discuss and draft a statement of the issue in small groups and present an example to the class.

For example:

Under 18 U.S.C.A. § 924(c)(1)(A), which imposes a mandatory prison sentence for carrying or using a weapon during the commission of a violent or drug-related crime, was Smith "carrying a firearm" when he had a handgun locked in the glove box of the truck he was using to transport marijuana for sale?

To answer the question posed, students must attempt to interpret the statutory language. Students should consider: Is the statute ambiguous, or is its meaning plain? If ambiguous, how should a court resolve the ambiguity?

The statute specifies the subject, the direct object (the firearm), and requires a connection to a drug trafficking crime. However, it is unclear how the defendant must "use" or "carry" the firearm.

Students can discuss whether Smith was "carrying" a firearm and how the interpretation of "carrying" will affect the determination of Smith's actions.

The professor can either provide some case information, or have the students research it. For a shorter, in-class exercise, providing students with the case information below would provide information they could use to create a synthesized rule applying the statutory language.

The statute has been reviewed by the U.S. Supreme Court on several occasions. In 1993, the Court held that the statute did not require use of the firearm as a weapon. *Smith v. United States*, 508 U.S. 223 (1993). To reach its decision, the court looked to the ordinary meaning and consulted two dictionaries. The Court reasoned that "it is one thing to say that the ordinary meaning of 'uses a firearm' *includes* using a firearm as a weapon," "[b]ut it is quite another to conclude that, as a result, the phrase also *excludes* any other use." *Id.* at 230. The Court held that if Congress had intended that the firearm must have been used as a weapon for the enhanced punishment to apply, it could have included the words "as a weapon" in the statute. *Id.* at 229.

Then, in 1995, the Court held that "use" requires the firearm be actively employed by the defendant. *Bailey v. United States*, 516 U.S. 137 (1995). There the Court determined that the dictionary definitions of "use" implied action and implementation. Thus, the action of putting a gun in a place to protect drugs or protect himself was not "use."

In 2007, the Court held that the meaning of "uses" turns on how it is normally spoken. *Watson v. United States*, 552 U.S. 74 (2007). Based on its own understanding of common usage, the Court reasoned that dictionary definition of "use" that may include receipt of a firearm in a transaction for drugs is inconsistent with how the word is generally used.

Students can use this case information to apply the synthesis concepts from Chapter 4, pp. 4-6.

PRACTICE EXAMPLE – CHAPTER 4, PAGES 6-7

Student should complete a synthesis chart using the case information provided in the exercise. Students can do as homework and then work in small groups to compare before discussing as a class.

Example completed synthesis chart

	New York Times Co. v. Sullivan	*McCoy v. Hearst Corp.*	*Live Oak Publishing Co. v. Cohagan*
Date of Opinion	1964	1986	1991
Jurisdiction	US Sup. Ct.	US Sup. Ct.	Cal. App. 3d

			District
Key Facts	Sullivan, an elected commissioner of the city, brought a civil libel action against NYT for advertisement it published.	Defendant newspaper published allegations that Plaintiff McCoy engaged in corrupt police and prosecutorial activities. It was later determined the information given to the reporters who published the story was false.	Plaintiff newspaper published a letter from Defendant reader as an advertisement, which later turned out to contain false information. Defendant claimed she believed the statements made in the letter were true.
Holding	The evidence presented by Plaintiff was constitutionally insufficient to support judgment in his favor.	Plaintiff failed to prove that Defendant acted with actual malice.	Plaintiff could not establish actual malice.
Reasoning	It is important that public discuss the character and qualifications of candidates. The importance to the state and to society outweighs the inconvenience of private persons.	Defendant reasonably believed the information reported was true. The fact that it failed to investigate further and the fact that it may have harbored ill will toward Plaintiff was not sufficient to prove malice.	Defendant actually believed the statements when she made them. Although there was proof that she harbored some animosity, that ill will toward Plaintiff was only circumstantial evidence of actual malice. Ill will without knowledge of falsity does not

			amount to actual malice.
Legal Principle from the case that has predictive value for your legal issue	A public official cannot recover damages for a defamatory falsehood relating to his official conduct unless he proves that the statement was made with "actual malice," that is, the statement was made with knowledge that it was false or with reckless disregard of whether it was false or not.	Investigatory failures and evidence of ill will does not necessarily amount to "actual malice" for purposes of defamation.	Evidence of ill will is not sufficient to establish actual malice without knowledge of falsity of the statement made.

Once students have completed the synthesis chart, they should draft a synthesized rule that has predictive value for their client's case. This can also be done in a small group exercise.

Example synthesized rule

To recover in a defamation action, a public official plaintiff must prove the statement at issue was made with "actual malice." Actual malice means the defendant made the statement with reckless disregard for whether it was true. Proof of failure to investigate the truth does not necessarily amount to actual malice. Further, ill will is insufficient to prove actual malice absent evidence that the defendant was aware the statement was false.

Ultimately, the facts seem to support that even though she may have been angry with him, thus evidencing ill-will, that alone will be insufficient to prove actual malice.

Chapter 5

Legal Reasoning and Analysis Toolkit

■ ■ ■

By Stephanie J. Thompson

The purpose of this chapter is to introduce students to the various types of rules, explanations, and analysis used in both objective and persuasive legal writing. In this chapter, the concepts are described generally so professors using this text can implement his or her own examples and exercises. Some ideas for exercises are provided below and there are various sample memos and briefs provided throughout this Teacher's Manual. This chapter should can be presented either as the first class on legal writing generally or it can be presented after a specific type of writing has been introduced (See Chapters 8, 9, 10, 14, 15).

Because this likely is the first introduction of these concepts, it might be best to start with a general PowerPoint presentation to review the chapter (as the students will have been assigned to read it before class). This allows the professor to give a general review of the reading assignment as well as expand upon the material included in the chapter.

After spending one class on a general introduction to the broad concepts of the toolkit, it probably would be best to teach each tool in the toolkit separately, starting with the Rules. I tend to dedicate 1 or 2 classes to each individual tool.

Rules

The introduction to Rules can be done using the PowerPoint provided below:

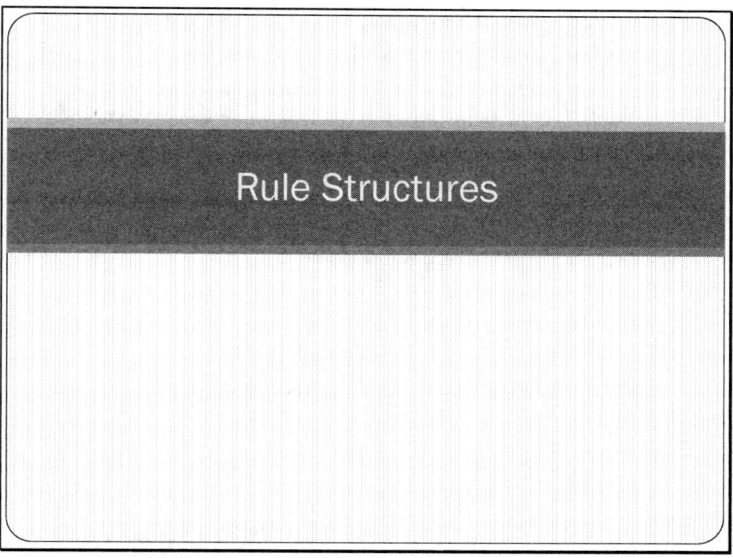

The Rule of Law
- Legal analysis is anchored by the rule of law.
- Without a rule to be applied, there cannot be any analysis of a legal issue.
- Finding and writing the rule of law may be the most important step in building your legal analysis.

Finding the Rule of Law

- The rule of law will be derived from primary authority.
- To determine the applicable rule of law, you will conduct research to find the relevant primary authorities.
- Once you have found the relevant primary authorities, you will need to determine if those authorities provide a clear and simple rule or if you need to combine, or synthesize, several primary authorities to develop a complete rule.

Synthesizing the Rule of Law

- Synthesis typically is the binding together of several cases to create a complete rule of law or expression of policy.
- Synthesis is not merely mentioning one case after another.
  - For example, it is not synthesis to describe Case A, Case B, Case C, Case D, and then Case E.
  - This is nothing more than an amplified list.
- Synthesis requires binding the cases together.
- You need to step back and ask yourself what the cases really have in common.
- Focus on the reasoning and key facts that the cases have in common to find and explain a collective meaning that is not apparent from the individual cases themselves.

The Types of Rules

- There are various types of rules.
- The most common types of rules will be discussed, but be aware that not all rules fall into one of these types of rules — they may be a combination of these types of rules or something that has yet to be categorized.

Types of Rules (or tests)

- Simple declarative rule
- Conjunctive rule
- Disjunctive rule
- Factors test
- Balancing test

Simple Declarative Rule

- A simple declarative rule is a rule that has no sub-parts, elements, factors, exceptions, or other considerations.
- EXAMPLE:
  - To be valid, a will must be signed.

Conjunctive Rule

- A conjunctive rule, or an "and" test, requires the satisfaction of two or more parts. The rule cannot be satisfied unless all of the parts of the rule are satisfied.
- A conjunctive rule typically has elements, or is referred to an elements test.
- EXAMPLE:
- To revoke a will, a testator must have the intention to revoke the will and must take some action that demonstrates that intent.

Conjunctive Rule

- When working with a conjunctive rule, there are important strategy considerations to keep in mind.
  - Specifically, for the party trying to prove the rule, all parts of the conjunctive rule must be satisfied for it to apply.
  - However, the party opposing the application of the rule needs only to disprove or defeat one part of the rule.

- To revoke a will, a testator:
  - Must have the intention to revoke the will AND
  - Must take some action that demonstrates that intent.

Disjunctive Rule

- A disjunctive rule, or an "either/or" test, requires the satisfaction of only one part of the test.
- The rule can be satisfied if one or the other part of the test is met.
- EXAMPLE:
- A lawyer shall not collect a contingent fee in a criminal matter OR a divorce.

Disjunctive Rule

- When working with a disjunctive rule, there are important strategy considerations to keep in mind.
  - Specifically, if you are writing for the client who wants the rule to be satisfied, you only need to be able to prove either one part or the other part of the rule for it to apply.
  - However, if you are writing for the client who does not want the rule to apply, then you need to disprove or defeat both parts of the rule.

- A lawyer shall not collect a contingent fee in a criminal matter OR a divorce.

Factors Test

- A factors test is a rule that requires the court to evaluate a non-exclusive list of factors.
- EXAMPLE:
- Child custody cases shall be decided based on the best interest of the child. Factors to consider in deciding the best interest of the child are: the fitness of each possible custodian, the appropriateness of the lifestyle of the possible custodian, the relationship between the child and the possible custodian, the placement of the child's siblings, living accommodations, the child's school, proximity to other family and friends, religious issues, and any other factor's relevant to the child's best interest.

Factors Test

- Child custody cases shall be decided based on the best interest of the child. Factors to consider in deciding the best interest of the child are:
  - the fitness of each possible custodian
  - the appropriateness of the lifestyle of the possible custodian
  - the relationship between the child and the possible custodian
  - the placement of the child's siblings
  - living accommodations
  - the child's school, proximity to other family and friends
  - religious issues
  - any other factor's relevant to the child's best interest.

Balancing Test

- A balancing test is where the rule requires the court to balance various factors.
- Typically a balancing test has an exclusive list of factors to be considered by the court.
- However, no one factor carries more weight than another factor.
- Instead, the factors are considered in light of the other factors.
- Specifically, a court would look at the quality of the support for each factor, the number of factors that support one side or the other, and the overall factual and policy-based impact each factor has on the case.

Balancing Test

- EXAMPLE:
- A party must respond to properly propounded interrogatories unless the burden of responding outweighs the questioning party's legitimate need for the information.

- Burden of responding vs. Legitimate need for the information

Rule Structures

- Knowing the type of rule you have will help you decide how to explain the rule, how to apply the rule, and also how many CREACs you will need to organize your analysis.
- Keep in mind that identifying the type of rule is to help you organize and analyze your rule; the goal is not to give it a label.

After a general introduction, exercises designed to have the students "see" the concepts in action can be done in class. Below are some ideas on how to help students see and understand the various types of rules used in both objective and persuasive legal writing:

1. I provide examples of the various types of rules or I use the examples in the book or in the sample memos/briefs provided in Chapters 9, 10, and 15 this Teacher's Manual. I then ask the students to identify the type of rule that is provided. After they identify the type of rule, we discuss why it is that type of rule and what each party needs to prove for this rule to be satisfied or to show that the rule fails. It is important that students can see how the rule works from both sides of the issue.

2. Another rule exercise is to give the students a statute and have them break it down and determine the type of rule (simple declarative rule, conjunctive, disjunctive, balancing test, factors test). This relates to the content and exercises in Chapter 4 on Statutory Interpretation and Rule Synthesis.

California Penal Code § 459. Burglary

Every person who enters any house, room, apartment, tenement, shop, warehouse, store, mill, barn, stable, outhouse or other building, tent, vessel, as defined in Section 21 of the Harbors and Navigation Code, floating home, as defined in subdivision (d) of Section 18075.55 of the Health and Safety Code, railroad car, locked or sealed cargo container, whether or not mounted on a vehicle, trailer coach, as defined in Section 635 of the Vehicle Code, any house car, as defined in Section 362 of the Vehicle Code, inhabited camper, as defined in Section 243 of the Vehicle Code, vehicle as defined by the Vehicle Code, when the doors are locked, aircraft as defined by Section 21012 of the Public Utilities Code, or mine or any underground portion thereof, with intent to commit grand or petit larceny or any felony is guilty of burglary. As used in this chapter, "inhabited" means currently being used for dwelling purposes, whether occupied or not. A house, trailer, vessel designed for habitation, or portion of a building is currently being used for dwelling purposes if, at the time of the burglary, it was not occupied solely because a natural or other disaster caused the occupants to leave the premises.

California Penal Code § 460. Degrees

(a) Every burglary of an inhabited dwelling house, vessel, as defined in the Harbors and Navigation Code, which is inhabited and designed for habitation, floating home, as defined in subdivision (d) of Section 18075.55 of the Health and Safety Code, or trailer coach, as defined by the Vehicle Code, or the inhabited portion of any other building, is burglary of the first degree.

(b) All other kinds of burglary are of the second degree.

One possible breakdown is as follows and it is a conjunctive rule structure:

To convict a defendant of 1st degree burglary, the prosecutor must prove:
1. person
2. enters
3. inhabited dwelling house
4. with intent to commit
    a. grand or petit larceny
    b. or any crime

Explanations

The introduction to explanations can be done using the PowerPoint provided below:

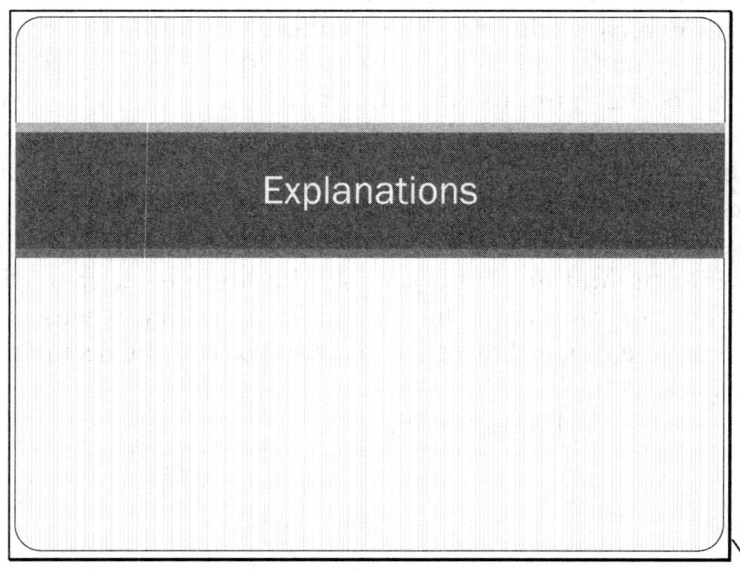

CREAC Review

- CREAC is the objective organizational paradigm
- CREAC=
  - Conclusion
  - Rule
  - EXPLANATION
  - Analysis
  - Conclusion

Types of Explanations

- Types we will learn this year
  - Case illustrations
  - Parentheticals

Case Illustrations

- A case illustration is a detailed description of a precedent case that provides the reader with an example of how the rule was applied in an-other case.
- In describing the precedent case, the case illustration should include information regarding the issue before the court, the facts, the holding, the reasoning, and the conclusion of the precedent case.

Case Illustrations

- However, that a case illustration is not a case summary.
- When providing information about the issue before the court, the facts, the holding, the reasoning, and the conclusion of the precedent case, the information provided must be focused only on the particular legal issue being explained.

Case Illustrations

- Case Illustrations Are Used in Three Situations:
  - To explain the whole rule
  - To explain part of the rule
  - To give an example of how the court has applied the rule

- A case illustration is NOT a case summary — it is an explanation (or an example) of a specific part of a precedent case to show how a rule has been treated by another court.

Case Illustrations

- **Case Illustration Components:**
  - Thesis Sentence stating *the specific legal issue*
  - Issue before the court on *the specific legal issue*
  - Facts relating to *the specific legal issue*
  - Holding relating to *the specific legal issue*
  - Reasoning on *the specific legal issue*
  - Conclusion on *the specific legal issue*

Case Illustrations

- **Example No. 1 (the R in the CREAC is in italics):**
- *A celebrity may have a common law right of publicity claim when his or her identity has been appropriated without consent.* White v. Samsung Electronics, 971 F. 2d 1395, 1397 (9th Cir. 1992). A celebrity's identity has been appropriated where there is little doubt as to who is being depicted. Id. For example, in White, the plaintiff, Vanna White, brought a common law right of publicity claim against the defendant for attempting to capitalize on her fame in an advertisement without her consent. Id. at 1396. The advertisement included a robot wearing a blonde wig, a formal gown, and jewelry chosen to resemble the plaintiff's style, and was standing in the plaintiff's well-known stance next to a game board recognizable as the Wheel of Fortune. Id. *Based on these facts, the court held* the defendant had appropriated the plaintiff's identify. Id. The court examined the advertisement and *reasoned* that while the individual aspects of the advertisement said little, when viewed together, there could be no other conclusion than that the robot was meant to depict the plaintiff. Id. *Thus*, where there is little doubt as to who is being depicted, the celebrity's identity has been appropriated. Id. at 1397.

Case Illustrations

- **Example No. 1 (the R in the CREAC is in italics):** *A work is entitled to First Amendment protection when it "adds significant creative elements so as to be transformed into something more than a mere celebrity likeness or imitation."* Comedy III Prods. Inc. v. Gary Saderup Inc., 25 Cal. 4th 387, 391 (2001). *This is known as the "transformative test."* Id. In Winter v. D.C. Comics, the court determined whether DC Comics' unauthorized use of the Winter Brothers' likeness in its comic book had sufficient creative elements to protect it under the transformative test. 30 Cal. 4th 881, 885 (2003). DC Comics published a comic book miniseries containing an outlandish plot involving worm-like creatures and singing cowboys. Three characters in the comic book, called the "Autumn Brothers," parodied some well-known musicians, the Winter Brothers. The "Autumn Brothers" were half-worm and half-human creatures with features resembling the Winter Brothers. Id. The court held that the comic books contained creative elements that transformed the Winter Brothers beyond a literal or conventional depiction. Id. at 889. The court reasoned that it was readily observable that the comic book characters were not literal depictions of the Winter Brothers, but were "distorted for purposes of lampoon, parody, or caricature." Id. at 890. It further reasoned that the depictions of the Winter Brothers were "but cartoon characters . . . in a larger story, which itself [was] quite expressive," such that the Winter Brothers were "only part of the raw materials from which the comic books were synthesized." Id. For these reasons, the court held the comic book had sufficient creative elements to protect it under the transformative test. Id.

Case Illustrations

- **Brainstorming Questions**
- What is the specific legal principle you plan to explain with the case illustration?
- What was the specific legal issue before the court in the precedent case as it relates to the specific legal principle you plan to explain with the case illustration?
- What are the specific facts in the precedent case as they relate to the specific legal principle you plan to explain with the case illustration?
- What is the holding in the precedent case as it relates to the specific legal principle you plan to explain with the case illustration?
- What is the reasoning in the precedent case as it relates to the specific legal principle you plan to explain with the case illustration?

Parentheticals

- A parenthetical is like a case illustration in that it provides the reader with an example of how the rule was applied in another case, but it is much shorter than a case illustration.
- A parenthetical can be thought of as a quick "hey-by-the-way" example, rather than an example you want the reader to focus on, such as a case illustration.

Parentheticals

- Because it is a short example, a parenthetical usually is not a complete sentence but only a short descriptive phrase that provides the holding of the court and the relevant facts.
- Additionally, it is called a parenthetical because it is included in parenthesis at the end of a citation.

Parentheticals

- **For a Parenthetical Rule Explanation to be substantively correct, it must <u>INCLUDE</u>:**
- A rule statement. What is the legal concept you are trying to explain to your reader?
- The relevant facts from the precedent case that are needed to support the rule statement.
- The key words and phrases from the precedent case that are needed to support the rule statement.

> ## Parentheticals
> - **Common Mistakes in Writing Parentheticals:**
> - Restating the Rule in the Parenthetical
>   - The parenthetical needs to explain the rule, not restate the rule. Thus, it likely will be more factually specific or a more nuanced aspect of the rule, not the rule itself.
> - Stating the Parenthetical Explanation in Overly Broad Terms
>   - A parenthetical needs to be a specific example of something, not broad generalizations.
> - Drafting Overly Long Parenthetical Explanations
>   - If you need more than one sentence to explain the point, you need to use a case illustration instead.

After a general introduction, exercises designed to have the students "see" the concepts in action can be done in class. Below are some ideas on how to help students see and understand the various types of explanations used in both objective and persuasive legal writing:

1. For each type of explanations, provide the students 3-5 samples. Go through each sample and discuss why it does or does not provide the reader with the relevant information for that type of explanation. These samples can be drawn from the samples provided in Chapters 9 and 10 of this teacher's manual.

2. Another exercise would be to provide the students with each type of explanation and have them annotate the various parts of the explanation to ensure it is complete. Do one of these together as a class so the students understand what you are looking for them to find and then have them do one on their own.

The following are the parts to a case illustration: the issue before the court, the facts, the holding, and the reasoning of the case. In addition to including these parts, the emphasis should be on the case illustration being focused on the specific legal issue or rule the case illustration is explaining. Thus, students should be reminded that they are not writing a case summary or a case brief, but that there is a specific purpose needed when writing a case illustration. This discussion should be part of this exercise as well.

The following are the parts for a parenthetical: the facts and the holding. Similar to the discussion above, the exercise should focus on finding the necessary parts for a complete parenthetical but it also should be focused on the purpose of the parenthetical.

Analysis/Reasoning:

One overall approach to teaching analysis/reasoning is to teach the students to begin with a series of brainstorming questions to get them to think about how the client's case and the rule, precedent case, or policy relate to each other. The emphasis on these brainstorming questions is twofold. The first is to emphasize to the students the need to think objectively and let the rule, precedent case, or policy guide the analysis. Too often students read their facts and read the rule, precedent case, or policy and make a decision prematurely based on a gut-reaction or personal opinion. The brainstorming questions are designed for a methodical comparison of the client's case and the rule, precedent case, or policy to allow for a truly objectively comparison. The second is to prepare the students to write their analysis, putting repeated emphasis on the use of the rule, precedent case, or policy, and not just their personal opinion of how those things could be applied.

The following PowerPoint can be used in one of two ways. First, it can be used as a large introduction to all of the different types of analysis the students will learn – deductive reasoning, analogical reasoning, and policy-based reasoning. Second, it can be broken down into 3 separate presentations – one presentation (one class session) per type of analysis.

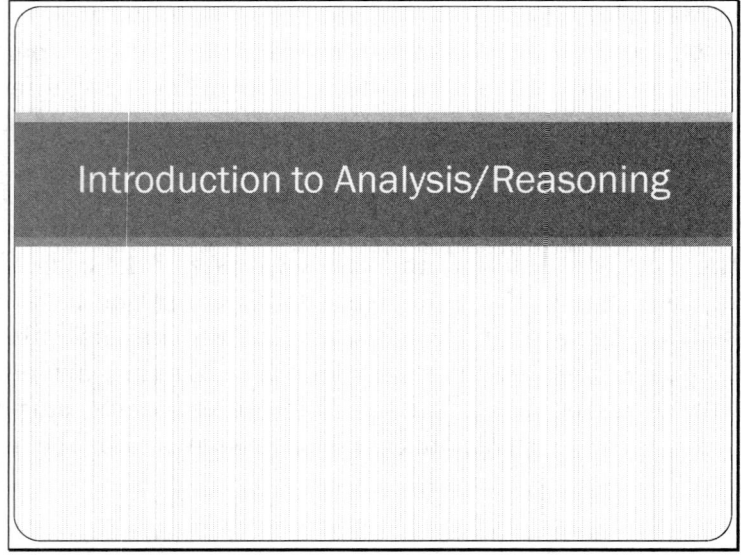

Types of Reasoning

- Types of reasoning we will learn this year
  - Deductive (rule-based) reasoning
  - Policy-based reasoning
  - Analogical reasoning

Deductive Reasoning

- Deductive reasoning justifies a result by directly applying a legal principle to the facts of the client's case.
- It is simple and direct without deep analysis.
- Deductive reasoning generally can be used where the legal principle or rule is clear and does not need any explanation.

Deductive Reasoning

- For example:
  - It is illegal for anyone under the age of sixteen to operate a motor vehicle. CITE. <u>Because the defendant was only 15 years old at the time he drove his father's car, he illegally operated a motor vehicle.</u>

Deductive Reasoning Components

- The legal principle or rule being applied.
- The legal conclusion sought to be established by the application of the legal principle or rule.
- The relevant facts from the client's case needed to justify the legal conclusion.

Deductive Reasoning Components

- 1. "In California, it is illegal for anyone under the age of sixteen to operate a motor vehicle. [legal principle or rule being applied]
- 2. The defendant illegally operated a motor vehicle [legal conclusion to be established]
- 3. because he was only 15 years old at the time he drove her father's car [relevant facts]

In-Class Exercise

- QUESTION: Did Mr. Gibson commit the crime of burglary when he entered Ms. Brown's home with the intent to take her personal property?
- What is the <u>rule of law</u> that applies to this issue?
  - In California, a person who enters the house of another with the intent to commit theft is guilty of burglary.
- What is <u>the legal conclusion</u> you seek to establish by the application of this rule?
  - Mr. Gibson is guilty of burglary.

People v. Gibson Example

- What are <u>**the relevant facts**</u> from your client's case that justify that legal conclusion?
  - Mr. Gibson entered Ms. Brown's house and took her personal property.

People v. Gibson Example

- Put it all together
- In California, a person who enters the house of another with the intent to commit a theft is guilty of burglary. [rule of law] Mr. Gibson committed the crime of burglary [legal conclusion] when he entered Ms. Brown's house with the intent to take her property and took her personal property.[facts]

In-class Exercise

Although celebrities have the right to First Amendment protection from the unauthorized exploitation of their photographs under the right of publicity, the statutory cause of action specifically exempts from liability the use of a photograph in connection with a matter in the public interest. California Civil Code § 3344(d) states that no prior consent is required for use of a photograph in the public interest, such as news, public affairs, or sports broadcast or account, or any political campaign. Public interest has been defined as "recent events or publications about people who, by their accomplishments, mode of living, professional standing or calling, create a legitimate and widespread attention to their activities." Dora v. Frontline Video, Inc., 15 Cal. App. 4th 536 (2nd Dist. 1993) (a 1987 surfing documentary that included footage of a famous surfer was in the public interest and no prior consent was needed); Gionfriddo v. Major League Baseball, 94 Cal. App. 4th 400 (1st Dist. 2001) (web cast of baseball statistics that included a photograph of a famous baseball player was in the public interest and no prior consent was needed). Because the use of Mr. Quarterback's photograph was in connection with his fourth Superbowl victory in the past ten years, it is in the public interest and his consent was not required.

In-class Exercise

- What is the legal principle or rule being applied?
  - Prior consent is not required for use of a photograph in the public interest, such as news, public affairs, or sports broadcast or account, or any political campaign. Public interest has been defined as "recent events or publications about people who, by their accomplishments, mode of living, professional standing or calling, create a legitimate and widespread attention to their activities."

In-class Exercise

- What is the legal conclusion sought to be established by the application of the legal principle or rule?
  - Mr. Quarterback's photo is in the public interest and his consent was not required for it to be used.
- What are the relevant facts from the client's case needed to justify the legal conclusion?
  - The photo was of his fourth Superbowl victory in the past ten years.

Policy-Based Reasoning

- It justifies a result by considering which result will be best for society.
- This rationale often considers a rules underlying purpose and/or the policy implications of how it might be interpreted.

Policy-Based Reasoning

- Policy-based reasoning begins with a rule.
  - Ask yourself: What is the rule being applied?
- To use policy-based reasoning, the purpose underlying the rule must be determined.
  - Ask yourself: What was the goal of the legislature or the court in creating the rule?
  - The purpose underlying the rule must come from the legislature, the court, legal commentary, etc. It can not come from your personal view of society or why you personally believe the rule was created.

Policy-Based Reasoning

- Once you have determined the purpose underlying the rule, then you need to evaluate how it does or does not apply to your client's case.
- Review the brainstorming questions for Worksheet No. 5.
- After you have answered the brainstorming questions for Worksheet No. 5, you should have a good idea of how the purpose underlying the rule does or does not apply to your client's case.
- Use the policy-based reasoning formula to help form your policy-based reasoning analysis.

Policy-Based Reasoning Formula

- Step 1: State the conclusion you will reach by applying the policy.
- Step 2: State the rule the policy justifies.
- Step 3: Identify and describe the purpose/policy behind the rule.
- Step 4: State whether the purpose/policy applies to the outcome you are predicting in the client's case.
- Step 5: Explain why the purpose/policy applies to the outcome you are predicting in the client's case.
- Step 6: Conclude by tying it all together.

In-class Exercise

- Read through the sample policy-based reasoning paragraph
- Identify the following:
    - The conclusion reached by applying the policy
    - The rule the policy justifies
    - The description of purpose/policy behind the rule
    - A statement of whether the purpose/policy applies to the outcome being predicted
    - Explanation of why the purpose/policy applies to the outcome being predicted
    - A conclusion sentence to tie it all together

In-class Exercise

The defendant's Civil Code § 3344(a) violation likely is not actionable because the defendant's use of Ms. Anchor's photograph on its t-shirt provided commentary on a matter in the public interest and, therefore, consent was unnecessary. California Civil Code § 3344(d) provides an exception to § 3344(a). It states that the use of a photograph in connection with "any news, public affairs, or sports broadcast or account, or any political campaign" does not require consent. The courts have explained that the purpose of this exception is to protect the public's right to know about things, events, and people, such as news, celebrity activities, and sports. Thus, the right of a celebrity in her image is not absolute, but must be balanced against the public interest in dissemination of news and information. It is for this reason that the use of a celebrity's photograph on a matter in the public interest is exempt from the consent requirement of § 3344(a).

Ms. Anchor's claim is not furthered by the statutory purpose of protecting matters in the public interest. Rather, the defendant's use of Ms. Anchor's photograph with the Mayor's photograph as a miniature devil on her shoulder furthers the purpose because the t-shirt is part of an expressive comment on the unethical reporting on politics in Los Angeles. This is the type of information the public interest exception was designed to protect. Thus, it is likely the use of Ms. Anchor's photograph on the t-shirt as a political and social commentary is not actionable due to the nature of the policy protecting the dissemination of information in the public interest.

Analogical Reasoning

- This is a more sophisticated technique
- It justifies a result by making direct fact comparisons between the facts of a decided case & the facts of the clients case with a specific focus on the reasoning of a decided case

Analogical Reasoning

- Begin with a series of brainstorming questions to think about how the client's case and the precedent case fit together.
- The brainstorming questions are designed for a methodical comparison of the client's case and the rule, precedent case, or policy to allow for a truly objectively comparison.
- They also are designed to keep the focus on how the precedent case and your client's case compare, not just your their personal opinion of how those things could be applied.

Brainstorming Questions for AR

- What is the issue from the client's case that you plan to use analogical reasoning to address?
- What precedent case do you intend to use to address this issue?
- What is the holding from that case?
- What is the reasoning from that case?
- What are the relevant facts from that case?
- What are the relevant facts from your client's case?
- How are those facts similar or different?
- Are those similarities or differences legally significant? Do they directly relate to the holding or reasoning of the precedent case?

After my general introduction, I introduce exercises designed to have the students "see" the concepts in action. Below are some ideas on how to help students see and understand the various types of analysis/reasoning used in both objective and persuasive legal writing:

1. Similar to the other exercises above, samples can be provided to review as a class and have the students find the various parts of the different types of reasoning.

2. The most complicated topic to teach is analogical reasoning. Below is an exercise that can be used to introduce analogical reasoning in a fun, but law-focused, way. The important point to emphasize to the students is that it is not just about the comparisons of the facts but more about the opinion of the judge and why the comparison of certain facts is important.

Introduction to Analogical Reasoning – Is a Burrito a Sandwich?

In 2006, the Worcester Superior Court determined the important question of whether a burrito is a sandwich. The article below discusses that case:

http://www.sunjournal.com/story/184707/NewEnglandNews/Judge_Burrito_not_a_sandwich (Saturday, November 11, 2006).

Is a burrito a sandwich?

Panera Bread Co. says yes. But a judge said no in settling a food fight over the bakery cafe chain's attempt to keep a Mexican restaurant from selling burritos in a Shrewsbury shopping mall.

Worcester Superior Court Judge Jeffrey Locke ruled that an exclusivity clause in Panera's lease restricting the White City Shopping Center from renting to another sandwich shop doesn't prohibit the mall from adding a Qdoba Mexican Grill.

Locke cited Webster's Dictionary as well as testimony from a chef and a former high-ranking federal agriculture official in ruling that Qdoba's burritos and other offerings shouldn't be considered sandwiches, The Boston Globe reported Friday.

The difference, the judge ruled, comes down to two slices of bread versus one tortilla.

"A sandwich is not commonly understood to include burritos, tacos, and quesadillas, which are typically made with a single tortilla and stuffed with a choice filling of meat, rice, and beans," Locke wrote in a decision released last week.

The judge ruled against Panera's request to halt Qdoba's plans to move into the shopping center because Panera failed to stipulate that burritos and tacos be covered in the sandwich exclusivity clause.

Panera spokesman Mark Crowley declined to comment on the ruling to The Associated Press on Friday, and would not say whether the St. Louis-based chain of more than 900 bakery-cafes planned to appeal.

In court filings, Panera argued for a broad definition of sandwich, saying a flour tortilla is bread, and that a food product with bread and a filling is a sandwich.

In defending its case, Qdoba - owned by San Diego-based Jack in the Box Inc. - called food experts to testify on its behalf.

Among them was Cambridge chef Chris Schlesinger, who said in an affidavit, "I know of no chef or culinary historian who would call a burrito a sandwich. Indeed, the notion would be absurd to any credible chef or culinary historian."

Judith Quick, a former division deputy director at the Department of Agriculture, said in her affidavit, "The USDA views a sandwich as a separate and distinct food product from a burrito or taco."

The case was about more than just the definition of a sandwich, observers said.

Panera Bread, with 31 Massachusetts locations, is trying to fend off upstart Qdoba, which plans to build at least nine new stores in the state next year, up from eight now.

"It shows you how competitive the business is when a bakery cafe feels like it's in direct competition with a Mexican chain," said Ron Paul, president of Technomic Inc., a restaurant consulting firm in Chicago.

Assignment 1:

You recently took a job as a research attorney for the Worcester Superior Court. A new case has come before Superior Court Judge Jeffrey Locke concerning the same White City Shopping Center and its exclusivity clause. In the new case, the restaurant Pita Pit (see the website for Pita Pit for menu information (http://www.pitapitusa.com/main.php?page=9)) was attempting to negotiate a lease with White City Shopping Center to open a restaurant in the same food court as in the previous case. Panera Bread Co., still upset about the court's prior decision, has challenged

White City Shopping Center's potential lease to Pita Pit. Thus, the question you need to address is: *Is a pita a sandwich?*

Using the above article as your "legal authority," please provide your recommendation to the judge on how he should rule in this new case. Please support your recommendation with specific fact-to-fact examples comparing Pita Pit to the facts in the Panera Bread Co. and Qdoba case and with specific reference to reasoning of the court in the Panera Bread Co. and Qdoba case.

Assignment 2:

After your research and suggestion to the judge, you obtained a connected case. Specifically, Qdoba's lease negotiations with White City Shopping Center resulted in an exclusivity clause in its lease restricting the White City Shopping Center from renting to another burrito shop. Thus, the question you now need to address is: *Is a pita a burrito?*

Using the above article as your "legal authority," please provide your recommendation to the judge on how he should rule in this new case. Please support your recommendation with specific fact-to-fact examples comparing Pita Pit to the facts in the Panera Bread Co. and Qdoba case and with specific reference to reasoning of the court in the Panera Bread Co. and Qdoba case.

Another Teaching Approach:

When I teach the tools of this toolkit, I use brainstorming and organizational structures for each type of explanation and analysis. Those brainstorming and organizational tools are included LEGAL WRITING EXERCISES: A CASE FILE AND FORMULA-BASED APPROACH TO LEGAL REASONING (West 2010), which can be used as a companion to the GLOBAL LAWYERING SKILLS book.

CHAPTER 6

THE PROCESS OF LEGAL WRITING

■ ■ ■

By Mary–Beth Moylan

The purpose of this chapter is to introduce the students to the process of outlining and organizing their ideas in a framework appropriate for all types of legal writing. This chapter should be assigned before the students focus in on any of the other particular types of legal writing discussed in Chapters 8, 9, 10, 13, 14, 15, and 17. While nuances in structure will be necessary depending on the particular legal document being drafted, good organizational skills and outlining practice are necessary for all forms of legal writing.

Any number of in-class exercises can be used to work on outlining, drafting, brainstorming, and organization. Sometimes using familiar topics can help the students to become aware of the different organizational categories that their writing must conform to when writing for a legal audience. The following exercise focuses on drawing out the Rule Explanation and Rule Application components of the CREAC structure, but it can also be used to teach outlining skills. In case any students are not familiar with the story behind the exercise, a brief synopsis of the background story can be provided and is included following the exercise.

<u>In Class Exercise:</u>

Hansel & Gretel v. Stepmother

202 F. Rptr. 16 (2008)[1]

Grimm, Chief Justice

Stepmother appeals from a judgment following trial in the Superior Court finding that Stepmother was liable in damages to Hansel and Gretel, her stepchildren, for the tort of "being evil." Appellant Stepmother asserts that the trial judge erred in allowing the jury to consider the case because, as a matter of law, she is not evil. We disagree.

On June 2, 2006, Appellant Stepmother caused her two stepchildren, Hansel and Gretel, to be led deep into the forest by their father, Woodsman. Appellant disliked Hansel and Gretel intensely, simply because they were the children of Woodsman and his late wife. She argued to her husband constantly that the children ate too much, needed new clothing too often, and were noisy and disrespectful to her. His replies that the children performed all of the household tasks on the order of Stepmother, were excellent students, and were always respectful to her in his presence, fell on deaf ears. Simply stated, Stepmother hated Hansel and Gretel and resolved to remove them from the family home. Claiming that it was "those brats or me," she induced her husband to lead them deep into the woods, where she hoped they would run afoul of the local witch, who lived in a gingerbread house.

Hansel and Gretel were indeed lured to the witch's house by hunger. She trapped Hansel in a cage and attempted to "fatten him up" to roast him for Sunday lunch. She made Gretel do all the housework while she sat conjuring spells to lure more children to her clutches. Through their native cleverness, the children managed to incinerate the witch in her own oven and return to their father. Reunited with their father, the children sued Stepmother, claiming the common law tort of "being evil."

---

[1] Please note this is not a real reporter citation. All references to the F. Rptr are the Fairytale Reporter in the jurisdiction of Fairytale Land. Thus, because the "F" signifies the jurisdiction, there is no need for a court reference in the court and date parenthetical.

The tort of "being evil" is a relatively new tort in this jurisdiction, which demonstrates a shift from older public policy of denying legal redress to child victims of evil in favor of simply making them the subject of numerous uplifting tales for youngsters. The modern approach is to allow the injured children to seek damages at law. The outlines of the tort were established by our Supreme Court eight years ago in the landmark case of <u>Snow White v. Wicked Queen</u>, 126 F. Rptr. 639 (2000). In order to prevail, plaintiffs must prove "the defendant had a duty of care to the child plaintiff based on marriage into the plaintiff's family." <u>Id.</u> at 642. Although the Court cast this element in gender-neutral language, it is perhaps instructive that none of the defendants in succeeding cases has been a stepfather. Second, the plaintiff must show that the defendant breached that duty of care by treating the child plaintiff like dirt in preference either to her own well-being, or to the well-being and advancement of her natural children and herself. <u>Id.</u> at 643. Third, the plaintiff must show that the defendant stepmother's breach of duty was the cause of extreme, often life-threatening danger or disgrace to the plaintiff. <u>Id.</u> Finally, the plaintiff must show he or she was injured, either physically or by reputation.

The instant case appears to be precisely the kind of situation for which the Supreme Court created this cause of action. By marrying Woodsman, Appellant assumed a duty to care for Hansel and Gretel as the children of the marriage. Her constant complaining about the children eroded Woodsman's support and care for his children. In addition, she required the children to do all housework, such as cooking and cleaning, tending to the family's animals, and fetching gallons of water every day for her own luxuriant bath. These onerous burdens of housework she imposed on them clearly demonstrate the breach of that duty. Finally, there is no question that Appellant's actions were at least the proximate cause of Hansel and Gretel being put in mortal danger of being roasted and eaten by the local witch, and that said danger caused physical injuries to the children, including cuts and scrapes from being lost in the woods, and a case of almost morbid obesity in Hansel, whom the witch first tried to fatten for the oven.

Appellant argues that the children were not led into the woods, but instead ran away from home and became lost on their own. The jury was entitled to give greater weight to the testimony of Hansel, Gretel, and Woodsman that the father led the children into the woods at the direction of his wife. Similarly, although Appellant argues that the training she gave them in household tasks is what saved the children by teaching them the rudiments of nutrition, cooking, and housecleaning, the jury instead credited Gretel's testimony that it was her native intelligence that helped her fool the witch for weeks into believing that Hansel was not gaining weight. These findings of fact and determinations of credibility were decisions uniquely within the province of the jury, and we will not overturn them.

For these reasons, we affirm the judgment below.

Dated: August 29, 2008

Justices Goose and Andersen join Chief Justice Grimm in this opinion.

Assume you are representing Cinderella in a suit against her Stepmother in Fairytale Land. The facts of the Cinderella story are provided below in case your recollection of the details is hazy. You have been asked to write a memo to a senior partner at your firm concerning the breach element of the tort of "being evil." The rule you have pulled from the Hansel & Gretel case is:

> Forcing a child to labor around the home as if the child were a servant satisfies the legal definition of a breach in support of the tort of "being evil" as such forced labor amounts to "treating the child . . . like dirt." Hansel & Gretel, 202 F. Rptr. 16, 18 (2008).

1. In free form writing complete the rule explanation paragraph of a memo to the partner you are working with on the case.

2. Now, apply the facts of Cinderella to the rule developed in Snow White and further explained in Hansel & Gretel (Be sure to cite to the cases when you compare them).

3. Draft an outline of the Discussion section of the Memo using both the rule explanation and the rule application ideas you have generated above.

Cinderella (A Refresher)

Once upon a time, a gentleman had a lovely wife who fell ill and died. He later married a woman who was very beautiful, but proud and haughty. She had two daughters, and they were like her in every way. The man had a daughter of his own, and she was without equal in sweetness and goodness. In this, she took after her mother.

The wedding was scarcely over when the stepmother's evil temper erupted. She couldn't bear the girl's good nature, which made her own daughters seem even more hateful. She gave her the dirtiest of the housework. The girl washed the dishes, scrubbed the stairs, and swept her stepmother and stepsisters' rooms. The girl slept in the attic on a dirty mattress while her sisters stayed in rooms with parquet floors, fashionable beds, and mirrors that showed them from head to toe. The poor girl did not complain to her father. He would have scolded her, for he always did what his wife told him.

When her work was done, she would go to the fireplace and sit in the ashes. This is why everyone called her Cinderella. Nonetheless, Cinderella, for all her tattered clothes, was still a hundred times more beautiful than her sisters, no matter how magnificently they dressed.

And it happened that the king's son gave a ball and invited all the finer folks. The stepsisters were invited, for they had quite a reputation around about. The stepsisters were please and delighted because the prince would be choosing a bride. Cinderella also wanted to attend the ball, and she begged her stepmother to give her permission. The stepmother refused saying "You cannot come with us, for you have no proper clothes and cannot dance. You would put us to shame."

At last the happy day arrived. Her stepmother and stepsisters left. Cinderella followed them with her eyes as long as she could. When she could see them no longer, she started to cry.

Instructions:

In this Hansel & Gretel exercise, the first prompt requires the students to practice free form writing. This means that they will write out the explanation of the Rule provided in a stream of consciousness way. The hope is that they will explain that there are four elements to the tort as articulated in the Snow White case and as applied in the Hansel & Gretel case. Specific examples from the Hansel & Gretel case should be used to show how the rule has been applied in the past. For example, the students might point to the finding in Hansel & Gretel that the burden of household tasks can be used – at least in part – to meet the second element of breach of the duty to care by treating children like dirt.

In the second prompt, the students are asked to make direct comparisons between Hansel & Gretel and Cinderella. Direct comparisons can be made for all the elements, and some comparisons may also be able to be drawn to the references to Snow White within the Hansel & Gretel opinion. Again, this prompt allows for a free flow form of writing out the comparisons. Students should be encouraged to generate as many direct comparisons of the facts as possible.

Since the second prompt also asks for citations to the cases being compared, this part of the answer can be used to discuss the appropriate placement of citations in analogical reasoning. Many students do not understand the proper placement of attribution in the context of analysis.

Finally, the students are then asked in the third prompt to commit their free form writing and ideas to an outline. The outline should look something like this:

Discussion

Conclusion: Cinderella is likely to be able to recover against her step-mother under a "tort of being evil" claim because her case is similar to Hansel & Gretel and Snow White.

Rule: The tort of being evil required the satisfaction for four elements: (1) duty of care for the child through marriage; (2) breach of the duty by ill treatment; (3) causation of harm through the breach of the duty; and (4) physical or reputational injury. Snow White v. Wicked Queen, 126 F. Rptr. 639 (2000). Forcing a child to labor around the home as if the child were a servant satisfies the legal definition of a breach in support of the tort of "being evil" as such forced labor amounts to "treating the child . . . like dirt." Hansel & Gretel, 202 F. Rptr. 16, 18 (2008).

Explanation: Excessive household chores, abandonment, and mistreatment in favor of others all constitute breach of the duty of care when a step-parent situation is present. H&G, 202 F. Rptr. at 18. The cases of H&G and Snow White both demonstrate that breach of duty, causation, and injury can exist when a step-parent places a child in danger and demonstrates animosity towards the child. Id.

Application:

Compare Cinderella duty to Hansel & Gretel and Snow White: marriage by step-mother to father of victim in all cases. H&G, 202 F. Rptr. at 18; Snow White, 126 F. Rptr at 642.

Compare breach element: excessive household chores for Cinderella similar to situation in H&G. 202 F. Rptr at 18.

Compare causation: Cinderella's step-mother was engaging in open campaign against her similar to both H&G and Snow White. H&G, 202 F. Rptr. at 19; Snow White, 126 F. Rptr at 643.

Compare injury: While not physically harmed like H&G, Cinderella experience psychic and reputational harm similar to the damage done to Snow White. 196 F. Rptr. at 644.

Conclusion: All elements are likely satisfied and Cinderella should be able to bring a viable claim.

The completed outline should show the students how to transition from the free flow of ideas to an organized CREAC structure if the writing assignment is an objective one.

Outlining exercises can be made more difficult by including synopses and rules from real cases and by making the facts more complicated. A more difficult outlining exercise is provided below, although this is still a beginning exercise and contains a much reduced closed-universe so that the students can focus in on the outlining and analysis skills, as opposed to the research and processing skills that they will also need to develop.

In Class Exercise:

Facts

A Canadian Actor named Hugo Clarke has contacted you about representation in a case in California. Hugo is fairly well known in Canada and has appeared on several television series that only air on Canadian channels. He has also appeared in several U.S.-based movies and T.V. series that were shot in Vancouver (like "The X-files" and "The Highlander"). Hugo lives in Vancouver and is a Canadian citizen.

Over the twenty year span of his acting career, Hugo has tried to secure an agent in Hollywood, but he has never been successful. One reason for his failure to secure an agent or U.S. work has been his inability to obtain a work visa in the U.S. As a result, all of his work on U.S.-funded films has taken place in Vancouver.

Hugo recently auditioned for a commercial by submitting a video-monologue to a website over the internet. The California producers of the commercial thought he would be perfect for the part of the villainess character who steals some coffee from an unsuspecting and very tired mother. The commercial is for a new San Francisco brand of coffee that hopes to push Peet's and Starbucks out of the market. After being emailed a copy of the agreement to accept the part, Hugo placed an electronic signature on the document and emailed it back. There was no forum selection clause in the agreement, and he did not read the fine print which said he was obligated to appear with a work visa in hand to shoot the commercial in San Francisco on a date certain. When Hugo realized that the contract required him to do work in the U.S. he explained to the producers that he had no work visa. They sued him in California.

At this point, Hugo has only received notification of the lawsuit through a copy in the mail. He has not been served or appeared in this case. In fact, he believes that there may be a problem with personal jurisdiction over him in California, so he has simply ignored the lawsuit so far. However, one of his best friends is having a huge 50th Birthday party in L.A. next week. Hugo would like to attend. He has been to California a few times before to visit friends and relatives who live in the state. Hugo is afraid to attend the party for fear that the plaintiffs will serve him with process and he will be forced to defend the breach of contract lawsuit in California. What should he do?

Law[2]

California Long-Arm Statute:

California Code of Civil Procedure § 410.10 - A court of this state may exercise jurisdiction on any basis not inconsistent with the Constitution of this state or of the United States.

Asahi Metal Industrial Co. v. Superior Court, 480 U.S. 102 (1987): "The Due Process Clause of the Fourteenth Amendment limits the power of a state court to exert personal jurisdiction over a nonresident defendant." To comport with due process, the defendant must have "purposefully established 'minimum contacts' in the forum State." Id. (citations omitted). A state may exercise jurisdiction where the defendant purposefully avails himself of the protections and laws of the State or where there is a substantial connection with the State. Id.

International Shoe Co. v. Washington, 326 U.S. 310 (1945): Minimum contacts between the defendant and the forum state are enough to satisfy the due process clause for the assertion of personal jurisdiction. "Minimum contacts" may mean a single act directed to the forum if that act is related to the cause of action being sued on. Id. Alternatively, "minimum contacts" may mean a systematic and continuous relationship with the forum state that is sufficient to establish jurisdiction even for claims unrelated to the contact. Id.

World-Wide Volkswagen Corp. v. Woodson, 444 U.S. 286 (1980): In addition to minimum contacts, assertion of jurisdiction must be reasonable. Id. The reasonableness inquiry requires the court to look at factors such as "the burden on the defendant, the interests of the forum state, . . . the plaintiff's interest, . . . the interstate judicial system's interest in . . . efficient resolution of controversies . . . and [furtherance] of fundamental social policies." Id.

Graduate Management Admissions Council v. Raju, 241 F. Supp. 2d 589 (E.D.Va. 2003): The Zippo test (created in the case Zippo Manuf. Co. v. Zippo Dot Com, Inc., 952 F. Supp. 1119 (W.D.Pa. 1997)) focuses on

---

[2] Synopses of cases pulled from edited versions reported in Steven C. McCaffery & Thomas O. Main, *Transnational Litigation in Comparative Perspective: Theory and Application*, pp. 81-104 (Oxford University Press 2010).

"the nature and the quality of commercial activity that an entity conducts over the Internet." Passive websites don't satisfy the constitutional requirement for personal jurisdiction, but where a defendant is clearly doing business over the Internet and is directing electronic activity into the state with the intention of engaging in business, and someone is harmed as a result of the contact, there may be sufficient contacts to establish personal jurisdiction. Id. While there was not sufficient particularized direction toward the state of Virginia in the GMAC case, the court found an alternate basis in Fed. R. Civ. P. 4(k)(2).

Assignment

1. Outline the Rule you would apply to Hugo Clarke's case relating to personal jurisdiction.

2. List the relevant facts that you would want to include in your analysis.

3. Outline the CREAC or CREACs (if you would use more than one) you would write in the discussion section of a memo about this case.

After the students have drafted an outline for an in-class exercise, I like to have them work together to help them see that different people might view the same problem differently. Peer review exercises can be helpful to the reviewer and the reviewed, but they do need to be carefully monitored and directed. Reading the work of another person and writing "good job" is ineffective for both parties. For an objective outline using the CREAC formula, the following peer editing checklist is helpful to direct the student reviewer and to target some specific areas for feedback.

Outline Peer Edit Comment Sheet

As the reviewer . . .

1. Comment below on the large-scale and small-scale organization of the outline. Your comments should focus on whether the organization is fundamentally sound, whether all essential steps are taken, and whether the steps are in a logical order. (You may write on the outline itself to show how the comments here fit into it.)

   Consider the following:

   - Is the outline divided into appropriate major issues and sub-issues?

   - Does the outline effectively use the CREAC structure?

   - Does the outline reference factual information from the cases that support the predictions?

   - What makes the organization that the student chose logical and complete?

   - If the organization used is not logical or complete, what essential steps or pieces are missing?

   - What alternative organization would you suggest and why?

2. Comment below on one or two specific parts of the outline that need re-thinking or more complete development. These comments should not simply repeat the comments you made in response to Question No. 1. In other words, what can you add that will help the writer draft a better memo?

For example:

- Identify specific steps in the outline where sub-issues, facts, or law are missing

- Identify specific steps that appear to be based on inaccurate or incomplete statements of fact or law

- Make specific suggestions for improvement

Summary Comments

The questions so far have focused on the individual components of the outline. This question requires you to consider the outline as a whole: If the student asked you to identify the three most important things the student could do to improve the outline, how would you respond?

1.

2.

3.

As the Author of the Outline, how will you revise after the review?

Now that you have your own outline returned to you, please answer these questions:

1. Identify any major organizational problems in your own paper.

2. How can you address these organizational problems? Be specific.

3. Identify any major content problems in your own paper.

4. How can you address these content problems? Be specific.

CHAPTER 7

KNOWING YOUR AUDIENCE

■ ■ ■

By Stephanie J. Thompson

The purpose of this chapter is to get students to really think about their audience and how knowing their audience will influence their written work product. Students need to understand that they are not writing for themselves but always for someone else and sometimes for multiple audiences. This chapter introduces students to the different audiences they will write to and the nuances specific to those audiences. Students should be assigned to read this chapter around the time they are working on their first writing assignment and it can be re-assigned for each writing assignment. It is a good idea to develop this concept with them early. Additionally, when discussing the purpose and benefits of knowing one's audience, you may also want to discuss intercultural competence for lawyers in Chapter 3.

The following is an In-Class Exercise that can start the discussion of the concept of knowing your audience:

1. View the 1:48 minute video clip of blind man. If you do not have link, you can find by typing "YouTube Power of Words blind man" into search line.

http://www.youtube.com/watch?v=qIWDHsbUiow

2. Assuming effectiveness of one's message is to have one's audience do what one asks in one's message, would everyone agree that the video seems to show that the second sign was more effective than the first sign. It persuaded more people to help the blind man by donating money.

3. Can anyone explain why the second sign was more effective?

4. Who is the blind man's audience? Is it blind people or is it the sighted community?

a. If his audience is the blind community, stating "I am blind. Please help" would have all kinds of unspoken messages and meanings, perhaps including the heartache of being unable to have meaningful work. Do you have to be blind to understand his message and be compelled to act? No. There are certainly others who are not blind who have insight into what it means to be blind and will be compelled to donate. (This clip may also have a secondary lesson in cultural competence.)

b. The blind man's audience is the sighted community, most of who likely do not know what it means to be blind. When asked by the blind man, "what did you do to my sign, the woman responds, "same message, only different words." The woman's words on the sign speak to the sighted community—her words resonate with those of us who can see and enjoy the beauty of the day. Her words help us to understand and empathize with the blind man and compel us to help him in a way that his words do not.

Another way of asking "Who is my audience?" is "who am I marketing my message to?" Once you identify your audience, the next step then is to create a message that will resonate with that audience that will persuade them to take the action that you seek, to grant the relief you or your client is requesting.

<u>Creating an Audience</u>

One way to have this concept come to life is to create a cast of characters that will be the audience for your students' work throughout the course. This helps take you, the professor, out of the equation. Then, when discussing the assignment in class, you never need to refer to what you want. And, when commenting, you do not need to refer to a generic reader or yourself, but you can refer to the character by name. For example, in my class, the supervising attorney for a memo assignment was named Emily Johnson. Thus, during class I talked about Emily's background and what she would need to know to understand the student's analysis. Then, when commenting, my comments would ask if Emily would understand something or my comments would indicate that a section in their writing needed more depth because Emily does not have a certain level of knowledge of the facts. This forced the students to think of the assignment more like a 'real' assignment to a 'real' audience rather than a school project that is read by a professor.

The cast of characters can be created in several different ways. One way is for you to create them before the school year begins. You know what your assignments will be in advance; thus, you can decide what characters you need and what traits they have. The other way is to let the students create the characters. You can decide how many characters you need (based on the assignments you know the students will have during the course) and then assign each character to groups of students. The students will then get to use their creativity and develop these characters. One year my students even created Facebook pages for their characters.

To start this exercise, have the students brainstorm the list of things they would want to know about a reader. The list of traits that I have used to include: education (levels and where), work experience (type and length), gender, race/national origin, sexual orientation, age, political affiliation, religion (if any), marriage status, children, and where they live and where they are from. This is not an exhaustive list and all of the items do not need to be addressed; it is just a starting point to developing the characters. It is interesting to see the list developed by the students and what they think is relevant. For each trait identified by the students have them explain why they think the trait is relevant.

PRACTICE EXERCISE

The *Practice Exercise* in this chapter provides:

Using the search engine of your choice or one of the sources suggested in this chapter, research a judge in your local jurisdiction or a judge identified by your professor. Make a list of the information that would help you "know your audience" if you were submitting a brief to this judge.

This exercise can begin with the same brainstorming exercise described above. Next, direct the students to possible websites they can use to locate information about judges, arbitrators, and mediators. Here are a few suggestions:

- Federal Judicial Center, Biographical Directory of Federal Judges, 1789—present,
  http://www.fjc.gov/history/home.nsf/page/judges.html (last visited Dec. 2012);
- The Recorder, Judicial Profiles,
  http://www.law.com/jsp/ca/judicial_profiles.jsp (last visited Dec. 2012); ARC Mediation, Mediator Profiles,
  http://www.arcmediation.com/mediator_profiles (last visited Dec. 2012);

- LinkedIn, American Arbitration Association Arbitrators, http://www.linkedin.com/title/arbitrator/at-american-arbitration-association (last visited Dec. 2012);
- JAMS, Neutrals, http://www.jamsadr.com/neutrals-search/ (last visited Dec. 2012);
- American Arbitration Association, Arbitrators & Mediators, http://www.adr.org/aaa/faces/arbitratorsmediators (last visited Dec. 2012).
- Additionally, most state court websites also have judicial profiles available.

Once the students have gathered the relevant information about their judge, re-group as a class and discuss what they found and why knowing that information would be helpful to them in writing to that particular judge.

Chapter 8

Objective Legal Writing

■ ■ ■

By Stephanie J. Thompson

The purpose of this chapter is to introduce students to the concept of objective legal writing and the objective writing paradigm. This chapter should be assigned in advance of the class session that introduces these topics and followed by the chapters on formal memorandums and short-form memorandums (Chs. 9 &10).

Some in-class exercises on how to present objective writing and the objective paradigm are as follows:

1. Introduce objective writing by having a brainstorming session on the broader question of: *what do lawyers do?* Make a list on the board of everything students think a lawyer does. After the list is complete, then explain the difference between objective writing and persuasive writing. Ask the students to identify the type of writing a lawyer might need for each item on the list on the board of the things lawyers do. You can then follow-up this group discussion with a short lecture on the purpose of objective writing and the various types of objective writing (objective memos, correspondence, bench briefs). This can track the materials in the chapter. The discussion here should be focused on both the purpose of an objective document as well the different types of objective documents.

2. The next step is introducing the objective paradigm and its various components. This book uses CREAC, but there are other acronyms that serve essentially the same function. Using an objective paradigm is a hard concept for students to grasp at first because they are used to more free-form writing. They will feel the paradigm is restrictive and controlling. It is a good idea to explain to them that it is merely a structure to help keep them organized and to "write like a lawyer." This can relate back to Chapter 7 Knowing Your Audience and how law-trained readers expect information to be delivered in a specific and familiar organization. This introduction can be done by drawing the paradigm on the board, giving a PowerPoint presentation, or calling on students to explain each part of the paradigm based on their reading of the chapter before class.

3. Giving a visual for the objective paradigm is critical. The students need to "see" the paradigm in action. There are two simple ways to do this. One is to distribute the Discussion section of an objective memo. First, have the students read the memo. Second, as a class, identify the paradigm components and write them in the margins. After this has been done as a full class and the students have "seen" the paradigm, distribute a second Discussion section of an objective memo and have the students, on their own, identify the paradigm components and write them in the margins. Re-group as a class and discuss the paradigm components in that second example. The other approach to having the students "see" the paradigm is to have them turn to a case in one of their casebooks for a non-LRW course. Courts almost always write using the objective paradigm. To be sure, it might be a good idea to pre-select the cases you know are in a casebook that they likely will have with them in class or, instead, bring copies of court opinions to class. The same exercise described above would be used. You can then challenge your students to "see" the objective paradigm in all cases they read for their other classes.

4. Another approach is to have the students organize the paradigm themselves. To do this, take a complete CREAC, cut it into its component parts, and randomly number them. Mix them up and hand them to the students. The students then need to organize the cut-up excerpts into a properly organized CREAC. Review the proper order of the information to ensure the students put the material in proper CREAC organization.

There are several sample memorandums in Chapters 9 and 10 of this Teacher's Manual that can be used for any of the exercises described above. When selecting the memo you will use, be sure to consider whether you want to use a memo that has a single issue (one CREAC) or multiple issues (multiple CREACs).

CHAPTER 9

THE FORMAL MEMORANDUM

■ ■ ■

By Gretchen Franz

The purpose of this chapter is to provide students with the necessary information to write a predictive office memorandum which evaluates the strength and weaknesses of a potential client's case.

In most legal arenas, whether a law firm, government agency, prosecutor's or public defender's office, or corporate in-house legal department, to name a few, attorneys will be presented with legal issues. A common process usually follows: the attorney researches the facts and relevant law to objectively evaluate the case and predict how a court would likely resolve the issue. This information is then memorialized in the Formal Memorandum.

This chapter explains the basic structure and general substance that should be included in the Formal Memorandum. While different legal employers may have unique formatting requirements, the information in this chapter should provide students with a general framework that can be adapted to meet any employer's expectations for a Formal Memorandum.

<u>Preparation for Writing The Formal Memorandum</u>

Prior to assigning this Chapter, students should have read Chapter 4, Rules: An Overview of Statutory Interpretation and Synthesis; Chapter 5, Legal Reasoning & Analysis Toolkit; Chapter 6 The Process of Legal Writing; Chapter 7 Knowing Your Audience; Chapter 8 Objective Legal Writing; and Chapter 22 Research Strategies.

It is very important that students understand the concepts explained in those chapters. Students must be able to read and understand the law, craft rules, explain the law in the most appropriate manner, and employ analogical, deductive (rule-based), and policy reasoning. Unless and until students have focused upon, practiced, and achieved some success implementing these concepts, students will be unable to write a coherent, well-organized, and effectively analyzed predictive Formal Memorandum.

Students can write a Formal Memorandum project prior to learning research. Professors can provide students with a "closed universe" of authorities relevant to the issue presented in the assigning memorandum for the project.

Teaching Methods for The Formal Memorandum

1. Exercise to get Students Thinking

One of the great challenges of teaching students predictive writing, is guiding students to look at an issue from all perspectives and consider how the law could support different arguments. It has been my experience that first year law students have difficulty stepping back from an issue to evaluate it globally. Students seem to latch on to one side of the argument and struggle to grasp the different arguments that result from the flexibility that is inherent in the law.

"Jim and the Luxury Car", is a fun exercise to get students thinking "globally" about an issue. This exercise can be used for predictive and persuasive writing, and challenges students to look at "both sides of the coin." For predictive writing, it helps students to see that there may be two strong arguments. Although students are engaging in persuasive fact presentation, rule-making and argument, the exercise helps students to understand how the facts and law can lend itself to different arguments. This exercise is provided at the end of this chapter.

2. Samples

Provide students with at least one sample Formal Memorandum. Walk through the sample with the students so they become familiar with the components of The Formal Memorandum. Samples are discussed in more detail under 5.a below – Teaching Materials.

3. The "Teaching Memorandum" versus The Graded Formal Memorandum

Professors may wish to teach the components of the Formal Memorandum separately by using a "teaching problem" that is not the same as the problem that students will work with to write the Formal Memorandum which is graded. This can be done by providing students with a memorandum which sets forth a problem which the students will analyze. Professors may choose to provide students with a statute and three or four cases - "a closed universe of authorities." Students work on writing different components of the Formal Memorandum in class using the "teaching problem," and then work on the graded memorandum outside of class.

By doing this, professors can concentrate on the various components of The Formal Memorandum and provide in-class feedback which students can transfer to their graded assignment. For instance, using the "teaching problem", professors can first have students read the fact pattern and brief the cases. During class, students can be assigned groups (it is very helpful to change the groups each class to allow different students to work together and develop relationships). After the group has had time to discuss the cases, the professor can direct a class wide discussion.

For the next class, the professor can instruct the students to craft a Question Presented for the "teaching problem". Again, class time can be used for students to discuss their Questions Presented in groups with the professor then showing examples on a screen and leading a class-wide discussion of the strengths and weaknesses of each example. This process can continue for each of the components of The Formal Memorandum.

Class-time is also well used to conduct peer edits of students' written work. Students exchange their written product - such as the Question Presented for the "Teaching Problem". Once students critique each other's work, they discuss the critique amongst themselves. This is a good opportunity for students to (1) get used to other people reading their written product and (2) to see other students' written work.

4. <u>Multiple Evaluations of The Formal Memorandum</u>

Professors may elect to assign the Question Presented and Discussion sections of The Formal Memorandum as a pass/fail assignment (with or without proper citations). Professors then critique the pass/fail assignment and provide detailed comments as to how the student can improve the re-write of the Memorandum. For the re-write, students include the Brief Answer, Facts, Conclusion and citations, for a grade. This process has worked well for the first year Global Lawyering Skills class at Pacific McGeorge.

5. Materials for Teaching The Formal Memorandum

   a. <u>Samples</u> It is helpful to provide students with examples of the type of written product they are expected to produce. There are two Formal Memoranda at this end of this chapter which can be used as examples, and with the Practice Exercises set forth in Chapter 9. Another sample is provided at the end of Chapter 14. Professors may wish to copy or post these samples for students use with Chapter 9.

   b. <u>Practice Exercises in Chapter 9</u>

      i. Facts, page 86. Have students review one or more sample Formal Memoranda and discuss whether all the Facts used in the Discussion section of the memo are included in the Facts section of that memo.

      ii. CREAC, page 87. Using one or more samples, have students:

      -identify the C, R, E, A, and, C for each issue.

      -identify the different types of rule explanations in each E of the CREAC.

      -identify the different types of analyses used in each A of the CREAC.

      -verify that the rule explanations match with the manner in which the rule is used in the analysis.

   c. <u>The Formal Memorandum Checklist</u>

   An example of The Formal Memorandum Checklist referred to on page 89 of the Global Lawyering Skills book is provided at the end of this chapter. The checklist is a great resource, and teaching tool, for three reasons:

      i. It provides students with a condensed outline of the format and substance expected in the memorandum.

      ii. It can be used for classroom exercises. Professors can have students evaluate sample memoranda, or individual components such as Questions Presented, Brief Answers, etc., and discuss whether the memoranda comply with the guidelines set forth in the checklist as follows:

    iii. Students can use the checklist to proof their own memorandum to ensure it complies with formatting and substantive requirements.

    d. <u>The "'White Glove' Inspection" - Read, Edit, Re-Write ...</u>

Professors should stress to students that good writing requires a lot of time, effort, and attention to detail. The writing process involves revision, revision and revision. Students must start the process early in order to complete the research (if there is no "closed universe" of authorities provided) and allow themselves time to carefully consider the different ways in which the law might apply. Students should be encouraged to write, re-read, edit, re-read, edit, re-read…again, and again…

When students have developed their formal memorandum to a nearly complete product, Chapter 25 The Last Critical Task: The 'White-Glove' Inspection, will prove invaluable. Students should plan to complete their Formal Memorandum a few days prior to the due date. This will allow students to properly "White Glove" their written work to ensure that they are submitting the most professional product possible.

    e. <u>Citations in The Formal Memorandum</u>

Chapter 24 "The Citation Requirement" may be incorporated into the lessons on writing a Predictive Office Memorandum.

For students' first Formal Memorandum, professors may elect to have students omit proper citation format. An abbreviated form can be used and citation format introduced at a later time. By doing this, students can focus on the substance of the memorandum. Citations can be introduced when writing a second Formal Memorandum.

Another approach is to teach citation along with the writing process. An effective way of doing this is to begin with citing statutes and cases. As students progress with their writing, the professor can require that other resources, such as secondary resources, be included, and cited in The Formal Memorandum.

In-Class Exercise: "Jim and the Luxury Car"[3]

Facts for Students

Consider the following:

Jim, a 17-year-old high school junior, wants to borrow his parent's luxury car to take his girlfriend to the junior prom. He is normally allowed to use only the family's "second" car, a beat up old Chevy.

Jim has asked his parents if they will allow him to make his case, and they have agreed to have an open discussion, even though they are not initially disposed to grant his request.

Here is the factual background that exists regarding Jim's request:

- Jim has an older sister and a younger brother. From the time his sister was fifteen, the parents have made it clear to all three children that the only car they would be allowed to drive (unless the parents were present) was the "second" car.

- Jim's sister was allowed to use the luxury car for her senior prom. At the time, she had been driving for two years and had a spotless record (no accidents or citations).

- Jim has been driving for fifteen months. In the first six months, he had four accidents, two of which were clearly his fault. (The other two probably could have been avoided if Jim had been more careful, but the other driver was also negligent.) Jim also received two citations (one for speeding, the other for running a red light) in the first three months. Since those incidents, Jim has had a clean driving record.

- At the time of Jim's last accident, his father told him that he was responsible for his own actions and that the increase in

---

[3] This exercise was originally created by Edward Telfeyan, Pacific McGeorge School of Law.

his insurance rates would come out of his allowance. Jim's father stressed that Jim should expect to be "punished" for bad performance in life, just as he should expect to "rewarded" for good performance.

- o Since that discussion with his father, Jim has come back under the insurance company's "Good Driver Discount." (The company is especially lenient with new drivers.) In addition, Jim now qualifies for a "Good Student Discount," by virtue of his excellent grades in the last year.

- o When Jim first received his license, he asked his mother if he could use the family's luxury car to take his girlfriend on a date. At that time, his mother told him that she did not consider a simple date important enough to justify a departure from the family's rules about use of the family cars.

- o Both of the parent's closest friends have children who are Jim's age. These parents are allowing their children to use the nicer cars that they own. In one family, the child was recently cited for speeding. That child is a marginal student, but is the captain of the football team and is active in the local church. In the other, the child has a clean driving record and is a top student.

- o Jim's parents would concede that they are thrilled with the growth and maturity that Jim has displayed in the last year or so. They are also very fond of his girlfriend.

Professor Instructions for The Formal Memorandum

1. Divide the class into small groups. Groups are assigned to represent Jim or the parents. Since working in small groups provides individual students a better opportunity to participate in the exercise, there can be more than one group representing each side.

2. Distribute the fact pattern.

3. Give students 20-30 minutes to "brainstorm" how precedent in the family, family policy, and custom and practice of family friends support the side the students are assigned to represent.

4. Students can formulate rules regarding precedent, policy, and custom and practice. If the group represents Jim, the rules could be something akin to:

   a. The luxury car can be used for special occasions and the prom is a special occasion.

   b. The parents' policy is to reward good behavior.

   c. The custom of family friends is to allow use of the luxury car to drive to the prom.

   If the group represents the parents, the rules could be something akin to:

   a. The luxury car can only be used for the senior prom when the child has a good driving record and good grades.

   b. Although the parents' policy is to reward good behavior, the child must have a good driving record and good grades for a significant period of time.

   c. Although family friends may allow use of the luxury car to drive to the prom, it is only when the child has a good track record.

5. Students then use the facts to support each rule to craft arguments.

6. The class then reconvenes as a whole, and the professor leads a discussion by calling on each group to present their arguments.

Student Instructions when using exercise for The Formal Memorandum

1. You will be divided into teams of three students each. The teams will be assigned to represent Jim or the parents. If your team represents Jim, you will argue in favor of Jim taking the luxury car to the prom. If you represent the parents, you will argue that Jim should not be allowed to take the luxury car to the prom.

2. Please prepare a short:

   a. Argument. Your argument should focus on three main points:

      i. Precedent

      ii. Policy

      iii. Custom and Practice

   b. Craft rules to support your argument.

   c. Make sure to use the facts to support your argument.

   d. Try to consider and address how the "other" side may argue the facts.

SAMPLE FORMAL LEGAL MEMORANDUM[4]

TO: Senior Attorney
FROM: Law Clerk
RE: Arnold and The Aquarter; Parody Toys; Transformative Test

---

QUESTION PRESENTED

Under the First Amendment, is Parody Toys entitled to protection against a right of publicity claim based on the transformative test when its product, "the Aquarter," includes a cartoon-like image of Governor Schwarzenegger wearing a sash that says "Governor," holding up an image of then-Governor Gray Davis by the neck, and standing in front of the California State Capitol with the phrase "The Total Recall" above them?

BRIEF ANSWER

Probably yes. When creative elements predominate a work, the unauthorized use of a celebrity's identity will not be actionable. A work is entitled to First Amendment protection when it adds sufficient transformative elements such that it is more than a literal or conventional depiction of the celebrity. It is likely that the cartoon-like image and conduct of Governor Schwarzenegger on "the Aquarter" is sufficient to transform his image to parody which is beyond a literal or conventional depiction warranting First Amendment protection.

FACTS

During the California gubernatorial recall election of Gray Davis, Parody Toys manufactured and sold "the Aquarter." The Aquarter is the same size as a real quarter, feels like a real quarter, and the "heads" side looks like a real quarter. The "tails" side of the Aquarter has an image of Mr. Schwarzenegger wearing a sash that says "Governor" and holding up an image of then Governor Gray Davis by the neck with the phrase "The Total Recall" above them. The images are standing in front of a likeness of the California State Capitol building. The images are not drawn to scale.

---

[4] Adapted from Sample Memorandum prepared by Stephanie Thompson, Assistant Director of Global Lawyering Skills, Pacific McGeorge School of Law.

Parody Toys recently received a letter from Mr. Schwarzenegger's attorney demanding Parody Toys immediately cease and desist from the production, advertising, marketing, promotion, and sale of the Aquarter. Parody Toys seeks advice as to the merits of the demands of Mr. Schwarzenegger's attorney. This memo specifically addresses whether Parody Toys' product, the Aquarter, is protected under the First Amendment.

DISCUSSION

Parody Toys' First Amendment rights probably outweigh Mr. Schwarzenegger's right of publicity. A work is entitled to First Amendment protection when it "adds significant creative elements so as to be transformed into something more than a mere celebrity likeness or imitation" and does not take away from the celebrity's right of publicity. Comedy III Prods. Inc. v. Gary Saderup Inc., 25 Cal. 4th 387, 391 (2001); Winter v. D.C. Comics, 30 Cal. 4th 881, 885 (2003). This is known as the "transformative test." Id. The court developed this balancing test to resolve the conflict between the right of publicity and First Amendment rights. Comedy III, 25 Cal. 4th at 404. The transformative test considers "whether the new work merely supersedes the objects of the original creation, or instead adds something new, with a further purpose or different character" beyond a literal or conventional depiction of the celebrity. Comedy III, 25 Cal. 4th at 391; Winter, 30 Cal. 4th at 885.

A work is protected by the First Amendment only if it contains "significant transformative elements." Id. In Winter, the court determined whether D.C. Comics' unauthorized use of the Winter Brothers' likeness in its comic book had sufficient transformative elements to protect it under the transformative test. 30 Cal. 4th at 882. D.C. Comics published a comic book miniseries containing an outlandish plot involving worm-like creatures and singing cowboys. Three characters in the comic book, called the "Autumn brothers," parodied some well-known musicians, the Winter Brothers. The "Autumn brothers" were half-worm and half-human creatures with features resembling the Winter Brothers. Id. The court held that the comic books contained creative elements that transformed the Winter Brothers beyond a literal or conventional depiction. Id. at 889.

Specifically, the court reasoned that it was readily observable from the facts that the comic book characters were not literal depictions of the Winter Brothers, but were "distorted for purposes of lampoon, parody, or caricature." Id. at 890. It further reasoned that the depictions of the Winter Brothers were "but cartoon characters . . . in a larger story, which itself [was] quite expressive," such that the Winter Brothers were "only part of the raw materials from which the comic books were synthesized." Id. For these reasons, the court held the comic books had sufficient transformative elements to protect them under the First Amendment. Id.

A work is not protected by the First Amendment, however, if it does not contain "significant transformative elements." Comedy III, 25 Cal. 4th at 391. In Comedy III, the court determined whether The Three Stooges' right of publicity had been violated when an artist created an original charcoal drawing of the trio, produced the image on t-shirts and lithographic prints, and, without consent, sold the t-shirts and lithographs for profit. Id. at 392. The court held that the image of The Three Stooges violated the Three Stooges' right of publicity. It explained that the image was an actual depiction of The Three Stooges and the court could "discern no significant transformative or creative contribution" to the drawing; it was merely a "literal, conventional depiction" of The Three Stooges. Id. at 394. The court found that when literal and imitative elements predominate in the work, a defendant cannot pass the transformative test. Id. It reasoned that the right of publicity essentially is an economic right. Id. When artistic expression takes the form of literal depiction or imitation of a celebrity for commercial gain, the interest in protecting the celebrity outweighs the expressive interest of the imitative artist. Id. at 405. In this case, the court found that the artist's literal and conventional depiction of The Three Stooges was done to exploit their fame. Id. at 409.

To determine whether Parody Toys is entitled to a First Amendment defense, the key inquiry is whether there are significant creative elements on the Aquarter for it to be more than a literal or conventional depiction of Mr. Schwarzenegger. Because the Aquarter contains more than a literal or conventional depiction of Mr. Schwarzenegger, it probably warrants First Amendment protection under the transformative test.

The image of Mr. Schwarzenegger on the Aquarter is probably not a literal depiction. The depiction of Mr. Schwarzenegger on the Aquarter goes beyond the literal depiction in Comedy III. Unlike the literal drawing of The Three Stooges sold on t-shirts and lithographs in Comedy III, the Aquarter, in contrast, did not use a literal depiction of Mr. Schwarzenegger. 25 Cal. 4th at 394. Specifically, the image on the Aquarter shows an inhuman and almost cartoon-like sized disparity between Mr. Schwarzenegger and the image of Gray Davis and between Mr. Schwarzenegger and the California State Capitol. It also has Mr. Schwarzenegger strangling Mr. Davis and wearing a "Miss America" style sash that says "Governor." These are not literal depictions of Mr. Schwarzenegger. Instead, the depiction of Mr. Schwarzenegger on the Aquarter more closely resembles the distortion of the Winter Brothers in the comic book series. Both transformed the identity of the celebrities. In Winter, the Winter Brothers were called the "Autumn brothers" and were half-human and half-worm creatures with features resembling the Winter Brothers. 30 Cal. 4th at 882. The court reasoned that because of the distortion of the Winter Brothers' images for "purposes of lampoon, parody, or caricature," they were not literal depictions. Id. at 889. Here, Mr. Schwarzenegger's image also was distorted, showing him as an inhuman and almost cartoon-like sized figure strangling another person wearing a "Miss America" style sash, such that he too was distorted for "purposes of lampoon, parody, or caricature." For these reasons, the image of Mr. Schwarzenegger on the Aquarter is probably not a literal depiction.

The image of Mr. Schwarzenegger on the Aquarter probably contains "significant transformative elements" because it is part of a larger story. Like the comic books in Winter where the depictions of the Winter Brothers were part of a larger expressive story, id. at 890, the image of Mr. Schwarzenegger on the Aquarter is part of a larger expressive story, including the California State Capitol, Gray Davis, the "Governor" sash, and the phrase "The Total Recall," all designed to parody the California recall election. As such, the use of Mr. Schwarzenegger's image is only "part of the raw materials from which the product is synthesized," as were the images of the Winter Brothers in Winter. Id.

For these reasons, the image of Mr. Schwarzenegger on the Aquarter is probably more than a literal or conventional depiction of Mr. Schwarzenegger.

CONCLUSION

Parody Toys' use of Mr. Schwarzenegger's image on the Aquarter probably contains sufficient transformative elements such that it warrants First Amendment protection. When creative elements predominate a work, the unauthorized use of a celebrity's identity will not be actionable. Instead, when a work adds sufficient transformative elements such that it is more than a literal or conventional depiction of the celebrity, it is entitled to First Amendment protection. It is probable that "the Aquarter," parodying the California recall election with a cartoon-like image of Governor Schwarzenegger wearing a sash that says "Governor," holding up an image of then-Governor Gray Davis by the neck standing in front of the California State Capitol with the phrase "The Total Recall" above them, is sufficient to transform Governor Schwarzenegger's image beyond a literal or conventional depiction. For these reasons, Parody Toys' "the Aquarter" is entitled to First Amendment protection against Governor Schwarzenegger's right of publicity claim.

SAMPLE OFFICE MEMORANDUM

TO: Supervising Attorney
FROM: Student Submission
RE: Joanne Hunter: Drunk Driving & Moral Turpitude

QUESTIONS PRESENTED

1. Under the California statutory code prohibiting driving under the influence, does Hunter's conduct violate the drunk driving statute, when she was arrested for sitting in her legally parked vehicle while intoxicated, listening and dancing to music with the engine off and key turned only to auxiliary?

2. Under the California rules governing attorney discipline, does Hunter's conduct establish moral turpitude per se, when she was arrested for driving under the influence because she is an attorney?

BRIEF ANSWERS

1. Probably no. An individual who drives a vehicle while intoxicated may be arrested for driving under the influence only when there is evidence showing the driver asserted a sufficient degree of control over the vehicle causing a volitional movement. The movement must be directly witnessed by an officer or established through circumstantial evidence. There is not any direct evidence of a volitional movement because Hunter was not asserting control over the vehicle in the officer's presence. The engine was off and the parking break was engaged so it would have been impossible for the officer to directly witness any vehicular movement forward. Additionally, there is not circumstantial evidence to prove movement occurred because Hunter's vehicle was legally parked in a neighborhood, the engine was off, and Hunter was sitting in the vehicle for the sole purpose of listening to music with a friend. Therefore, there is not any direct or circumstantial evidence proving Hunter was driving so her conduct does not violate the drunk driving statute.

2. No. A drunk driving conviction does not establish moral turpitude per se under the California rules governing attorney discipline. Therefore, Hunter cannot be punished for her conduct as an attorney because a drunk driving conviction does not establish moral turpitude per se.

FACTS

Joanne Hunter is an attorney who was arrested by a police officer for driving under the influence on September 1, 2012. Hunter is currently working with a public defender to challenge the arrest because she does not believe her conduct of sitting in her car while intoxicated and listening to music constituted driving. Furthermore, the California State Bar seeks to punish her conduct as moral turpitude by suspending her license for twenty-four months, placing her on five years of probation, and requiring her to attend a thirty-day outpatient alcoholism program. Hunter seeks to reach a reasonable agreement with the State Bar regarding punishment for her conduct during her upcoming adversary proceeding with the State Bar Court.

On the night of the arrest, Hunter was attending a house party in a residential neighborhood. Upon arrival, Hunter legally parked her car next to the curb on the street. While attending the party, Hunter wanted to share a song with a friend and suggested they listen to the song inside her car. After situating herself in the driver's seat, Hunter turned the key to auxiliary. Never starting the engine or disengaging the parking brake, Hunter and her friend listened and danced to the song. Hunter proceeded to tap her foot on the brake pedal causing the brake lights to flash.

An officer approached the vehicle after seeing the flashing brake lights and the vehicle "moving." Hunter explained that her vehicle was only rocking, not moving, due to their dancing so the officer checked the hood to see if it was warm, but admitted it was not. After Hunter proceeded to stumble out of her car, the officer subjected her to a breathalyzer test, in which she blew a 0.12 percent blood-alcohol level. The officer then arrested her for driving under the influence.

Hunter asserts that her drunk driving arrest was unlawful because she does not believe sitting in a vehicle while intoxicated constitutes driving. Therefore, Hunter would like to challenge her drunk driving arrest and work out an agreement with the State Bar regarding punishment for her conduct.

DISCUSSION

Hunter's arrest for driving under the influence most likely does not violate the drunk driving statute nor does her conduct establish moral turpitude per se. An individual who drives a vehicle while intoxicated can be arrested for driving under the influence but cannot be punished for moral turpitude per se if she is an attorney. Cal. Vehicle Code § 23152 (West 2012); In re Kelley, 52 Cal. 3d 487, 494 (1990). It is illegal to drive a motorized vehicle while intoxicated if a person has .08 percent or more, by weight, of alcohol in her blood. Veh. Code § 23152. In California, driving requires an individual to actively assert a sufficient degree of control over the vehicle causing a volitional movement. Mercer v. Dep't of Motor Vehicles, 53 Cal. 3d 753, 768 (1991); Henslee v. Dep't of Motor Vehicles, 168 Cal. App. 3d 445, 451-452 (6th Dist., 1985). For an individual to be lawfully arrested an officer must witness a volitional movement. However, for a valid conviction, circumstantial evidence can be used to prove movement occurred. Mercer, 53 Cal. 3d at 769; People v. Wilson, 176 Cal. App. 3d Supp. 1, 9 (1985). If an attorney is convicted for drunk driving, her conduct does not constitute moral turpitude per se. Kelley, 52 Cal. 3d at 494.

I. Hunter should not be convicted for drunk driving because although she was intoxicated, there is not any direct or circumstantial evidence to establish she was driving by causing a volitional movement of her vehicle.

Hunter must have been both intoxicated and driving for her conduct to violate section California Vehicle Code Section 23512. To establish the element of "driving," an officer must directly witness a volitional movement of the vehicle to make a lawful arrest or he must use circumstantial evidence of a volitional movement to sustain a drunk driving conviction. Mercer, 53 Cal. 3d at 762, 769; Wilson, 176 Cal. App. 3d Supp. at 9. In determining whether Hunter's actions constitute drunk driving, this memorandum will address whether (1) she was intoxicated, (2) there was direct evidence of her driving, and (3) there was substantial circumstantial evidence to establish she was driving.

    A. Hunter was intoxicated because her blood-alcohol level was over the legal limit.

Hunter was intoxicated under Vehicle Code Section 23512. An individual is considered intoxicated if she has .08 percent of alcohol in her blood. Veh. Code § 23152. When subjected to a breathalyzer test, Hunter blew .12, higher than the .08 limit. Therefore, Hunter was intoxicated under the drunk driving statute.

B. <u>Hunter was not lawfully arrested for drunk driving because there is not any direct evidence of her driving.</u>

The element of driving cannot be established for a lawful arrest where the officer does not directly witness a volitional movement. <u>Mercer</u>, 53 Cal. 3d at 769. A volitional movement occurs when an individual actively asserts a sufficient degree of control over the vehicle, taking every necessary step to resume travel, and causing a slight vehicular movement to occur in which the vehicle moves forward at least a few inches. <u>Henslee</u>, 168 Cal. App. 3d at 452 (holding there was direct evidence of a volitional movement established in the officer's presence because Defendant placed the vehicle's transmission in drive causing the vehicle to move forward several inches). There is not any direct evidence of a volitional movement when an officer does not witness an individual asserting a sufficient degree of control over her vehicle causing a slight vehicular movement. <u>Mercer</u>, 53 Cal. 3d at 769 (holding there was no direct evidence of a volitional movement because the officer found Defendant sleeping in his legally parked car and never witnessed a movement of the vehicle).

While the officer did see Hunter's vehicle rocking, the engine was not running, the parking brake was still engaged, and the car was not in gear. Thus, she could not cause a volitional movement nor was she taking every necessary step to resume travel. Therefore, it was not possible for the officer to have directly witnessed a volitional movement because Hunter did not cause a forward movement of the vehicle in his presence. Hence, because there was not any direct evidence of a volitional movement, she was not lawfully arrested for drunk driving.

C. <u>Hunter should not be convicted for drunk driving because there is not substantial circumstantial evidence to establish she was driving.</u>

There is probably not substantial circumstantial evidence to establish Hunter had been driving so she should not be convicted for drunk driving. Circumstantial evidence may be used to convict an individual for drunk driving when there is substantial evidence allowing a reasonable person to infer a volitional movement occurred while the driver was intoxicated. <u>Wilson</u>, 176 Cal. App. 3d Supp. at 7. The combination of circumstances, such as the location of the vehicle, status of the engine, and position of the driver while being the sole occupant in the vehicle, can show the intoxicated driver placed herself in that position by driving her vehicle to the place she was found. <u>Id.</u> For example, in <u>Wilson</u>, there was sufficient evidence to establish a volitional movement had occurred: Defendant's vehicle was illegally parked on the highway shoulder with the rear portion of the vehicle partially obstructing a lane. Id. at 3. The officer approached Defendant's vehicle, noticed the engine running, headlights on, and Defendant sleeping behind the steering wheel alone in his vehicle. Id. After Defendant performed poorly on sobriety tests, the officer concluded that Defendant was intoxicated and inferred he had recently caused a volitional movement of his vehicle. Id. at 4. The court ruled that Defendant was lawfully convicted for drunk driving after Defendant challenged his drunk driving arrest. Id. at 7. The court reasoned that due to the combination of circumstances, including the location of the vehicle, status of the engine, position of the driver, and the driver's sole occupancy in the vehicle, there was substantial evidence to infer the vehicle could have only been in that location from Defendant previously driving the vehicle. Id. Thus, the court held that Defendant was lawfully convicted for drunk driving based on substantial circumstantial evidence. Id.

Hunter's actions most likely do not constitute driving because there is not substantial circumstantial evidence to infer a volitional movement based on the location of her vehicle, status of the engine, and her position in the vehicle with a passenger next to her. Hunter's case is distinguishable from Wilson based on the lack of circumstantial evidence. In Hunter's case, her vehicle was legally parked on the street when the officer approached. She and a friend were listening and dancing to music while sitting in her vehicle. The engine was off, the parking brake was engaged, the car was in park, and the hood was not warm so it is not known when her vehicle materialized at that particular location.

Hunter's case is distinguishable from Wilson where there was substantial circumstantial evidence to infer volitional movement and sustain a drunk driving conviction. Defendant was sleeping behind the wheel of his illegally parked vehicle that was protruding into a highway lane, with the headlights on, and the engine running. Id. at 3. The officer concluded that Defendant could have only gotten his vehicle to that location by driving. Id. at 8. This circumstantial evidence in this case is distinguishable from the circumstantial evidence Hunter's case for four reasons. First, the location of the vehicle- Wilson's vehicle was illegally parked on a highway whereas Hunter's vehicle was legally parked on a street. Id. at 3. Second, the status of the engine- Wilson's engine was running while Hunter's engine had not been started and it was not warm, indicating that it had not recently been running. Id. Third, the position of the driver- Wilson was sleeping behind the wheel whereas Hunter was awake and dancing to music. Id. Fourth, the presence of a passenger- Wilson was the sole occupant while Hunter was accompanied. Id. at 8.

Thus, Hunter should not be convicted for drunk driving due to the lack of circumstantial evidence necessary to make an inference of a volitional movement. The circumstances regarding the location of the vehicle, status of the engine, and position of the driver does not indicate that there was intoxicated driving. Id. at 7. Because Hunter's vehicle was legally parked, both Hunter and her friend were dancing in the front seat, and the engine was off, in park, the parking brake was engaged, and the engine, the officer could not make a reasonable inference that a volitional movement had recently occurred. Therefore, Hunter's actions do not constitute driving so she should not be convicted for drunk driving.

II. Hunter's conduct does not establish moral turpitude per se because driving under the influence is not punishable behavior by the State Bar.

Hunter's conduct does not establish moral turpitude per se. "Convictions for drunk driving do not per se establish moral turpitude" for purposes of attorney discipline. Kelley, 52 Cal. 3d at 494; Cal Bus. & Prof. Code § 6101 (West 2012). Because driving under the influence is not moral turpitude per se and Hunter is an attorney who was arrested for driving under the influence, she cannot be punished by the State Bar for moral turpitude per se.

CONCLUSION

Hunter most likely cannot be convicted for drunk driving or punished for moral turpitude per se. Under the California statutory code prohibiting driving under the influence, it is illegal for an individual to drive a motorized vehicle while intoxicated. Driving requires an individual to assert a sufficient degree of control over her vehicle causing a volitional movement. There must be direct or circumstantial evidence to show the driver caused a volitional movement while intoxicated. In this case, although Hunter was intoxicated, there is no evidence to establish she was driving. There is not any direct evidence because the engine was off and the parking brake was engaged so the officer could not have witnessed a volitional movement. There is not substantial circumstantial evidence to show Hunter was driving because the officer could not reasonably infer when Hunter's vehicle materialized at that particular location. Hunter was sitting in her legally parked with a friend and the engine was off. For these reasons, Hunter likely cannot be convicted for drunk driving so she should be advised to continue challenging her arrest.

Additionally, Hunter's conduct does not establish moral turpitude per se. As an attorney, the State Bar cannot punish Hunter because convictions for drunk driving do not establish moral turpitude. Therefore, Hunter should be advised that her conduct does not establish moral turpitude per se and she should use this rule of law against the State Bar in her upcoming adversarial proceeding.

FORMAL MEMORANDUM EDITING CHECKLIST[5]

1. **<u>Entire Memorandum</u>**

    ☐ Locate the following section headings and put a check next to them (NOTE: all of these categories may not be required for all assignments – check the assignment instructions):

    - Question(s) Presented (does it need to be plural?)

    - Brief Answer(s) (does it need to be it plural?)

    - Facts

    - Discussion

    - Conclusion

    ☐ Are all of the section headings:

    - In ALL CAPS

    - Centered on the page

    - <u>Underlined</u>

2. **<u>Questions Presented</u>**

    ☐ For each Question Presented, identify and label the 3 <u>substantive</u> components (these components are the same for the Under-Does-When QP or the Narrative Question Presented):

    - The relevant facts

    - Summary of the relevant law

    - The legal question(s) to be addressed

---

[5] Adapted from Objective Legal Writing Memorandum Checklist prepared by Stephanie Thompson, Assistant Director of Global Lawyering Skills at Pacific McGeorge School of Law.

☐ For each Question Presented, confirm the <u>technical</u> requirements are met:

For the Under-Does-When Question Presented

- It is only one sentence
- It ends with a question mark
- It follows the under-does-when formula
- Uses the words "under," "does," and "when" or the equivalents

For the Narrative Question Presented:

- It is more than one sentence
- It is no more than 100 words
- The last sentence ends with a question mark

3. **Brief Answer**

☐ For each Brief Answer, identify and label the 3 <u>substantive</u> components (these components are the same whether the Question Presented is in the Under-Does-When or Narrative format)

- The short statement of the answer (<u>only</u> can be Yes, Probably Yes, No, or Probably No/Not)
- Summary of the relevant law
- Summary of the reasoning

☐ For each Brief Answer, confirm the <u>technical requirements</u> are met (if any are not met, make a note to fix it):

- There is a Brief Answer for each Question Presented
- The Brief Answer answers the Question Presented and includes the "because"

- The short statement of the answer is its own sentence with a period at the end

- The organization of the Brief Answer matches the organization of the Discussion section

4. **Facts**

☐ Locate the <u>first paragraph</u>. Locate and CIRCLE the following information:

- The parties and the client

- The client's problem or goal

- The general time and location of events

- Any procedural history or status of the case [this could be in the last paragraph instead]

☐ Locate the <u>legally significant</u> <u>facts</u>:

- Turn to the Discussion section and highlight all the facts that relate to the client's case

- Turn back to the Facts section and make sure that all of the facts just highlighted in the Discussion section are included in the Facts section. If any are missing, make a note to fix it

- Now, highlight the facts used in the Discussion section in the Facts section as well. If there are facts that are not highlighted in the Facts section, look at the <u>background facts</u> section below.

☐ Locate the <u>background</u> <u>facts</u>:

- Turn to the Facts section

- Read all facts that are not highlighted – highlight them in a different color

- Evaluate whether they are necessary background facts by asking:

- Why are they included?
- Are they necessary to support the relevant facts?
  - If yes, keep them
  - If not, delete them

☐ Locate the <u>last paragraph</u>. Identify and label the following information:

- Closure to the Fact section – a sentence or phrase at the end of the Facts section to prevent the Fact section from ending abruptly, such as the procedural stance of the case or the client's problem or goal

☐ Identify the type of <u>organization</u> used – chronological, topical, combination

- Read the Fact section looking only at organization
- Identify the type of organization used
- Write the type of organization next to the FACTS section heading

☐ Turn to the facts/case file provided in the assignment packet

- In those documents, highlight all facts used from those documents in the Facts section
- Compare the highlighted facts in the assignment packet to the facts in the Facts section and ask the following questions:
  - Are the facts accurately stated?
  - Are the facts described in a neutral tone?
- Go back to the facts provided for the assignment
  - Review the facts that are NOT highlighted

- Evaluate why these facts were not included in the Facts section and whether they should be included

5. **Discussion**

    - **Umbrella**

        ☐ Locate each umbrella in the memo

        ☐ Read it and identify the following (if any of these are missing, make a note to fix it)

        - The statutory rule or rules or synthesized common law rule or rules

        - The purpose or policy of those rules

        - A quick definition of those rules

        - Any part of the rules that will not be discussed and a quick explanation as to why it will not be discussed

        - A organization sentence describing how the analysis is structured

        - A statement of the overall conclusion of the section the roadmap precedes

        - A brief statement of the reasons for that conclusion (only if it can be done succinctly)

        The flow of information should be presented with the big rules or legal concepts first working down to the specific legal issues the memo is addressing

- **Predictive Point Headings and Sub-headings** (NOTE: this may not be required for all assignments – check the assignment instructions)

☐ Locate each heading and sub-heading in your memo

☐ For <u>each</u> heading and sub-heading, check the <u>substantive</u> compliance:

- Read the section the heading or sub-heading represents and CIRCLE key legal terms
  - Check to see that those legal terms are included in the heading or sub-heading.

- Read the section the heading or sub-heading represents and <u>underline</u> the key facts used in that section
  - Check to see that those key facts are included in the heading or sub-heading.

- Read the heading and <u>label</u> each part of the heading formula:
  - The legal prediction
  - Because or because equivalent
  - The part of the rule justifying the legal conclusion
  - The key relevant fact(s)

- **Rule Explanations**

☐ Locate rule explanations

☐ Determine whether the explanation is sufficient – i.e. if the explanation is used for analogical reasoning, it must be an in-text rule explanation; if the explanation is only to provide examples, it should be a parenthetical explanation.

- **Analysis/Application**

    ☐   Locate the analysis/application paragraph

    ☐   If the analysis is rule based, identify and label each component:

    - A rule of law

    - The predictive conclusion reached by the application of the rule of law

    - The relevant facts from the client's case needed to justify that result

    ☐   If the analysis is based on policy, identify and label each component:

    - Thesis sentence that makes a prediction about the issue

    - Statement of the rule that is the basis of the policy-based reasoning

    - The relevant policy or purpose for the rule the paragraph will apply and cite to the relevant authority

    - The legally relevant facts from the client's case

    - Connection between the legally relevant facts from the client's case and the policy (Statement of whether the underlying policy or purpose does or does not apply to the client's possible outcome(s))

    - Explanation of how or why the possible outcome(s) for the client will or will not further the underlying policy or purpose of the rule

    ☐   If the analysis is based on analogical reasoning, identify and label each component:

- A thesis sentence that makes a prediction about the case that is topic-focused, rather than case-focused

- Statement that the precedent case(s) and the client's case are similar or different

- Specific facts from the precedent case(s)

- Specific facts from the client's case

- Clear discussion as to *why* the facts are similar or different

- Clear discussion as to *why* the comparison/distinction is <u>legally</u> <u>significant</u> (this is where the reasoning from the precedent case is applied directly to the facts of the client's case)

- Conclusion that closes the discussion

- **Conclusions at the end of each section** (NOTE: this does not apply to a single CREAC memo; only multi-CREAC issues)

☐ Locate the last sentence at the end of each section (it should be the last sentence prior to the heading for the next section or the big CONCLUSION at the end of a memo)

☐ Read the last sentence of the section. Is it the last C in a CREAC?

- If there is only 1 CREAC, this is okay

- If there is more than one CREAC, then there needs to be a separate conclusion sentence to sum up the multiple CREACs before moving onto the next section

6. <u>Conclusion</u>

☐ Read the overall CONCLUSION at the end of the memo:

- Does it provide the conclusion on each issue addressed in the memo?

- Does it provide overall advice or a prediction of the client's situation.

- Does the organization of the CONCLUSION track the organization of the Discussion section? Does the section summarize the analysis in the A section or sections? Does it omit any new information?

Chapter 10

The Short-Form Memorandum

■ ■ ■

By Hether C. Macfarlane

The purposes of this chapter are to introduce students to the evolving use of shorter memoranda in law practice, the use of parenthetical explanations of the law, and some information about using email as a medium of conveying legal analysis to lawyers and clients. The chapter should be assigned once you believe your students have a solid understanding of objective writing and the traditional office memorandum. The discussion of parenthetical explanations is also appropriate, of course, as part of the later discussion of persuasive writing in Chapter 14.

The most difficult part of this chapter may be convincing your students that they did not waste their time in learning the traditional format for an objective memorandum of law. The first paragraph of the chapter is designed to address this issue.

Choosing which sections of a traditional memo to include in a short-form memo depends largely on what you think your students need more practice on at this point in the semester or year. For example, if you believe your students need additional practice in writing a Question Presented, by all means have them do it again in this assignment. On the other hand, if you believe they have mastered the skill of framing that kind of issue, you can eliminate that section and have them start the memo with something like, "You have asked me to research X."

Many students will need practice shortening their full case illustrations, particularly after the earlier emphasis on including all the necessary parts as completely as necessary. The chapter includes one example of "before" and "after." It will probably be easiest for the students to work with a case or cases with which they are already familiar. They can rewrite their own prior case illustrations to shorten them, or they can work on a sample case illustration you provide.

Writing a good explanatory parenthetical is a skill that takes a great deal of practice to master. Again, after looking at the example and reading the text, the students can work on writing a rule and a parenthetical for a case with which they are already familiar. Alternately, of course, they can read a short case or a created-case, extract the relevant rule, and then write the accompanying parenthetical.

Ultimately, you can have them shorten a memo they have already handed in for a grade by editing the case illustrations and converting some of them into rule statements with parenthetical explanations. Or, you can simply assign a new memo and have them turn in a short-form memorandum for a grade or as the first draft of a graded memorandum.

If you choose to have them draft an email analysis, be sure to pick a topic with a very clear answer whose analysis and recommendation or conclusion can fit on a single computer screen. For example, you can have them research what a person must do to legally change his or her name in your state. For California, the applicable statute is in the Civil Procedure Code §§ 1275-1279.5, in particular § 1276.

We have included several examples of short-form memos. All of them were written by our students, but we have combined the work of different authors in each sample. We did not, however, correct errors other than typographical ones. Because the short-form memo is assigned after the students have practiced the longer format, our short-form memos usually involve more sophisticated or complex problems. These examples may not look particularly short, but they are considerably shorter than they would be if they were written in the longer format.

Note that the first sample, "Smith County v. Steven Hydekov," uses the narrative question presented. The second sample, "Valenzuela Move-Away Case," uses the "under, does, when" format. And the third sample, "Claim of sexual harassment of wholly-owned subsidiary of a Japanese corporation," dispense with both the Question Presented and a Facts section, replacing them with an "Executive Summary."

OFFICE MEMORANDUM

TO: Supervising Attorney
FROM: Legal Intern
DATE: February 19, 2012
RE: Smith County v. Steven Hydekov; Case No. 11-0615

QUESTIONS PRESENTED

1. The Fourth Amendment protects a person from unreasonable searches and seizures that are not supported by an articulable suspicion. While a passenger in a vehicle that was involved in a traffic stop, Hydekov was arrested on an outstanding warrant and possession of marijuana following a warrant search for suspected underage drinking. Will Hydekov's motion to suppress the evidence of possession of marijuana obtained pursuant to his arrest succeed?

2. Article thirty-six of the Vienna Convention on Consular Relations (VCCR) ensures that a foreign national who has been arrested may contact his embassy. After Hydekov was arrested, he acknowledged that he understood the standard Miranda rights, including his right to not incriminate himself, and then informed the arresting officer he is a Russian national. Will a motion to suppress incriminating statements he made prior to contacting his embassy succeed?

DISCUSSION

Hydekov will likely succeed in his motion to suppress evidence and dismiss the charges against him for possession. In State v. Worwood, the court held that evidence should be excluded which was obtained by violating an individual's constitutional rights, and when there is a connection between the violation and the evidence. State v. Worwood, 2007 UT 41, ¶¶ 42-44. To establish the grounds for a motion to suppress, this analysis will focus on whether Hydekov's rights were violated when he was searched and arrested by the Utah Highway Patrol. Hydekov's rights under the Fourth Amendment will be analyzed first, and then his rights under article thirty-six of the VCCR.

I. **Extending a search to Hydekov as a passenger is reasonable, but the warrant check is unreasonable because the search should have been limited to investigating underage drinking, and a warrant search is not necessary to check Hydekov's age.**

This analysis will focus on whether Hydekov's rights were violated under the Fourth Amendment. The Fourth Amendment ensures "[t]he right of the people to be secure in their persons, . . . against unreasonable searches and seizures, shall not be violated, and no warrants shall issue, but upon probable cause, . . . particularly describing the place to be searched, and the persons or things to be seized." U.S. Const. amend. IV. First, the court will probably find that when Officer Hand suspected underage drinking, his search was properly extended to Hydekov who was only a passenger in the vehicle. However, the court will most likely find that the warrant check on Hydekov was unreasonable because it was not needed to ascertain whether Hydekov was under the legal drinking age.

A. The court will likely find that extending the search to Hydekov was supported by an articulable suspicion because the officer smelled alcohol and had a reasonable suspicion that the occupants of the vehicle could be under the age twenty-one.

The court will probably find that Officer Hand had an articulable suspicion of underage drinking which supported his investigation into the ages of the vehicle's occupants, and it is reasonable to extend the search to Hydekov. The search and seizure of a vehicle passenger should be reasonably connected to the original scope of the traffic stop with an articulable suspicion of criminal activity. State v. Johnson, 805 P.2d 761 (Utah 1991). Investigation of the criminal activity may be expanded beyond the original purpose of a traffic stop if objective information is obtained supporting the suspicion of the criminal activity. United States v. Kitchell, 653 F.3d 1206 (10th Cir. 2011) (holding that inconsistent statements from the occupants of a vehicle to a Utah State Trooper gave rise to a reasonable suspicion of criminal activity, and further detention was reasonable).

A police officer should have an articulable and reasonable connection, from the original scope of the traffic stop to suspected criminal activity, to search and seize the passenger of the vehicle. In State v. Johnson, the court determined if the detention of a passenger was justified beyond the original purpose of the traffic stop. Johnson, 805 P.2d 761 at 764. The police officer pulled over the vehicle, in which Johnson was a passenger, for a faulty brake light. Id. at 762. Upon learning the driver of the car was not the registered owner of the vehicle, the police officer suspected that it may be a stolen car. Id. at 762. Without asking who owned the vehicle, the officer ran a license and outstanding warrant check on the driver and Johnson. Id. at 762. The warrant search on Johnson revealed that she had outstanding warrants and she was placed under arrest. Id. at 762. A search during the arrest procedure produced drug paraphernalia and she was charged with possession of a controlled substance. Id. at 762.

Hydekov can argue that the suspicion of underage drinking unreasonably expanded the original scope of the traffic stop for a speeding violation. Hydekov's claim is similar to Johnson because Officer Hand's request for identification to verify the age of Hydekov was not related to the traffic stop of a speeding vehicle. Johnson was a passenger in vehicle traffic stop, and the police officer ran an outstanding warrants check for her name because he suspected the car she was a passenger in could have been stolen. Id. at 762. Hydekov was also a passenger in a vehicle involved in a traffic stop, and Officer Hand ran an outstanding warrant check of Hydekov because he suspected underage drinking. In Johnson, the defendant was arrested because the officer found outstanding warrants when he ran a warrants check, and Johnson was additionally charged with possession of a controlled substance when drug paraphernalia was discovered in a search of her bag. Id. at 762. Hydekov was also placed under arrest when an outstanding warrant was discovered in a warrants check, and he was later charged with possession of a controlled substance for concealing marijuana in his sock.

The court in Johnson reasoned that Johnson's detention was beyond the original scope of the traffic stop, was not justified with a specific suspicion of a crime, and the evidence of drug paraphernalia should be suppressed. Id. at 764. Likewise, Hydekov could argue that evidence obtained pursuant to his arrest should be suppressed because investigating underage drinking was not reasonably related to the original scope of the traffic stop for speeding.

The State will likely argue that Officer Hand obtained objective information which supported his suspicion of criminal activity, beyond the speeding violation, and was justified in requesting identification from Hydekov. Investigation of criminal activity may be expanded beyond the original purpose of a traffic stop if objective information is obtained supporting the suspicion of the criminal activity. Kitchell, 653 F.3d 1206 at 1217-8. Officer Hand detected the odor of alcohol coming from the passenger side of the vehicle, the driver admitted to having a beer earlier, and it can be assumed Officer Hand had a concern the occupants may be under 21 by their appearance. UHP R. by Officer Hand ¶ 2, Aug. 13, 2011.

The odor of alcohol and the admission of the driver of consuming one beer earlier are objective observations, which Officer Hand could use to conclude that consumption of alcohol had been taking place. However, Officer Hand did make an assumption as to the age of the occupants of the vehicle by physical appearance. At the time of arrest Hydekov was twenty-two years and nine months old, and the other occupants of the vehicle were over twenty-one years old as well. It is unknown if Officer Hand suspected one or all of the occupants of underage drinking. If Officer Hand decided to just check identifications for all the occupants, and did not suspect Hydekov specifically of underage drinking, then his suspicion may not support expanding his search to Hydekov. But, the court will probably find that it was reasonable to suspect Hydekov was under the age of twenty-one, deferring to Officer Hand's judgment at the time.

The court will probably conclude that Officer Hand extending the search to Hydekov was supported by an articulable suspicion of underage drinking and checking identifications for age was justified.

B. <u>The warrant check on Hydekov was unreasonable because it should have been limited to investigating underage drinking, and a warrant search was not necessary to check Hydekov's age.</u>

The court will most likely find that the warrants check of Hydekov was unreasonable because it was beyond the scope of Officer Hand's articulable suspicion, and a motion to suppress the evidence found on Hydekov should succeed. A police officer may run a warrants check on an individual, if it is limited to an articulable suspicion, and must cease when the suspicion is dispelled. <u>State v. Chism</u>, 2005 UT App 41 (holding that Chism's further detention was unreasonable when the police officer's suspicion of underage tobacco use was dispelled by checking Chism's age on a state issued driver's license). The purpose of allowing a police officer to run a warrant check is to protect the officer from unknown risks of dangerous confrontations, and to serve the government interest to bring offenders to justice. <u>United States v. Burleson</u>, 657 F.3d 1040 (10th Cir. 2011) (holding that a police officer's warrants check and arrest of an individual, who had an outstanding warrant, accomplished the government interest in bringing an offender to justice, when there was a risk of a dangerous confrontation with the detainee).

The State may argue that the warrants check on Hydekov was justified because he did have an outstanding warrant, and it is good public policy to bring offenders to justice. The purpose of a warrant check is to identify if a detainee has an outstanding warrant to protect the police officer from a potentially dangerous situation, and to serve the public interest by bringing offenders to justice. <u>Id.</u> at 1051. One level of protection for Officer Hand is to identify a threat to his safety by checking if any of his detainees have a potential to resort to violence to avoid arrest for an outstanding warrant. Officer Hand's warrant check successfully identified a fugitive from justice because Hydekov did have an outstanding warrant, although it was not for a violent offense. Hydekov Warrant Check Doc., Aug. 13, 2011. Therefore the government interest of bringing offenders to justice was served by the warrant check and arrest of Hydekov.

However, the court should find the warrant check was unreasonable because Officer Hand's investigation should have been limited to his articulable suspicion, and should have ceased once Hydekov's age was verified to be over twenty-one. A police officer may run a warrant check on an individual, but he must limit the investigation to his articulable suspicion and cease his investigation when his suspicion is dispelled. State v. Chism, 2005 UT App 41 at ¶ 15. Officer Hand's articulable suspicion was that underage drinking was taking place. Hand R. ¶ 2. In his report, Officer Hand did not articulate any suspicion of a threat to his safety, or that Hydekov may have been a fugitive from justice. Officer Hand's investigation should have been limited to identifying the ages of the occupants of the vehicle. Once his suspicion of underage drinking was dispelled, his investigation should have ceased, prior to running a warrants check.

The court will probably conclude that the suspicion of Hydekov's underage drinking was dispelled when Officer Hand checked his age, and a warrant check was beyond the scope of his suspicion of criminal activity.

II. **The court will likely find that Hydekov's status as a Russian national does not provide an additional right to suppress the evidence of his statements to police because the VCCR does not provide a suppression remedy, and Hydekov was informed of his right to not incriminate himself.**

As a foreign national, Hydekov will likely not be able to suppress his statements to police because the statements were made prior to his embassy being notified of his arrest. Under Article 36 of the Vienna Convention on Consular Relations, (VCCR), if requested, "the competent authorities of the receiving State shall, without delay, inform the consular post of the sending State if . . . a national of that State is arrested . . . ." Vienna Convention on Consular Relations & Optional Protocol on Disputes art.36, para. (1)(b), Apr. 24, 1963, 21 U.S.T. 77, 596 U.N.T.S. 261. Under the Article thirty-six of the VCCR, paragraph (2), "the rights referred to in paragraph 1 of this article shall be exercised in conformity with the laws and regulations of the receiving State." Vienna Convention on Consular Relations & Optional Protocol on Disputes art.36, para. (2), Apr. 24, 1963, 21 U.S.T. 77, 596 U.N.T.S. 261. This analysis will address whether

Hydekov's statements to police should be suppressed because they were made prior the Russian embassy being notified of his arrest.

The court will probably find that Hydekov does not have an additional right to suppress his statements made prior to contacting his embassy. Where the VCCR treaty does not provide an express or implied remedy to a violation, the court should not impose one that does not conform to the existing remedies in the United States. Sanchez-Llamas v. Oregon, 126 S.Ct. 2669 (2006) (holding that the rights provided in Article thirty-six of the VCCR should be exercised in conformity with the laws of the United States, which already provides the right to an attorney and protection against self-incrimination).

The court should find that the rights of Hydekov are already protected by existing state law, and that Article thirty-six of the VCCR does not provide an additional remedy to suppress his statements. In Sanchez-Llamas v. Oregon, the Supreme Court held that if a treaty does not expressly or implicitly provide a remedy of a violation, then it is not up to the federal courts to impose a remedy that intrudes on the existing constitutional rights of every person residing in the United States. Id. at 347. The VCCR does not provide any protections against unreasonable gathering of evidence, only the right of a foreign national to have his embassy notified of his arrest. Id. at 349. Before being transported to jail, Hydekov was read the standard Miranda rights, which informed him of his right to an attorney, as well as his right to protection against self-incrimination. It was only after Hydekov acknowledged that he understood his rights that he informed Officer Hand that he is a Russian national. In the event Hydekov had not understood the Miranda rights, the Russian embassy could have assisted with translation services to make sure he did understand. Hydekov's acknowledgement that he understood his rights is also his acknowledgement that he knew he had rights of protection beyond any rights granted to a foreign national by the VCCR.

The court should find that the rights of Hydekov are already protected by existing state law, and that Article thirty-six of the VCCR does not provide an additional remedy to suppress his statements.

RECOMMENDATION

Hydekov should file a motion to suppress the evidence of possession of marijuana found pursuant to his arrest. The motion should be based on the fact that Hydekov's Fourth Amendment right was violated by an unlawful warrants search which was directly followed by the discovery of Hydekov's possession of marijuana. A motion based on the VCCR should not be filed because it does not provide a remedy to suppress the evidence.

OFFICE MEMORANDUM

TO: Andrea Langworthy
FROM: Lauren Taylor
DATE: February 10, 2013
RE: Case 13-1045: Valenzuela "move-away" case

QUESTIONS PRESENTED

I. Under the Hague Convention on the Civil Aspects of Child Abduction, can a non-custodial parent seek the return of a child if the custodial parent moves to Canada when the moving parent has sole physical and legal custody and the non-moving parent only has visitation rights?

II. Under California law, is a court likely to change a woman's custody order if she moves to Canada with her son when she has a good relationship with her ex-husband and is moving to accept a better job?

FACTS

Emily Valenzuela and her ex-husband, Robert Chung, divorced in 2009. Ms. Valenzuela received sole legal and physical custody of their son, Justin, now 12; Mr. Chung received visitation rights. Since the divorce and the subsequent move from Davis to Sacramento, Justin sees a counselor who has commented that Justin seems adaptable—likely arising from having a close relationship with both of his parents—and makes friends easily. Mr. Chung, a musician, has changed professions within the last few years, enabling him to spend more time with Justin recently, including helping to coach Justin's soccer team, bringing them closer. Father and son see one another every other weekend, if Mr. Chung is in town, and share an interest in the guitar. When Mr. Chung is unable to take Justin, Ms. Valenzuela is flexible in allowing Mr. Chung make up the time, demonstrating the civility of their relationship.

Recently, Ms. Valenzuela received an offer for a job in Vancouver that would provide her and Justin increased financially security, ensuring they could maintain their current standard of living, which includes computers in the house, internet access and smartphones. When asked how he feels about the potential move of roughly 900 miles, Justin wavers over with which parent he would like to stay, and has expressed more concern over leaving behind his soccer team than he has about the relationship with his father suffering.

As Mr. Chung has stated that he will oppose the move because it will affect his ability to see his son, this memorandum addresses the issue of whether, under either international or California law, Mr. Chung can either restrain Ms. Valenzuela from moving or have the custody order changed. Each of these issues will be discussed separately.

DISCUSSION

I. Ms. Valenzuela and Justin can move.

There is no domestic or international law that would effectively prohibit Ms. Valenzuela from accepting the job in Canada, nor would she violate any laws by taking Justin with her. While the Hague Convention on the Civil Aspects of International Child Abduction, (the Convention,) signed by both the United States and Canada—drafted to ensure that the rights of custody and rights of access of one Contracting State are respected in other Contracting states, (Oct. 25, 1980), T.I.A.S. No. 11670—does include a return remedy where children are wrongfully taken in breach of rights of custody, there are no such remedies available for parents who have only visitation rights. Hague International Child Abduction Convention; Text and Legal Analysis, 51 Fed. Reg. 10494-01 (March 26, 1986). As Mr. Chung has only visitation rights, the Convention does not provide him with remedies for keeping either Justin or Ms. Valenzuela in California, or forcing their return. As a result, Mr. Chung cannot prohibit the move nor force Justin's return.

II. Ms. Valenzuela's custody rights will not likely change.

In order for Mr. Chung to succeed in getting the custody order changed he would need to: (1) get a hearing granted, requiring an initial, substantial showing that the move would be detrimental to Justin, and (2) present sufficient evidence at the hearing that a change in custody is in Justin's best interests. *In re Marriage of LaMusga*, 32 Cal 4th. 1072, 1078 (2004).

A. <u>Getting a hearing granted will not be easy.</u>

In California, "[a] parent entitled to custody . . . has a right to change the residence of the child" unless the move would negatively affect the welfare of the child. Cal. Fam. Code Ann. § 7501 (West 2004). It is the non-custodial parent who bears the burden of making the substantial showing that the move represents a detrimental change. *In re Marriage of Burgess*, 13 Cal. 4th 25, 38 (1996). This policy reflects the State's interest in ensuring judicial economy and the stability of custody agreements.

LaMusga, 32 Cal 4th. at 1088 (citing *Burchard v. Garay*, 42 Cal. 3d. 531 (1986)). Changes sufficient to warrant a hearing include those that could result in severe physical or emotional harm to the child. *In re Marriage of Melville*, 122 Cal. App. 4th 601 (1st Dist. 2004) (holding that a hearing should be granted because a lack of access to adequate medical care, or a developmentally-disabled child potentially having trouble transitioning to a new school at the new location constitute sufficient detriment); but see *In re Marriage of Edlund*, 66 Cal. App. 4th 1454 (1st Dist. 1998) (reasoning that although the child would be "significantly negatively impacted" by the separation from her father, the move would not constitute detriment.) Additionally, although viewed sometimes as a factor evaluated at the hearing, courts have held that if a move is being made in bad faith, for example as an attempt to frustrate visitation, a hearing should be granted. *In re Marriage of Brown and Yana*, 37 Cal. 4th 947, 964 (2006) (denying a hearing because of the lack of bad faith). The courts have, however, specified that a move pertaining to employment is made in good faith. *Id.* at 954 (reasoning that it was good faith for the custodial parent to relocate because her new husband accepted a job elsewhere); see also *Edlund*, 66 Cal. App. 4th at 1470.

The court will probably find that Ms. Valenzuela's move poses no detriment to Justin's welfare. Not only is she moving to accept a more secure job, Vancouver has a universal health care system, so unlike the child in *Melville*, Justin's access to health care will not diminish. As Justin does not suffer from developmental disabilities, and demonstrated an ability to adapt when he moved from Davis to Sacramento, there is little chance he will be subjected to the type of severe emotional harm that potentially disallowed the move in *Melville*. Because Justin seems more upset about leaving behind his soccer team than his father, any emotional harm Justin might suffer falls short of even that of the Edlund child. As the *Edlund* court reasoned that despite the child being "significantly negatively impacted" by the move there was no detriment, *id.*, and the *Brown* court reasoned that as there was no evidence of bad faith, and therefore no potential detriment, in a move based on employment opportunities, 37 Cal. 4th at 963, a court should likewise reason that Ms. Valenzuela's move poses no detriment. Applying the same reasoning that led the *Brown* court to deny a hearing, a court will likely deny Mr. Chung's request for a hearing.

B. Assuming that Mr. Chung is able to convince a court to grant a hearing, it is unlikely the court will change the custody order.

In evaluating the issue, California courts balance several considerations. It is public policy that children should have frequent and continuing contact with both parents. Cal. Fam. Code Ann. § 3020(b) (West 2004). However, in "move-away" cases "a change of custody is not justified simply because the custodial parent has chosen . . . " to move, *Burgess*, 13 Cal. 4th at 38, unless the move would "prejudice the . . . welfare of the child." Cal. Fam. Code § 7501 (West 2004). This determination of whether a change in circumstances would negatively affect the child's well-being looks to several factors including:

> [1] the children's interest in stability and continuity in the custodial arrangement; [2] the distance of the move; [3] the age of the children; [4] the children's relationship with both parents; [5] the relationship between the parents . . . [6] the wishes of the children if they are mature enough for such an inquiry to be appropriate; [7] the reasons for the proposed move; [8] and the extent to which the parents currently are sharing custody.

LaMusga, 32 Cal 4th. at 1101.

Several of these factors are not relevant in the Valenzuela case. Although it is stated that the court should consider the "distance of the move," the factor does not carry much weight; even moves across the planet have not affected custody determinations. *In re Marriage of Condon*, 62 Cal. App. 4th 533, 562 (2d Dist. 1998) (holding that the custody order of a mother moving from California to Australia would not be changed.) Nor will the decision in this case turn on the "relationship between the parents" as the facts establish that the parents have civil relationship, or "extent the parents currently share custody," as Ms. Valenzuela has sole custody. Lastly, while the preference of a pre-teen usually carries weight, *Brown*, 37 Cal. 4th at 964 (reasoning the preferences of a 12-year old are important), and Justin is the same age as the *Brown* child, Justin has not expressed a definitive interest in staying with either parent. As a result, the court cannot currently evaluate how the "child's preference," (usually discussed alongside the "age of the child,") will affect the outcome of a hearing.

The determination of whether a change of custody is in Justin's best interests will fall to the remaining factors. Most importantly, there is a presumptive, "paramount need for continuity and stability in custody arrangements . . . [which] weigh heavily in favor of maintaining ongoing custody arrangements [with the primary caretaker]," *Burgess*, 13 Cal. 4th at 32-33 (holding the court would not change the custody agreement in order to protect the established bonds developed during the four years the mother had sole physical custody.) This interest is so strong that the *Burgess* court posited that the interest "will most often prevail" in matters concerning custodial placement. *Id.* at 39. To reconcile this policy of stability with the policy of ensuring frequent and continuing contact with the non-custodial parent, the court has clarified that it does not "specify a preference for a particular form of contact." *Id.* at 38. The melding of these two policies allows the application of the reasoning in *Burgess*, which involved a move of only 40 miles, *id.* at 30, to long-distance moves. See *Edlund*, 66 Cal. App. 4th at 1459 (reasoning the stability established by a custody agreement in which the mother had had primary physical custody, but shared legal custody, for two years outweighed the difficulties of a 2,300-mile move hindering frequent in-person contact with the non-custodial parent). *Edlund* ultimately held that without a substantial showing of detriment, a change in the custody order would run contrary to California Supreme Court decisions stating that in the interest of permanency, the primary caretaker will most often prevail. 66 Cal. App. 4th at 1472. That holding only makes sense if it can be inferred that frequent telephone, email and/or internet contact between the child and the non-custodial parent is sufficient.

The greatest challenge facing custodial parents who wish to move without their custody orders being affected is ensuring the child maintains a good relationship with both parents. The courts feel it is of "primary importance" that the move not have a detrimental effect the child's relationship with the non-custodial parent. *LaMusga*, 32 Cal 4th. at 1093. In *LaMusga*, the parents had a history of verbal violence towards one another and the non-custodial father felt that the mother did not foster a healthy relationship between the father and the children. *Id.* Because the court feared that if the children moved, the father could lose any relationship he had with the children, it changed the order to award custody to him. *Id.* at 1079.

The Valenzuela case raises many of the same issues *Burgess*, *Brown* and *Edlund* did. Ms. Valenzuela has had custody of a 12-year old for four years. Her economic situation is such that she can allow Justin ready access to electronic means of communication with Mr. Chung, ensuring Justin maintains frequent contact and a good relationship with his father. She provides flexibility in the visitation schedule, and allows Justin to play a sport his father coaches and to play the guitar. In doing so, she fosters an environment towards her ex-husband of neutrality, if not positivity. Given the time she has spent as Justin's primary caretaker, her bonds with Justin are equally as established as the bonds in *Burgess*, and perhaps more established than those of Ms. Edlund. Additionally, as Justin is 12, the same age as the Brown child, it is likely the depth of his emotional dependence on that primary caretaker relationship and his ability to rely on modern technology as a means of staying in touch with his father can be equated to the situation in *Brown*. Further, as the circumstances surrounding the relationship between Justin and Mr. Chung are significantly different from the father/son relationship in *LaMusga*, the court should not worry that Mr. Chung would have "no relationship" with Justin after a move. Because of the strength of the primary caretaker bond, the ability for Justin to stay in touch with his father, and that there is little concern the father/son relationship could be seriously jeopardized, we can apply the same reasoning the *Edlund* court used, concluding that there would be no detriment. For that reason, the court will almost certainly uphold the current custody agreement absent any issues raised in the evaluation of the "international factors."

C. <u>Concerns regarding an international move</u>

Additional scrutiny of the move is warranted where a child is potentially being relocated internationally. In such cases, in addition to the factors mentioned above, the court will evaluate cultural and jurisdictional enforcement issues. *Condon*, 62 Cal. App. 4th at 546-547. American custody orders lack enforceability in many foreign jurisdictions. *Id.* at 557. Noting that "[a]n unenforceable order is no order at all," the court recognized that a non-custodial parent has an interest in maintaining a relationship with his child that needs protecting, which can only be accomplished if the moving parent concedes the continuing jurisdiction of the California court. *Id.* at 562. Further, "to move a child [internationally] is to subject him or her to [different] cultural conditions [such as the permissibility of genital mutilation or, simply, an unfamiliar language] . . . or to deprive the child of important protections and advantages [like opportunities for higher education] . . ." *Id.* Citing these concerns, the court allowed Mrs. Condon, the custodial parent, to relocate with the children (1) to Australia (where they speak English), but not France (because of the difference in language), *id.* at 554, and (2) only after conceding the jurisdiction of the California court, *id.* at 561.

Applying the policies above to the facts of our case, we can conclude that just as Mrs. Condon could not take the children to Australia without conceding jurisdiction, Ms. Valenzuela will not be allowed to take Justin to Canada without conceding jurisdiction. Because the culture of Canada is similar to that of the United States—English-speaking, first world countries, which share the same views on bodily autonomy and equal opportunities for all citizens—the court will likely reason that a move to Canada does not pose a detriment to Justin's welfare much the same way it reasoned the welfare of the Condon children would be unaffected.

    D.   <u>Overall "factor" evaluation</u>

Assuming that Ms. Valenzuela does concede jurisdiction, most, if not all, of the other factors weigh in favor of the court maintaining the current custody agreement. As discussed above, there is little evidence a long-distance move will substantially affect Justin's welfare. As Canada is a country with a nearly identical culture to America, the court will almost certainly conclude that the mere fact that the move is international is not a sufficient detriment either. Should a hearing be granted, there is little chance the custody agreement will be altered.

CONCLUSION

There are no international or California laws that would affect Ms. Valenzuela's ability to move to Canada with Justin. While it is highly unlikely that Mr. Chung would be able to successfully lobby the court to grant a hearing at which it could change the custody order, should a hearing be held, Ms. Valenzuela has a very strong case supporting the current arrangement.

OFFICE MEMORANDUM

TO: Supervising Attorney
FROM: Student Submission
RE: Claim of sexual harassment at wholly-owned subsidiary of a Japanese corporation

EXECUTIVE SUMMARY

This memo addresses whether Audrey Stadler, a receptionist at Global Business Solutions (GBS), has a valid claim for hostile environment sexual harassment against Charlie Murray, a market manager at GBS and whether GBS will be liable if Mr. Murray has committed sexual harassment. Under California's Fair Employment and Housing Act (the FEHA) it is unlawful for anyone to harass someone because of their sex. To satisfy a claim of hostile work environment sexual harassment the plaintiff must be subject to unwelcome conduct based on her sex that is so severe or pervasive so as to alter the conditions of her employment and create a hostile or abusive working environment.

In this case, although the conduct was unwelcome and based on Ms. Stadler's sex, there is no evidence that the conduct was so severe or pervasive so as to alter the conditions of Ms. Stadler's working environment. There is evidence of unwelcome conduct because Ms. Stadler told Mr. Murray that she did not wish to talk to him. There is also evidence that Mr. Murray's conduct was based on sex because he made sexual advances toward Ms. Stadler. However, Mr. Murray's conduct was not pervasive enough to alter Ms. Stadler's working environment because it was not constant, systematic, numerous, repeated and did not have a set pattern, rather it was sporadic. Mr. Murray's conduct was also not severe enough to alter the conditions of Ms. Stadler's employment because in the absence of any pervasiveness, the severity of the conduct must be extreme. Mr. Murray's conduct failed to meet the extremity needed to alter the conditions of Ms. Stadler's working environment.

Additionally, GBS's liability depends on whether Mr. Murray is Ms. Stadler's supervisor. If Mr. Murray is Ms. Stadler's supervisor, than GBS is strictly liable for his conduct. If Mr. Murray is not Ms. Stadler's supervisor, than GBS will not likely be liable because liability is based on a negligence standard and GBS did not know and did not have reason to know of Mr. Murray's conduct prior to Ms. Stadler's complaint because the conduct always occurred in private. GBS can try to mitigate damages through a defense of avoidable consequences. It is unlikely that the defense will apply, however, because while GBS does have reasonable steps in place to prevent and correct sexual harassment, Ms. Stadler took advantage of the measures provided by GBS to report sexual harassment. While there is not likely a claim of hostile environment sexual harassment, GBS should continue to investigate Mr. Murray and continue to follow its procedures for a sexual harassment complaint.

DISCUSSION

I. **Mr. Murray's conduct was not likely hostile work environment sexual harassment because while the conduct was unwelcome and based on sex, it was neither so severe nor pervasive so as to alter the conditions of employment and create an abusive working environment.**

Hostile work environment sexual harassment under the Fair Employment and Housing Act (Cal. Gov't. § Code 12940) requires a plaintiff to show that, while in the workplace or during normal working hours, she was subjected to harassing conduct that was (a) unwelcome; (b) because of sex; and (c) sufficiently severe or pervasive to create an abusive work environment. *Lyle v. Warner Bros. Television Prods.*, 38 Cal. 4th 264, 278 (2006); *Myers v. Trendwest Resorts, Inc.*, 148 Cal. App. 4th 1403, 1421 (3rd Dist. 2007). The plaintiff must subjectively feel the conduct was unwelcome and show the conduct was objectively unwelcome via interactions with the perpetrator. *Meritor Sav. Bank, FSB v. Vinson*, 477 U.S. 57, 68 (1986); *Reiger v. Arnold,* 104 Cal. App. 4th 451, 459-461 (3d Dist. 2002). For the second element, a claim needs only to show that sex is a substantial factor in the discrimination, and that a plaintiff would not have been treated the same had she been a man. *Birschtein v. New United Motor Mfg., Inc.*, 92 Cal. App. 4th 994, 1002 (1st Dist. 2001). Finally, when the harassing conduct is not physically extreme or threatening, a plaintiff must show a pattern of harassment taking into consideration the context, frequency, and nature of the conduct, the number of days over which the conduct occurs, and whether the victim's work was unreasonably affected. *Lyle*, 38 Cal. 4th at 283-284; *Fisher*, 214 Cal. App. 3d at 610. On the issue of hostile work environment, California courts often refer to federal decisions and interpretation of Title VII of the Federal Civil Rights Act of 1964. *Id.*

A. **Mr. Murray's conduct was likely unwelcome because Ms. Stadler complained to Human Resources due to Mr. Murray's conduct and made requests to Mr. Murray not behave in that manner.**

Conduct is considered unwelcome if an employee did not solicit or invite it and the employee regarded the conduct as undesirable or offensive. *Meritor Savings Bank, FSB v. Vinson*, 447 U.S. 57, 68 (1986); *Williams v. Herron*, 687 F.3d 971, 975 (8th Cir. 2012) (finding that Plaintiff's suggestion to end the relationship and her attempt to avoid Defendant was sufficient to show Defendant's conduct was unwelcome). Ms. Stadler did not invite Mr. Murray to act in this way toward her, she expressed discomfort with the advances, and she did nothing to solicit Mr. Murray's conduct after their prior romantic relationship ended. When Mr. Murray asked her to talk privately, she attempted to resist until he threatened to make their situation known to their co-workers. When Mr. Murray called or texted her every 15 minutes, she did not answer. When Mr. Murray would give her hugs or caress her face, she did not reciprocate. Ms. Stadler complained to the human resources department about Mr. Murray's conduct; thus showing his conduct was undesirable to her. Mr. Murray's conduct was unwelcome because Ms. Stadler did not invite the conduct and she found it undesirable and offensive.

B. **The conduct complained of was likely based on sex because while Mr. Murray's comments were not based on Ms. Stadler's sex, Mr. Murray's actions were sexual advances.**

A hostile work environment sexual harassment claim only needs to show that sex is a substantial factor in the discrimination, and that Plaintiff would not have been treated the same had she been a man. *Birschtein*, 92 Cal. App. 4th at 1002 (holding that perpetrator's asking for dates, desire to "eat [victim]" remarks, and sexual bathing fantasies were based upon victim's sex). Here, Mr. Murray's remarks of "tease," "heartbreaker," and "bitch," crying, restricting hugs, saying, "Are you sure you don't want this?", and facial caresses, saying "Remember how I made you feel?" were because he was attracted to her. Mr. Murray is heterosexual, so he would not have so treated Ms. Stadler if she were a man. Therefore, sex was a substantial factor in Mr. Murray's harassing conduct as it was based on his sexual attraction.

C. **The conduct was not so severe or pervasive so as to alter working conditions and create a hostile or abusive working environment because the comments and conduct were not the kind that a reasonable person would find hostile or abusive even though Ms. Stadler did.**

Severity and pervasiveness are measured by both objective and subjective standards: an environment that a reasonable person would find hostile or abusive and the victim's subjective perception that the environment is abusive. *Myers,* 148 Cal. App. 4th at 1421. Ms. Stadler subjectively felt that her working conditions have been altered. She complained that her productivity was lowered because she is unable focus and must take numerous breaks to compose herself after her interactions with Mr. Murray. Ms. Stadler also stated that she feels anxious at work and has anxiety coming to work each day.

1. **Mr. Murray's conduct was likely pervasive because of the frequency and duration of the conduct directed at Ms. Stadler.**

To determine whether conduct was severe or pervasive enough to create a hostile or abusive working environment, the totality of the circumstances are evaluated. This includes looking at: the frequency of the conduct; the total number of days over which all of the conduct occurred; whether the conduct is physically threatening or humiliating, or a mere offensive utterance; and whether the conduct unreasonably interferes with an employee's work performance. *Herberg v. California Institute of the Arts,* 101 Cal. App. 4th 142, 149-150 (2nd Dist. 2002); *Lyle,* 38 Cal. 4th at 283. The conduct must be repeated, routine, or generalized in nature; not occasional, isolated, sporadic, or trivial. *Mokler v. County of Orange,* 157 Cal. App. 4th 121, 142 (2nd Dist. 2007).

In determining whether the Mr. Murray's conduct was repeated or isolated, the number of incidents and the frequency of the incidents over the period of harassment is significant. *Hughes v. Pair,* 46 Cal. 4th 1035, 1048 (2009) (holding a single telephone conversation and a brief statement to the plaintiff in person later the same day does not meet the standard of more than a few isolated incidents); *Fisher v. San Pedro Peninsula Hospital,* 214 Cal. App. 3d 590, 613-614(2d Dist. 1989) (finding the complaint contained no indication of the frequency or intensity with which the touchings or sexual comments occurred, and thus were more like isolated incidents); *Mokler,* 157 Cal. App. 4th at 144-145 (holding harassment of the plaintiff on three occasions over five weeks with no physical threats fell short of establishing a pattern of continuous, pervasive harassment).

The factors, when taken as a whole, must demonstrate the harasser's rude, inappropriate, and offensive behavior permeates the workplace with discriminatory intimidation, ridicule, and insult. Mokler, 157 Cal. App. 4th at 145. For example, in Mokler, the court determined whether the defendant's conduct was sufficiently pervasive to alter the employment conditions by evaluating the totality of the circumstances. Id. The defendant's harassing conduct occurred on three incidents over a five-week period. Id. at 144. The conduct consisted of: calling the plaintiff "aging nun," pulling the plaintiff to his body while asking her to "lobby" him, putting his arm around the plaintiff and in doing so rubbed her breast with his arm. Id. The court held that this conduct was isolated and did not create a pattern of pervasive harassment sufficient to alter the employment conditions. Id. at 145. It reasoned that the totality of the circumstances, including the nature of the unwelcome sexual acts, frequency of encounters, number of days the conduct occurred, and context in which the harassment occurred, did not amount to pervasive conduct. Id.

Mr. Murray's actions most likely are sufficiently pervasive to alter the employment conditions based on the sexual nature of his conduct, frequency of encounters, number of days his conduct occurs, and the context in which his harassment occurs. Ms. Stadler's case is distinguishable from Mokler based on the pattern of pervasive, and not isolated, harassment sufficient to alter the employment conditions and permeate the workplace with intimidation. In Ms. Stadler's case, she works with Mr. Murray on a daily basis in the same building as her where he has authority over her. Mr. Murray calls her names like "heartbreaker," "bitch," and "tease" in front of coworkers, makes aggressive statements toward her while caressing her face, and cries to her at work. The harassing conduct has occurred over five weeks and varies from hourly to once a week. This conduct has made Ms. Stadler uncomfortable and nervous at work.

This case is distinguishable from Ms. Stadler's case for three reasons. First, the nature of the unwelcome sexual acts- Mr. Murray's conduct includes sexual remarks and restrictive hugs whereas the defendant's conduct in *Mokler* only involved isolated sexual remarks and nonrestrictive touching. Id. Second, the frequency of offensive encounters- Mr. Murray's conduct occurs at least once a week while the defendant's conduct never occurred more than once a week. Id. Third, the total number of days over which the conduct occurs- while the conduct in both cases occurred over a five-week period, Mr. Murray's conduct has occurred a countless number of times whereas the defendant's conduct only occurred three times. Id.

Thus, unlike the offensive conduct in *Mokler*, Mr. Murray's sexual advances, based on the totality of the circumstances, are of an unwelcome nature, occur frequently and continuously, and occur at work that caused Ms. Stadler to feel uncomfortable and nervous. Therefore Mr. Murray's conduct is sufficiently pervasive.

> **2. Mr. Murray's conduct was not severe enough to alter Ms. Stadler's working conditions to create a hostile or abusive working environment because there it was not extreme and there were no physical threats.**

The severity of the harassment required varies inversely with the pervasiveness of the conduct. *Mokler*, 157 Cal. App. 4th at 142. A single incident of severe harassment may be sufficient to establish liability; however, the incident must be extremely severe and "generally must include either physical violence or threat thereof." *Herberg*, 101 Cal. App. 4th at 151. In determining the severity of the conduct, courts have reasoned that the less pervasive the conduct the more severe the conduct must be. *Hughes,* 46 Cal. 4th at 1049 (finding the defendant's threat to get the plaintiff on her knees and that he would "f**k" her one way or another could not be constructed as a physical threat; and thus was not severe enough to satisfy sexual harassment for an isolated incident); *Hergberg*, 101 Cal. App. 4th at 153 (holding the display of a painting that included the plaintiff naked and in a sexual act did not meet the severity of rape or violent sexual assault and thus was not severe enough to establish sexual harassment from the isolated incident); *Sheffield v. Los Angeles County Department of Social Services*, 109 Cal. 4th 153, 163 (2003) (finding the defendant's slamming of her fist into her palm was severe enough physical threat to alter the conditions of the work place for harassment that occurred over seven days and where the defendant was significantly larger than the plaintiff).

Mr. Murray's conduct does not reach the level of severity required given the lack of physical threats. Mr. Murray was never extremely physically violent with Ms. Stadler and never threatened her physically. And, Ms. Stadler does not feel that Mr. Murray is physically threatening. Thus, Mr. Murray's conduct was not severe enough to alter Ms. Stadler's working conditions to create a hostile or abusive working environment.

II. GBS may be liable for sexual harassment by Mr. Murray because GBS's liability depends on Mr. Murray's employment status as a supervisor or a co-worker.

To determine whether GBS will be liable for the sexual harassment by Mr. Murray, it must be determined whether he is Ms. Stadler's supervisor. FEHA imposes different standards of employer liability for sexual harassment depending on whether the alleged harasser is the victim's supervisor or a "nonsupervisory co-employee." *State Dep't of Health Servs. v. Super. Ct.*, 31 Cal. 4th 1026, 1040-1041 (2003).

If Mr. Murray is a supervisor, than GBS is strictly liable for any sexual harassment conducted by Mr. Murray. *Dep't of Health Servs.*, 31 Cal. 4th at 1034. If Mr. Murray is not a supervisor, GBS will likely not be liable for sexual harassment. An employer is liable for harassment conducted by a nonsupervisory co-employee under a negligence theory. *Id.* The employer is liable only if it knew or should have known about the harassing conduct and failed to take immediate and appropriate corrective action. *Id.* at 1041.

There is no evidence that GBS knew of the harassment before Ms. Stadler informed them. First, GBS did not know nor should have known of Mr. Murray's acts of sexual harassment before Ms. Stadler's report. Under FEHA, an employer will be held liable if it knew or should have known of the harassment through a manager's or supervisor's knowledge, due to the pervasiveness of the acts or remarks, or through other circumstances. §12940(j)(1); *Weeks*, 63 Cal. App. 4th at 1160-1161. Generally, an employer "knows" when a manager or supervisor receives a report. *Sheffield*, 109 Cal. App. 4th at 164. However, reports to coworkers do not give the employer knowledge. *Lappin v. Laidlaw Transit Inc.*, 179 F. Supp. 2d 1111, 1117, 1122 (N.D. Cal. 2001) (holding employer did not receive knowledge when victim spoke to coworkers about the incident). Ms. Stadler reported to human resources' management on January 2nd. Before that she told Suzanne Brown, a GBS temporary receptionist. Since Suzanne is a coworker this did not give knowledge to GBS. Thus, GBS "knew" on January 2nd when Human Resources received Ms. Stadler's report to which it immediately responded. Thus, GBS's likely did not know nor should have known about Mr. Murray's harassing conduct before Ms. Stadler's report on January 2nd.

Thus, GBS can likely defend against liability if Mr. Murray is not Ms. Stadler's supervisor because it did not know of the alleged harassment until Ms. Stadler reported it. Yet, if Mr. Murray is a supervisor, GBS will be strictly liable.

III. GBS likely can mitigate damages under the avoidable consequences doctrine because GBS had established effective sexual harassment policies and complaint procedures in place.

The avoidable consequences doctrine allows employers to mitigate damages when the employer took reasonable measures to prevent and correct workplace sexual harassment, the employee unreasonably failed to use the measures provided, and reasonable use of the measures would have prevented at least some of the harm suffered without undue risk, expense, or humiliation. *State Dep't of Health v. Super. Ct.*, 31 Cal. 4th 1026, 1044 (2003). Whether an employer has anti-harassment policies in place, communicated policies to employees, enforced policies consistently, sought to maintain confidentiality, and prevented retaliatory conduct will weigh in the court's determination. *Id.* at 1048-1049. The purpose of the avoidable consequences doctrine is to support Legislature's goal of harassment prevention by encouraging employers to establish effective policies and complaint procedures and encouraging employees to use employer-provided remedies to stop workplace harassment before it becomes severe or pervasive. *Id.* at 1039, 1046-1048.

Allowing Ms. Stadler to bar mitigation of GBS's damages because she reported in compliance with the establish procedures would not further the purpose of the avoidable consequences doctrine because it would not encourage employers to comply. GBS has a sexual harassment policy in place, communicates this policy to all employees, enforces the policy consistently, has sought to maintain confidentiality, and prevents retaliation against those who report. These are all the steps the avoidable consequences doctrine is purposed to implement. *Id.* at 1045-1046. If an employer does all that is required and takes every reasonable step to prevent sexual harassment, but is still fully penalized, the reward for compliance is diminished and employers have less incentive to establish effective policy and complaint procedures. Without such policies and procedures, employees would be less likely to report to their employers, employers would have less redress, and less harassment would be stopped, undermining both purposes of the doctrine. Thus, GBS should be able to mitigate damages because it established effective sexual harassment policies and complaint procedures which allowed Ms. Stadler to use employer-provided anti-harassment measures.

CHAPTER 11

INTERVIEWING THE CLIENT

■ ■ ■

by Kathleen Friedrich

For some students, client interviewing is a skill that appears to have many "moving parts" if their only exposure is a lecture on how to interview a client. It is important to remind/assure students that they have already learned to communicate with others. Students will find that client interviewing can be made more effective by taking those communication skills and tailoring to the primary mission of client interviewing—gathering and exchanging information between the client and the lawyer.

We know from learning theory, that much of what students read in this book about lawyering skills will be forgotten if students are not implementing the skill that they are being taught. Learning how to effectively and efficiently conduct a client interview is no different. Thus, the best way to teach a lawyering skill is to follow the precepts set forth in the following Chinese proverb: "I hear and I forget. I see and I remember. I do and I understand."

This skill should not be introduced until at least the end of students first quarter/semester in law school. Students will need to have some legal knowledge so that they can identify the legal issues that the client presents in the interview. They will not know what facts are relevant or what questions to ask the client without some foundation in the law.

To aid in presenting the material from this chapter in a lecture, I have included PowerPoint slides with explanatory notes.

EFFECTIVE COMMUNICATION SKILLS FOR CLIENT INTERVIEWING & COUNSELING

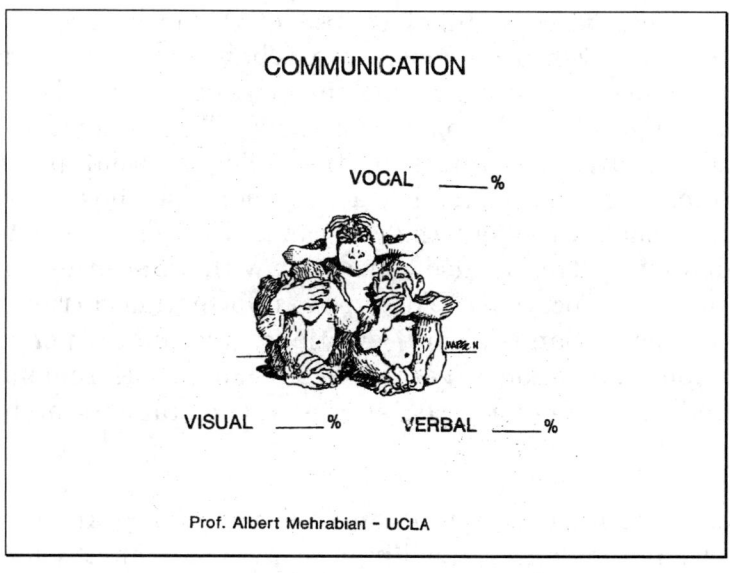

Dr. Albert Mehrabian, who taught in the psychology department at UCLA, did extensive study, research and writing in the field of non-verbal communication. Along with journal articles and other writings he is the author of <u>Nonverbal Communication</u> (1972) and <u>Silent Messages: Implicit communication of Emotions and Attitudes</u> (1981). According to Dr. Mehrabian, our face-to-face communications are made up of 3 domains:

- verbal channel = the actual words which appear in a transcript of what a person says

- vocal/voice channel = everything the listener/audience hears, *except* the actual words spoken. This channel includes tone, inflection (stress), volume (loudness/softness), pitch, rate of speech, pauses, silences, etc.
- visual channel: everything the listener/audience sees including body language, facial expressions, posture, territorial space, and dress

Using the graphic, ask students how much of the verbal, vocal and visual channel is involved in a face-to-face communication on a 100 point scale. (there may be students who were communication majors who may already know this or there may be students who have an intuitive sense of the percentages.)

According to Mehrabian, the verbal channel is only 7% of the message; the vocal/voice channel is 38% of the message and the visual channel is 55%. (Even if one wishes to debate the exact numbers, what Mehrabian's research reveals is the importance of the visual and vocal channels in our face-to-face communications. This is consistent with the studies and research by others in the field of social psychology and communication. Paul Ekman, a psychologist has studied facial expressions to such an extent that he can tell when a person is lying by observing his face. This is also consistent with what other psychologists tell us about communications. The type of information carried through the visual and voice channels are emotions, attitudes, personality and sincerity. Communication experts tell us that people remember longest attitudes and feelings—not facts, stories and metaphors or theories and principles.

Thus, it is important that an attorney convey an interest in the client's story /circumstances, a willingness to help, empathy for the client's problem. It will not be enough to say the words, "How can I help you?" if the message from the visual and vocal channel belie interest.

An attorney conveys interest, shows empathy, establishes rapport, and connects with the client by being an "active listener".

> **Facilitators of Communication**
>
> 1. Conveying empathetic understanding
>
> 2. Engaging in active listening
>
> 3. Encouraging communication through conveying expectations and recognition
>
> 4. Keeping open mind about what is relevant

Here are some key communication facilitators which aid in the free flow of information from the client to the lawyer. This is not an exhaustive list.

Clients will volunteer information to the attorney if they can connect with the attorney, if they can trust the attorney with the information, particularly sensitive or private, personal information, if they feel like they have a rapport/positive relationship with the attorney.

> **Inhibitors of Communication**
>
> -Fears of embarrassment or hurting the case
>
> -Anxiety, tension or trauma
>
> -Etiquette barriers and prejudices
>
> -Differing conceptions about relevant info

Inhibitors are "any social-psychological barrier" which impedes the flow of relevant information by making the client unable or unwilling to give it to the lawyer at the moment. There are inhibitors internal to the interview and inhibitors external to the interview. The lawyer cannot "fix" external inhibitors like the client's memory failure, but being cognizant of it will be beneficial to the attorney-client communications. The lawyer does have control over internal inhibitors such as "ego threat". Clients will withhold information from the lawyer when the lawyer does not engage in active listening, when the lawyer appears judgmental of the client or the client's circumstances or when the lawyer is not culturally sensitive.

4 Categories of Listeners

- Non- listener
- Marginal listener
- Evaluative listener
- Active listener

Experts say that there are 4 categories of listeners. This list identifies the listener from the lowest level to the highest level.

Why We Don't Hear Others

- Mind Reader
- Comparer
- Filterer
- Dreamer
- Identifier

- Rehearser
- Derailer
- Placater
- Sparrer

Communication experts tell us that some attorneys engage in a speech habit/behavior that destroys credibility—talking too much and not listening enough. Especially for the initial interview, experts say that attorneys should be listening 70-80% of the time and talking only 20-30% of the time.

Not all of the listening by the lawyer will be active listening-- that is mentally trying. Moreover, sometimes it is appropriate for the lawyer to evaluate/assess the client and the client's message.

But the lawyer needs to not mistake evaluative listening with active listening. This slide shows the variations of the evaluative listener.

- MIND READER- the lawyer will hear little or nothing as he/she thinks "what is this person really thinking?"
- REHEARSER- the lawyer's mental tryouts for "here's what I'll say next" tunes out the other person.
- FILTERER- some call this selective listening—hearing only what the lawyer wants to hear.
- DREAMER- drifting off during a face-to-face conversation can lead to an embarrassing "What did you say?" or "Could you repeat that?" from the lawyer.
- IDENTIFIER- if the lawyer is busy referring everything he/she hears to his/her own experience, the lawyer probably doesn't hear what is being said.
- COMPARER- when the lawyer is sidetracked assessing the client/messenger, he/she is sure to miss the message.
- DERAILER- changing the subject too quickly soon tells the client that the lawyer is not interested in anything the client has to say.
- SPARRER- the lawyer hears what is said but quickly belittles it or discounts it. That puts the lawyer in the same class as the derailer.
- PLACATER- agreeing with everything the lawyer hears just to be nice or to avoid conflict does not mean that he/she is a good listener.

Important Skills of Active Listener

- Sensing
- Attending
- Responding

Sensing

- Ability of the active listener to recognize and appreciate the silent message the speaker is sending
  - Verbal channel
  - Vocal channel:
    - Intonation, volume, pitch, rate of speech
    - Silences, pauses
  - Visual channel:
    - Body language, posture, dress
    - Facial expressions

> ## Attending
> - Refers to the verbal, vocal and visual messages that active listeners send to speaker to indicate attentiveness, receptiveness & acknowledgement of the speaker and message
>   - Verbal expressions: "uh-huh", "yes", "go on", "I see", "Keep going", "Continue….",
>   - Visual signs: eye contact, open body language, affirmative head nods, appropriate facial expressions, avoidance of nervous, bored, or angry gestures
>   - Establishment of receptive listening setting: creating atmosphere of privacy away from phone calls, people talking or people within earshot; no violation of speaker's "personal space"; elimination of communication barrier like large desk

Since not all clients are alike, the lawyer should not "attend" to each client exactly the same. A lawyer who is a good active listener, tailors his active listening skills to each client.

> ## Other Silent Messages
> - Note-taking
> - Dress—physical appearance

Too much note taking can be a barrier to communication. Clients generally expect and appreciate that the lawyer takes some notes during the interview because it means that they said something that is so important that the lawyer wrote it down to remember it. The best way for a lawyer to handle note-taking is to first hear the client's story, maintaining appropriate eye contact. After the client has given an overview of the circumstances and the lawyer is ready to ask follow-up questions, the lawyer can begin taking notes at that time. Some lawyers even comment about the note-taking by stating something like, "I know I can't remember everything that you have told me so I hope you don't mind if I jot down some notes before I forget."

What do students think about the lawyer using a computer to take notes? Is this more of a barrier to communication than a notepad?

What about dress? Do clothes make the person? Most lawyers would probably say that if they want to be treated as a professional, they need to dress as a professional. The lawyer who dresses professionally tends to have inherent creditability. The lawyer who dresses casually sends the silent message that they are treating the client and his/her message casually.

Responding

- Occurs when active listener tries to get feedback on the accuracy of the speaker's content and feeling, tries to keep the speaking talking, tries to gather more information, tries to make the speaker feel understood, and tries to get the speaker to understand herself and/or her problems or concerns better

    – Verbal expressions: "How did that make you feel?"; "I am really sorry to hear that...."; "I can understand why that made you upset...."

    – Visual signs: offering a tissue when speaker needs it; touching speaker gently to express; exhibiting signs that you are connecting with speaker

Affiliative Behaviors

- Lots of eye contact- 80% of conversation time
- Many gestures- head nods, smiles
- Forward body lean- when sitting, leaning toward listener
- No shoulder angle- body squarely facing listener
- Warmth in voice

Active listening skills are also sometimes referred to as affiliative behaviors. Affiliative behaviors are those that connect us to others and unaffiliative behaviors are those that turn us away from others.

Unaffiliative Behaviors

- Little eye contact- 40% or less of conversation time
- Few gestures
- Backward body lean- when sitting, leaning away from listener
- Shoulder angle- body angled 30 degrees away from listener
- Lack of warmth in voice

> **Value of Active Listening**
>
> People who display active listening skills are rated as being more:
> – Persuasive
> – Trustworthy
> – Expert
> – Well-informed
> – Sensitive to needs of client

This slide should be viewed as good news to law students because they already know how to be active listeners from everything they learned before they came to law school. They should bring all of their communication skills and talents with them to client interviews. They do not need to be the world's best expert on negligence or fraud or defending a criminal charge of burglary. They can be considered expert by their potential client by engaging in active listening, a skill that is not unique to attorneys, a skill that is not necessarily taught in law school, but a very valuable skill to be a successful lawyer. Students should continue to develop this skill with each new client that they interview.

Survey of Missouri Lawyers
Positive Factors

Clients
1. Friendliness
2. Promptness, business-like manner
3. Courtesy
4. Not condescending
5. Keeping client informed

Lawyers
1. Results
2. Honesty
3. Efficiency
4. Personality
5. Education

This survey of Missouri lawyers and clients was conducted in the 1980's. Similar surveys were conducted in other states with similar results.

When lawyers were asked what top five factors that they thought clients wanted from their attorney, they interestingly thought the number one thing that clients wanted was "results".

BUT when clients were asked what top five traits/characteristics they want from their attorney, they responded that the number one thing they wanted was "friendliness".

So, not only do psychologists and communication experts tell lawyers the importance of strong people skills in creating a successful attorney-client relationship, clients themselves tell us that is what they look for in an attorney. Clients want a lawyer who is an active listener, someone they can connect with and who will connect with them, someone who cares about them and their problem, someone who they have a rapport with....

Survey of Missouri Lawyers
Negative Factors

Client
1. Superior attitude
2. Bored/indifferent
3. Impatient, impersonal
4. Rude

Lawyers
1. Procrastination
2. Failure to inform
3. Lack of frankness
4. Lack of courtesy

- Ask questions and listen:
- "We were born with 2 ears and 1 mouth. As we use them in that proportion, we establish rapport and improve communication." – J. Douglas Edward

- Listen with ears, eyes and body:
- "People don't care how much you know until they know how much you care." -Anonymous

---

Additionally, you can show students examples of client interviewing and discuss what was effective and what was not and why. Here are 3 excerpts from Hollywood movies that highlight various aspects of client interviewing:

1. Initial client interview between Tom Hanks' character as a client and Denzel Washington's character as an attorney in <u>Philadelphia.</u> This clip is not intended to show bad client interviewing because the attorney does not take the client's case. Rather, it is an excellent clip to highlight non-verbal messaging. The client figures out that the attorney does not want to represent him even before the attorney states so as the interview draws to a close because of all of the non-verbal messages. Before I show the video clip, I set the stage and ask students to jot down each silent message that the attorney sends to the client eventually leading the client to recognize that the attorney will not take his case "for personal reasons". The clip is about 8 minutes and the discussion that follows can be about 20-30 minutes if you identify the 12 or so non-verbal messages. Time permitting, you can also discuss what the attorney does effectively in the interview. This clip provides a number of lessons: (1) how to conduct an organized client interview, including allowing the client to tell his version of the facts; (2) useful to remind students that they have already developed the skill of being able to "read" people, that they can identify non-verbal messages shows an awareness of this aspect of oral communications and should give them some confidence that they are not undertaking this lawyering skill completely from scratch.

2. Initial client interview between Halle Berry's character as client and Samuel L. Jackson's character as attorney in <u>Losing Isaiah</u>. This video clip shows ineffective client interviewing techniques displayed by the attorney. This is an excellent clip to highlight the interconnected concepts of active listening and rapport-building. The client states at one point in the interview, "You don't like me very much." What does the attorney do (or not do) that leads the client to say this? Before showing the video clip, ask the students to jot down each opportunity that the attorney had to build rapport and failed to do so. The clip is about 4 minutes and the discussion that follows can be about 20 minutes if you identify the various failed opportunities to connect with the client. Time permitting, you can also discuss what the attorney does effectively in the interview. This clip provides a number of lessons: (1) it is not enough that an attorney agrees to represent the client; clients want to know the attorney cares about them and their problem and will zealously represent their interests. (2) It is useful to remind students that they have already developed the skill of knowing what to say and what not to say in order to establish rapport with others; their ability to identify the attorney's failed opportunities to connect with the client shows an awareness of this aspect of oral communications and should give them some confidence that they are not undertaking this lawyering skill completely from scratch. (3) While the attorney and client have some cultural similarities, they also

have some cultural differences. What are they? Sometimes cultural similarities play a role in rapport-building. Individuals can connect with those with whom we share something in common. Do the cultural similarities between the attorney and client help establish rapport in this interview?

3. Scene between Susan Sarandon's character as attorney and Brad Renfro's character as a child client in The Client where the client wants to fire the attorney after he discovers that the attorney has a history of alcohol problems. This video clip shows effective client interviewing techniques displayed by the attorney, highlighting the concepts of active listening and rapport-building. At the beginning of the scene, the client wants to fire the attorney but by the end of the scene, he not only retains the attorney, but provides additional facts to the attorney. Near the end of the scene, the client trusts the attorney enough to reveal that he is scared. What does the attorney do to build (rebuild) the client's trust? Before showing the video clip, ask the students to jot down each verbal and non-verbal message that the attorney used to build rapport. The clip is about 8 minutes and the discussion that follows can be about 20 minutes if you identify the various things the attorney did and said to connect with the client. Time permitting; you can also discuss what the attorney does effectively in the interview. This clip provides a number of lessons: (1) it is not enough that an attorney agrees to represent the client; clients want to know the attorney cares about them and their problem and will zealously represent their interests. (2) It is useful to remind students that they have already developed the skill of knowing what to do and say and what not to do and say in order to establish rapport with others; their ability to identify each step the attorney takes to connect with the client shows an awareness of this aspect of oral communications and should give them some confidence that they are not undertaking this lawyering skill completely from scratch. (3) While the attorney and client have some cultural similarities, they also have some cultural differences. What are they? Sometimes cultural similarities play a role in rapport-building. Individuals can connect with those with whom we share something in common. Do the cultural similarities between the attorney and client help establish rapport in this interview?

4. If time does not permit viewing and discussing video clips in class, another method would be to assign students to view a client interview outside of class. As discussed more fully in the next chapter, you can purchase videotaped interviews of the 3 top-ranked national ABA Client Counseling Competition teams available on the ABA website. Each year the subject matter of the competition changes, so you can choose a

subject matter that may be more appropriate to your class. You can assign one 30-minute interview along with the 15-minute post-consultation session or assign all 3 interviews so that students can see several interviewing styles.

<u>In-Class Exercise No. 1:</u>

Create a client profile from an upcoming writing assignment so that students have a sense of where the facts of a case originate. Have a student from outside the class such as your teaching assistant role play the client. You may act as the supervising attorney in a law firm and your students can be identified as associates in the firm who will conduct the interview as a group. You may wish to begin the interview and have the students focus on obtaining the facts from the client. You can guide the interview by making sure that students have acquired all of the necessary information from the client on a particular topic before moving onto another topic, making sure that students begin with open-ended questions before moving to close-ended questions, and making sure that the questions are not too personal or probing for the client given the early stage of the attorney-client relationship.

<u>In-Class Exercise No. 2:</u>

In the event, you do not have an upcoming assignment that can be easily linked to a client interview exercise, attached are six different scenarios that can be used. Students can be given the opportunity to role play the client for one-half of a class session and to role play the attorney for the other half of class. Students who play the role of the client should be given the following instructions. Please do not "read" your profile to the attorneys interviewing you. Try to get into your role and imagine how your client may feel about his/her circumstances. You are free to invent the remainder of your client's story so that you can answer any questions that the attorney may ask.

CLIENT PROFILE OF BRAD O'NEILL

You are BRAD O'NEILL, an admitted baseball fanatic to the point that you attend every River Cats home game and follows 2 major league baseball teams' standings. You still collect baseball cards. And even though you have no children of your own, you coach your 8 year-old nephew's Little League team.

At the last game in July 2005, there was a very annoying parent from the other team who was heckling your team every time they took the field. You first tried to get the umpire to handle the parent but it didn't do any good–probably because the guy had been drinking beer. You felt the parent was being very disruptive to the sport, let alone stressing your team. You confronted the parent yourself. The discussion soon escalated into a heated verbal exchange and eventually into the drunken parent taking a swing at you. A physical fight ensued. You suffered a broken nose and 8 stitches above your right eye. Both you and the other man were arrested by police but charges were eventually dismissed against both.

You have come to lawyers to discuss whether you have a good civil lawsuit for personal injuries against the drunken man.

HIDDEN INFORMATION: *Only if the attorney specifically asks if you have ever had something like this happen before or ask if you have gotten in this kind of trouble before do you reveal your 2 prior arrests. One arrest is for a fight in a sports bar last year during the last game of the World Series. You pled to a charge of disorderly conduct and you are on informal probation. About the same time, your girlfriend filed a domestic violence charge against you when you threw an empty beer bottle at her during a baseball game. You didn't mean to hurt her–it was an accident. But she got 8 stitches above her eyebrow and the treating ER doctor reported you to law enforcement. You think you are in some kind of diversion program that if you complete a 52-week anger management class, the criminal charge will be erased.*

CLIENT PROFILE OF ELLA MAE MORGAN

You are ELLA MAE MORGAN, a widowed grandmother of 2 children, J.T., age 1 and Ellie, age 3, who live with you in your 3-bedroom house.

J.T. and Ellie's mother, Brenda, also lives with you off and on, mostly off these days. Brenda is a 22-year-old unemployed female. Brenda is a frequent drug user and a prostitute with a number of convictions. Brenda does not know the identity of either of the fathers of her children. Brenda's only source of income is welfare which she sometimes shares with you but most often she seems to use for drugs or alcohol as far as you can tell.

You have been making sure that your grandchildren are well-fed, well-clothed and that Ellie gets to preschool on time every day. So far you have been pretty successful. However, several days ago you and Brenda got into an argument. Brenda threatened that if you didn't "stay out of her business" she would move out of your house with the children and you would never see them again.

You are concerned that you cannot continue to protect your grandchildren from Brenda's lifestyle. Your friends tell you that you should seek a guardianship of your grandchildren.

HIDDEN INFORMATION: *Only if the attorney asks questions about your personal background do you reveal that you take Prozac for clinical depression. If the attorney asks appropriate follow-up questions you tell him/her about a car accident you got into about two months ago. You stupidly mixed drinking alcohol, taking Prozac and picking the kids up from school. The other driver told you that he could smell alcohol on your breath. You were scared so after exchanging information with the other driver you left–you did not stick around for the police to arrive since it was just a "fender bender".*

CLIENT PROFILE OF NICK/NICOLE BROOKS

You are NICK/NICOLE BROOKS. You have come to see a lawyer because you and your spouse are planning to open a day care business out of your home. You and your spouse have a 2 year old of your own with another one on the way. You felt it would be cheaper for one of you to stay home and run your own day care business rather than paying someone else to do so. But you do not know anything about running such a business. Do you need a business license? A written contract? You have a written contract with your current day care provider and you were wondering if you could get into trouble copying the contract for your own use. Are there rules about how much you can charge per week?

You live in a 3-bedroom fixer-upper with an above-ground pool in the backyard. (You and your spouse have not had time to maintain the pool so it has become more of a pond for mosquitoes.) Are there rules about how many kids you can watch? Are there rules about having a pool? Can the lawyers recommend a good business guidebook about opening a day care business?

HIDDEN INFORMATION: *Only if the attorney specifically asks you about whether your spouse will be involved in the day care business do you advise them of the following: your spouse is an employee in a local cannery. There are slow times during certain harvest times so you expect that your spouse will be home with you sometimes. But you quickly add that you are going to tell everyone that your spouse will never be there because a while back your spouse had his/her children from another relationship taken away from him/her by Child Protective Services for neglect.*

CLIENT PROFILE OF ALEX CARPENTER

You are ALEX CARPENTER. About 3 months ago you bought a "previously owned" 2006 Volvo sedan from a local car dealer. The car dealer let you test drive the Volvo and everything was working fine. The car dealer represented that the car had been repossessed from the previous owner so it only had about 4,000 miles on it. You agreed to buy the car for $28,000 "as is"; you couldn't afford to buy any extended warranties and as you understood it, all the standard factory warranties had run out before you bought the car. Your credit union that gave you the loan for the car reported that you probably paid too much for the car–you paid above Kelly bluebook.

The Volvo has been in for repairs 2 times during the past month. Apparently, it all has to do with its computer. The first problem was that the Volvo would stall at intersections whenever you had to stop. It was some kind of fuel injection problem that cost you $1,000. Last week you got another computer message on the dash that you had another problem with the engine. You don't speak auto mechanic lingo but it has something to do with replacing some parts in the engine. You were given an original estimate of $250 for parts and labor but you are fearful that this repair will exceed that amount. This car is not what it was represented to be. Can you cancel the contract and get your money back? You would be willing to pay fair rental value for the Volvo for the days you actually got to drive it.

HIDDEN INFORMATION: If you feel that the attorney is sympathetic to your plight, you tell them that you have lodged a written complaint against the car dealer with the Better Business Bureau and the Bureau of Automotive Repairs in the state Department of Consumer Affairs. The government moves too slowly for you. If the attorney seems interested in this part of your story, you also tell him/her that you saw 2 other attorneys who couldn't help you. So with the help of a computer geek friend of yours, you have created a website that trashes the car dealer–it is kind of like picketing the car dealer, but on-line. See if the attorney thinks that is a great way to get the dealer's attention.

CLIENT PROFILE OF CHRIS BARKER

You are CHRIS BARKER. Until about 2 days ago when you walked off the job in tears, you had been a paralegal at a local law office.

You have been a paralegal for about 5-6 years. This is the third law office that you have worked at. You started at your present job about 6 months ago and you thought everything was going great. You worked for 2 male attorneys who had even temperaments. Occasionally, they would ask you to come in on weekends or stay late, and you always accommodated them, in part because they were courteous with their requests.

Unfortunately, last month a new female attorney joined the firm. She had a temperament close to Meryl Streep's in her latest movie "The Devil Wears Prada". This attorney, Melissa, was always yelling at everyone, from the staff to opposing counsel to her clients. When she tried to bark orders at you, you told her that she could not speak to you in that tone of voice.

Two days ago there was a big scene because you had put one of her projects behind one of the other attorneys so she came into your office insisting on an explanation as why her "request" had not been completed. The discussion became heated and you recall her telling you that you were incompetent. All that you could think to do was call her a "bitch" and you ran out.

You want to know if you have to put up with such a hostile work environment. Do you have any rights? Melissa has caused you emotional distress and your doctor has prescribed medication for the anxiety.

HIDDEN INFORMATION: Only if the attorney asks you specific questions about the circumstances of your leaving your prior 2 jobs do you tell him/her that you left on "unfriendly" terms with both of those jobs too. You got some "severance pay" from the first employer after you sent a letter threatening to sue them. You filed a complaint with the state department of fair employment against your second employer because no attorney would take your case. The department is still investigating your complaint.

CLIENT PROFILE OF MALLORY SEACREST

You are MALLORY SEACREST, a single parent of Lindsay, a 13-year-old student in 8th grade at a local middle school. You are both confused and upset that she and you have been sued by a father and his 8th grade son following an altercation after school between Lindsay and the boy.

Your daughter, Lindsay, has been the subject of verbal teasing by a group of boys at the middle school for months. You have complained to the school administration. Lindsay was taken out of all the classes that the boys shared with her, but the taunting seemed to continue. They teased her about her weight, the clothes she wears and about her friends. Lindsay told you that 2 months ago the teasing began escalating into pranks, like pushing her into the lockers when they passed her in the hallways, trying to trip her in the lunchroom and following her to the school bus after classes.

You are proud of Lindsay because she is a scrappy girl who is not afraid to defend herself. You have encouraged your daughter to stand up for herself, especially when people do cruel and mean things like these boys.

Apparently last month, Darren Rogers, the ringleader of the boys who have been bothering her over the months, followed her to the bus stop after school was out. Lindsay reported to you that she repeatedly warned him to stop following her but he only laughed and kept getting closer and closer to her. Lindsay was fearful that he was going to try to physically hurt her so she reached into her backpack, pulled out a pair of scissors, turned around and scratched him in the face with the scissors.

Two copies of the summons and complaint were delivered to you at your one-bedroom apartment one evening last week. You did not bring the complaint with you but you read it. You do not understand much of it. It did say something about Darren having medical expenses for stitches to his face. It also asks you and Lindsay to pay $250,000 for Darren's injury.

You want to know if you can countersue Darren and his father for the months of harassment and torment they have caused Lindsay. You also want to know if you can sue the school for not protecting your daughter better.

HIDDEN INFORMATION: Unless the attorney specifically asks, you do not tell them that Lindsay has been in trouble at school before. She has been suspended for smoking cigarettes in the girl's bathroom during school. She has been kicked out of two different classes for being "insubordinate" to the teachers. She also has been reprimanded on 2 occasions for instigating physical altercations with a rival gang of girls. You downplay these incidents and repeat that Lindsay is a good kid who keeps getting picked on.

CRITIQUE FORMS:

Critique forms can be used by the student interviewer to self-critique an interview that has been videotaped for later viewing. The critique form can also be used so that outside observers can provide feedback as to what they saw as effective or successful.

CLIENT INTERVIEWING AND COUNSELING -INITIAL CONSULTATION

CRITIQUE OF STUDENT PERFORMANCE

PERSON BEING CRITIQUED:_____

PERSON CRITIQUING:_____

1. WORKING ATMOSPHERE: (Established the beginning of an effective professional relationship and working atmosphere? Did the lawyer demonstrate an interest in or engage in a strategy to put the client at ease? Did the lawyer appear to have an agenda or objectives in mind for the initial consultation? Did the lawyer provide the client with any information about what to expect during the initial meeting? When appropriate, did lawyer orient client to special nature of the relationship including confidentiality? Did lawyer respond to client's concerns, duration and plan of the initial meeting, discuss mutual obligations and rights, after hours availability, etc. in a courteous, sensitive and professional manner?)

_____
_____
_____
_____
_____
_____

2. GATHERING RELEVANT INFORMATION: (Did the lawyer gather basic information about the client in an effective way. Did he/she let the client tell his/her story using active and passive listening? Learned how the client viewed his/her situation, using a combination of listening and questioning, drawing out both information and feelings, as appropriate, to develop a reasonable complete and reliable description of the problem?)

_____
_____
_____
_____
_____
_____

3. CLIENT'S GOALS AND EXPECTATIONS: (Learned the client's goals and initial expectations, modified or developed these as necessary.)

_____
_____
_____
_____

4. PROBLEM ANALYSIS: (Analyzed the client's problem with creativity and from both legal and non-legal perspectives, resulting in a clear and useful formulation of the problem.)

_____
_____
_____
_____
_____
_____

5. DEVELOPING A CLIMATE OF TRUST: (What did the lawyer do to develop and maintain a climate of trust with the client? Did you observe any behavior on the client's part that suggested that he/she was effective? What, if anything would you have done differently?)

_____
_____
_____
_____
_____

6. OTHER COMMENTS: (Most positive aspects of this exercise; suggestions for improvement, etc.)

_____
_____
_____
_____
_____

(Note: The criteria used here to evaluate an initial client interview are adapted from the criteria used in the ABA Client Counseling Competition.)

CHAPTER 12

COUNSELING THE CLIENT

■ ■ ■

By Kathleen Friedrich

I. In the practice of law, there are many situations in which communication effectiveness is driven by much more than intellectual content. This is particularly true with client interviewing and counseling which require strong oral communication skills.

This chapter continues the theme contained in the prior chapter. There are three essentials of effective communication that sustain the working relationship between the client and the lawyer: genuineness, respect and empathy.

Here, genuineness is synonymous with authenticity, sincerity and transparency. The genuine, sincere, or transparent lawyer exhibits openness and allows the client to know what he or she is thinking and feeling. Being genuine provides the avenue for being viewed as a trustworthy person. Interactions between the lawyer and client will be smoother if both parties are open. And it is the lawyer who sets the stage for openness.

The characteristic of respect may also be defined as caring, acceptance, or people regard. Karl Menninger, a noted psychotherapist, speaks of this quality as a person's "patience, his fairness, his consistency, his rationality, his kindliness, in short—his real love." In the legal world, lawyers who are respectful of their clients generally receive the same treatment in return and allow for the free exchange of information.

Empathy is the third essential characteristic for effective communication. Achieving empathy is more difficult than becoming genuine and conveying respect. The first two qualities are behavioral. We can talk about our feelings. We can thank people for extra effort. We can show respect for people through active listening. Empathy, however, involves more heart, more intuition. Sympathy is feeling <u>for</u> someone and empathy is feeling <u>with</u> someone. In Milton Mayeroff's book <u>On Caring</u>, he notes: "To care for another person, I must be able to understand him and his world as if I were inside it. I must be able to see, as it were, with his eyes what his world is like... and how he sees himself." The listening habits of a person impact greatly on a person's ability to feel and express empathy. In addition, although the gift of empathy is a difficult personal characteristic to improve on, watching others being empathetic provides a foundation for learning this trait and improving our own performance of empathy.

II. Counseling is a skill that involves giving appropriate information to clients so that they can make informed decisions about what the best option is for them. In counseling, the lawyer weighs advantages, costs, risks and chances of success of one option against the advantages, costs, risks and chances of success of other options. Counseling is examining these variables with the client, explaining them to the client, and assisting the client to reach a decision about which of the options is best for the client. Thus, the lawyer needs to know something about legal remedies and the practicalities of each potential remedy. Counseling requires a more sophisticated understanding of not only what the client, in theory, can do, but also what in reality, the client should do. Students should not be introduced to this skill until they have completed a course on remedies, or at least the end of their first year in law school where they will have had exposure to remedies in their core courses such as torts, contracts and property.

III. LECTURE: To aid in presenting the material from this chapter in a lecture, I have included PowerPoint slides. Teachers should feel free to export some of the slides from the PowerPoint on client interviewing to remind students of the importance of active listening in oral communications.

Effective Techniques of Counseling and Advising

What is counseling?

- Counseling is the process in which lawyers help client reach decisions
- Counseling is a form of advice but not all advice is counseling.
- In counseling, lawyers weigh advantages, costs, risks & chances of success of 1 option against advantages, costs, risks & chances of success of another
- Counseling is working out those variables & explaining them to the client in a way that will help the client to decide

Client Counseling Process

- Two parts to counseling
  - 1. Preparation includes identifying client's goals & developing 2 or more alternative potential solutions that to varying degrees, might accomplish those goals
  - 2. Meeting with client where lawyer explains potential solutions so client can choose between or among them
- Interviewing & counseling can overlap in same meeting
  - Deadline
  - Emergency

Preparation

1. Identifying the problem
    a. Rank the client's goals
    b. Identify client's preferences
2. Gathering and evaluating information
3. Generating alternative potential solutions to problem
    a. Do not simply itemize solutions that are obvious
    b. Consider both legal & non-legal aspects & ramification of decisions
    c. What matters to client? business, financial, political, interpersonal or emotional factors
4. Evaluating each potential solution to measure its advantages, costs, risks and odds of success

Meeting with Client

- 1. Summarize client's concerns/goals
- 2. Demonstrate collaboration by beginning discussion of various options with "Let's brainstorm your situation together…" or "Let's discuss/analyze these concerns together…"
- 3. Prioritize into short-term goals/concerns and long-term goals/concerns
- 4. Choosing the best potential solution
  - Analyze legal consequences of options—lawyer's task
  - Analyze non-legal consequences of options—client's task
- 5. Acting on solution chosen

Counseling Techniques

- Involve the client so that you have a genuine conversation
- Give the client helpful respect
- Consider in advance how you will explain legal concepts & terminology
- Ignore your own emotional needs
- Explain the option neutrally
- Give the client empathy
- Face the harsh facts

Skills of a Good Counselor

- Need to be able to combine empathy & detachment
  - Empathy helps you understand clients goals and needs
  - Detachment helps you see the problem as it really is, without delusion
- Perspective: able to see client's situation from within & at same time, from a distance
- Give advice that is compassionate & objective

IV. VIDEO EXAMPLES OF COUNSELING

Each year, the ABA Law Student Division records the championship round of the three top-ranked national ABA Client Counseling Competition teams. The competition simulates a law office consultation in which law students, acting as attorneys, are presented with a client matter. They conduct an interview with a person playing the role of the client and then explain how they would proceed further in the hypothetical situation. Teachers can assign one 30-minute interview along with the 15-minute post-consultation session or assign all three interviews so that students can see several interviewing and counseling styles.

The ABA sells two versions – one containing the video of the round only; the other containing the video plus the complete regional and national competition problems, including the confidential information for competition judges. You may order online through the ABA website; DVD's may also be purchased through the ABA Service Center (800.285.2221).

Each year the subject matter of the competition changes, so you can choose a subject matter that may be more appropriate to your class. Here is a list of the subject matter of the counseling competition from prior years:

2011-12	K-12 Education/School Law
2010-11	Professional Responsibility of Lawyers and Judges
2009-10	White Collar Crime
2008-09	Negligence and Related Tort Claims
2007-08	Civil Rights/Civil Liberties

V. CLIENT COUNSELING EXERCISES:

COUNSELING EXERCISE #1

<u>Telephone Counseling Exercise:</u>

Students are randomly assigned to represent either the plaintiff or the defendant on two law and motion matters in the federal district court. Students for the party losing the motions are instructed to counsel their client about the meaning of the loss to their claim/defense and the next steps in the litigation including a possible appeal. Students for the party winning the motions are instructed to counsel their client about the meaning of the court's order to their claim/defense, the next steps in the litigation including a possible appeal, and options to avoid appeal. The students' professor acts as the client for both sides in this exercise.

Instructions for Telephone Counseling Exercise:

For this assignment, you will be required to telephone your client at an assigned time. The number to call for your client is XXX-XXXX. When you sign up for your call on TWEN, you will indicate which side you represent and a representative for that side of the case will answer your call.

Your job is to alert your client to the resolution of the relevant motion (e.g. Defendant's Motion for Summary Judgment) and explain to your client the appellate process. You should be prepared to counsel the client about the next steps she may pursue in this litigation, and explain the substance of the appeal.

You will have 8-10 minutes to discuss the case with the client. If you represent plaintiffs, you need to have authorization from the client to pursue the appeal by the end of the conversation. If you represent the defendant, you must prepare the client for the next steps and point out the strengths and weaknesses of the defendant's position on appeal.

After you have completed your phone call, you will receive brief feedback about the substance of your counseling, as well as your professional demeanor and your success at communicating information to the client.

Benefits of the Telephone Counseling Exercise:

This exercise may be the first and only time students deliberate about the motives of their respective clients in this litigation. Even this brief glimpse of who their respective clients are aids their ability to be zealous advocates in the appellate brief.

COUNSELING EXERCISE #2

Problem Summary**: Male student writes a letter during his summer vacation to his ex-girlfriend in which he threatens to rape and murder her. The letter is never delivered to the ex-girlfriend by him. Instead, a friend of the male student steals the letter and shares the contents with the ex-girlfriend after school begins. School officials learn of the "threatening" letter after a friend of the ex-girlfriend reports the incident to the school resource officer. The school principal investigates and decides to expel the male student for one year. The parents of the male student are challenging the principal's decision. (**Problem based on <u>John Doe v. Pulaski County Special School District</u>, 306 F. 3d 616 (8th Cir. 2002).)

Factual Background: M (male student) and F (female student) began "going together" the prior school year. They primarily saw each other at school and church. Their relationship was marked by multiple break-ups during the prior school year.

Sometime during their summer vacation, F broke up with M for the final time because she was interested in another boy. Frustrated by the break-up and upset that F would not go out with him again, M drafted 2 documents that expressed a desire to molest, rape and murder F. M intended to write a rap song with lyrics similar to Eminem, Juvenile and Kid Rock. Finding that his "song" fit no particular beat or rhythm, he penned the documents as letters, signing them at the end.

M prepared both letters at his home where they remained until M's best friend, (M2), discovered one of them approximately 1 month before school started. M2 found the letter in M's bedroom while he was searching for something on top of a dresser. Before M2 had a chance to read the letter, M snatched it from his hand. M2 asked to read the letter and M handed it back to him and gave M2 permission to read the letter. M2 asked for a copy of the letter but M refused to give him one.

It is unclear exactly when and how F learned about the existence and contents of the letter. M2 may have told her because M2 and F were friends. Shortly before the school year began, F discussed the letter with M during 2 or 3 telephone conversations—at first he denied authorship but M eventually admitted to F that he had written the letter. M made similar admissions to F's best friend who would likely convey information to her.

Concerned about the letter, F enlisted M2's help in getting the letter from M. About 1 week before the start of school, M2 spent the night at M's house, took the letter from M's room. M2 did so without M's knowledge or permission. M2 delivered the letter to F on the second day back from summer vacation and F read it in gym class in the presence of other students. One of the students immediately went to the school resource officer and reported that threats had been made against F. The officer found F in the gym, crying and frightened. The officer investigated and informed the school administration about the situation.

The principal also investigated. He recommended that M be expelled for the remainder of the school year based on violation of Rule 36 in the school district's Handbook for Student Conduct and Discipline.

Additional background facts: Before the break-up, M may have bragged to F, as well as her best friend, that he was a member of the "Bloods" gang which isn't likely to be true since he is a white male. Also, F reported that M once stated that he shot a cat during a telephone conversation.

M was a recipient of a certificate of honor from the local Chamber of Commerce, was a student in good academic standing with a record of good behavior. He did not possess any weapons.

A police report was filed on this incident, but the district attorney did not press charges.

M participated in church activities with F throughout the summer and he continued to have civil conversations with her even after she knew about the letters. After the investigation of the letters by school officials began, M apologized and hugged her and her mother at the church they attend together.

Counseling Exercise No 2- **School Rule 36**

HANDBOOK FOR STUDENT CONDUCT AND DISCIPLINE
(INSERT NAME) SCHOOL DISTRICT

Rule 36: Students shall not, with the purpose of terrorizing another student, threaten to cause death or serious injury or substantial property damage to another person or threaten physical injury to teachers or school employees.... Students will be suspended immediately and recommended for expulsion.

Counseling Exercise No. 2- **Student's Letter**

[PARTIAL TEXT OF STUDENT'S HANDWRITTEN DOCUMENT]

"F*** that bitch (female student's name)"

Student writer refers to female student as a "bitch", "slut", "ass", and "whore" over 80 times in 6 pages of handwritten text.

Student writer used "f***" word no fewer than 90 times and spoke frequently of a wish to sodomize, rape and kill female student.

In 2 passages, student writer expresses that female student should not go to sleep because he would be lying under her bed waiting to kill her with a knife.

[Document signed by student writer]

Instructions for Counseling Exercise #2:

Arrange for someone to role play the student and one of his parents and for someone else to role play the principal and a school district administrator. Both sets of actors should be given the problem background, the relevant school rule and the student's profane letter. Make extra copies of the rule and the letter so that the clients can share copies with their attorneys in the interview. Depending upon the backgrounds of the actors, teachers may need to discuss the non-legal consequences of certain solutions on each side. For instance, if the student has career plans that involve top security clearance, will the middle school expulsion impact such a career choice? On the other hand, the principal may want to be seen as a hero in his community and not a bully. Can the principal insist that he is keeping his school safe by making an example of this student?

Give the students who will act as attorneys a short memo about what their clients are coming in to see them about, i.e., expulsion from middle school, so that they can do some research on law of school expulsion in their controlling jurisdiction.

Divide the class in half so that one group represents the student and his parents and the other half of the class represents the principal and the school district. Each group should be given approximately 45 minutes to gather the facts and determine the goals of their clients concerning this problem. Teachers may need to guide the interview to make sure both side have gathered the bulk of the key facts and have obtained a copy of the relevant school rule and a copy of the student's profane letter. Allow the student attorneys to determine the goals of their clients and explore the non-legal consequences of each potential course of action. Are their economic consequences to both sides? Are there psychological consequences? Political consequences?

Short Version of Counseling Exercise # 2:

Bring all the attorneys and parties together to reflect on the exercise. Teachers should feel free to use the critique form provided below to guide the discussion. How did each side feel they did in counseling their client? Did they feel that any shortcomings in the counseling session where the fault of the attorney or the fault of the clients?

Longer Version of Counseling Exercise # 2:

Pair an attorney for the student and parent with an attorney for the principal and school district and have them attempt to negotiate a resolution of the problem. Each attorney should write down the terms of any settlement proposal that has been offered. After 15-20 minutes, bring all the attorneys and parties together to reflect on the exercise. Did those who represented the student and parent get the same set of facts as those who represented the principal and school district? Why might that be? Is this an issue in counseling the clients? Would any of the attorneys recommend to their respective clients the settlement offer proposed by the other side? Why or why not? As a follow-up, ask the client whether such a recommendation from the attorney suggests that the attorney heard and understands the client's goals and the non-legal consequences of such a solution. Teachers should feel free to use the critique form provided below to guide the discussion further.

VI. CRITIQUE FORMS:

Critique forms can be used by the student interviewer to self-critique an interview and counseling session that has been videotaped for later viewing. The critique form can also be used so that outside observers can provide feedback as to what they saw as effective or successful.

CLIENT INTERVIEWING AND COUNSELING

CRITIQUE OF STUDENT PERFORMANCE

PERSON BEING CRITIQUED:

PERSON CRITIQUING:

1. **WORKING ATMOSPHERE**: (e.g. Did the lawyer establish the beginning of an effective professional relationship and working atmosphere? Did the lawyer put the client at ease? Did he/she let the client tell his or her story using active and passive listening? When appropriate, did the lawyer orient the client to special nature of the relationship, including confidentiality? Did the lawyer respond to the client's concerns, discuss mutual obligations and rights, after hours availability, duration and plan of the consultation, in a courteous, sensitive and professional manner.)

2. **DESCRIPTION OF THE PROBLEM**: (e.g. Learned how the client viewed his or her situation, using a combination of listening and questioning, drawing out both information and feelings, as appropriate, to develop a reasonably complete and reliable description of the problem.)

3. **PROBLEM ANALYSIS**: (e.g. Analyzed the client's problem with creativity from both legal and non-legal perspectives, resulting in a clear and useful formulation of the problem.)

4. **MORAL AND ETHICAL ISSUES:** (e.g. Recognized, clarified and responded to any moral or ethical issues which may have arisen, without being prejudicial or judgmental.)

5. **ALTERNATIVE COURSES OF ACTION:** (e.g. Consistent with the analysis of the client's problem, developed a set of potentially effective and feasible alternatives, both legal and non-legal.)

6. **CLIENT'S INFORMED CHOICE**: (As appropriate, assisted the client in his or her understanding of problems and solutions and in

making an informed choice, taking potential legal, economic, social and psychological consequences into account.)

7. **CONCLUSION**: (e.g. Did the lawyer conclude the interview skillfully, leaving the client with a sense of confidence and understanding, and with a clear outline of the next steps to be taken and by whom?)

8. **THE MOST POSITIVE ASPECTS OF THIS EXERCISE WERE**:

9. **MY SUGGESTIONS FOR IMPROVEMENT INCLUDE**:

10. **OTHER COMMENTS**:

(Note: The criteria used here to evaluate the client interview are adapted from the criteria used in the ABA Client Counseling Competition.)

Chapter 13

Professional Correspondence

■ ■ ■

By Jeffrey Proske

This chapter is designed to provide students with a general overview of the range of considerations that come in to play in drafting professional correspondence, from the legal significance of the attorney client privilege and standards of professionalism, to practical considerations about the benefits of creating a clear history of a client matter, as well as instructions on specific information that must be included in basic correspondence. The chapter provides lists for the components of effective transmittal letters, advice letters and demand letters.

Because the content of an advice letter or a demand letter depends entirely on having performed an objective legal analysis, the Professional Correspondence chapter should be assigned after the students have covered objective legal writing and outlining in Chapters 6, 8, 9 and 10. Since a demand letter does require a more persuasive tone and analytical formula, it may be helpful to also assign Chapter 14 at the same time or just before this Chapter.

A useful way to help students master the task of drafting an effective advice letter or demand letter is to link the professional correspondence drafting component to the objective and predictive legal memorandum assignment. By having the students translate their findings from an objective legal memorandum to an advice letter to a non-attorney client, the students can demonstrate the ability to convey the essential advice arrived at from their legal analysis and view that legal analysis in the larger context of a client's representation. It's also a useful way of helping the students understand how sometimes arcane conclusions arrived at through legal analysis apply in the real-world in a meaningful and practical way, and how they translate into specific action items in the representation of the client.

Chapter 10 of this manual contains numerous sample objective legal memoranda that can serve as the foundation for an advice letter or demand letter exercise. Chapter 14 provides an objective memorandum and mediation brief sample based on the same problem as the sample demand letter addressed to Old Navy below.

Sample Advice Letter

Law Offices of Paul Levenson
3200 Fifth Avenue
Sacramento, CA 95817
February 20, 2013

Mr. Horatio Caine
1018-1020 Du Fort
Montreal, Quebec
H3H2B3
Certified Mail

Re: <u>Joint Venture Agreement with Rian Wolfe</u>

Dear Mr. Caine,

     You have asked me to research three questions regarding your joint venture agreement with Ryan Wolfe in connection with your recent purchase and sale of a property, The Inn, at Indian Wells. First, whether you had a right to rescind your joint venture agreement; second, whether you followed the proper procedure for rescinding the joint venture agreement; and third, whether a complaint can be served on you in Montreal, Canada.

     My opinions are based upon the following facts. You are a U.S. citizen that divides your time between your primary residence in California and your second home in Montreal. On November 1, 2011, you entered into a joint venture agreement with Mr. Wolfe for the purchase, renovations and sale of The Inn at Indian Wells, which had ten guest cottages. The agreement stipulated that you would make the down payment for the property, pay the mortgage tax, insurance, and maintenance costs and Mr. Wolfe would complete all the renovations by November 30, 2012.

     You purchased the property on November 15, 2011 and Mr. Wolfe began solely renovating the units, which he estimated would take approximately one month per unit. On June 25, 2012 Mr. Wolfe sent you a project update informing you he had completed nearly five of the ten units. On November 1, 2012, you visited the property to find that only six units had been completed. On November 2, 2012 you sent Mr. Wolfe a letter expressing your concern that the deadline would not be met and reminding him that you were carrying all the costs. Mr. Wolfe responded on November 3, 2012, apologizing for the delay, explaining that he temporarily abandoned the renovations for paying work, and promising to make every effort to finish the renovations by November 30, 2012. After receiving Mr. Wolfe's letter you decided to rescind the agreement. On November 5, 2012 you sent Mr. Wolfe a letter advising him that because you did not believe the renovations would be completed by the agreed upon date of November 30, 2012 the agreement was rescinded. You sold the property on December 29, 2012 for a profit and are now residing in Canada until May 2013.

Right to Rescind the Agreement

In determining whether a party has a right to rescind an agreement courts examine what was owed to the rescinding party under the contract and whether it failed in a material way before it was given to the rescinding party. Generally, courts have determined whether there was a material failure by looking at what the purpose of the contract was and whether the issue giving rise to the right to rescind went to that purpose. In the past, courts have found a material failure where one party purchases land from another party and the other party promises to make improvements by a given deadline and only completes a substantial portion of the improvements by the deadline.

Here, the ultimate purpose of your joint venture agreement with Mr. Wolfe was for both of you to make a profit. In order for you both to make a profit without losing money, Mr. Wolfe had to make the renovations by the agreed upon deadline of November 30, 2012, while you covered the costs. Since Mr. Wolfe had determined that it would take him approximately one month per unit, as he was solely performing the renovations, it follows that he probably would not have completed the renovations of four units in one month in order to meet the deadline. Because Mr. Wolfe would most likely not meet the deadline and the value of the completed units by the deadline was what you were paying for under the contract, in order for you both to make a profit, we should be able to prove you had a right to rescind the contract.

Procedure for Rescinding the Agreement

To properly rescind a contract, a party to the contract must give timely notice of rescission to the other party upon discovering the facts that entitle him to rescission and give to the other party everything of value which he has received under the contract or offer to give the other party everything of value which he has received under the contract on the condition that the other party does the same.

Your letter to Mr. Wolfe on November 5, 2012 stated your reason for rescinding the agreement and was sent within five days of your discovering the facts that entitled you to rescind (only six units complete by November 1, 2012). Between November 1, 2012 and November 5, 2012 you gave Mr. Wolfe a chance to explain why the renovations were behind and also allowed Mr. Wolfe to suggest a remedy. Because you notified Mr. Wolfe of the rescission within five days of discovering the facts that allowed you to rescind and you gave Mr. Wolfe the opportunity to explain himself we should be able to prove that you gave timely notice of rescission.

However, in your letter of rescission to Mr. Wolfe you made no offer to give him everything back you received under the agreement (Mr. Wolfe's labor). You also failed to give Mr. Wolfe back everything of value you received under the contract or offer to give Mr. Wolfe everything back of value you received under the contract after selling the property for a profit. Because you failed to give everything back of value you received under the contract to Mr. Wolfe and because you failed to even offer to do so you did not follow the proper procedure for rescinding the agreement.

Service of Process in Montreal

The United States and Canada are members of a convention that governs a U.S. citizen's ability to serve a complaint on someone residing in Canada. Under the convention, a U.S. citizen may serve a complaint on someone residing in Canada through personal service made by a sheriff or a hussier, however, in any place, if there is no sheriff or hussier within a radius of fifty kilometers, service may be made by any person of legal age or by registered or certified mail.

Since you will be residing in Montreal, Canada until May 2013, Mr. Wolfe will be able to serve a complaint on you there if he follows the proper procedures.

My opinions regarding the three issues discussed above are based upon the facts as stated above, and upon the law as it existed at the time I drafted this letter. Should you have knowledge of any additional information, please contact me immediately.

On the basis of the analysis in this letter, you did have a right to rescind the agreement. However, you did not follow the proper procedure for doing so. Because you did not follow the proper procedure Mr. Wolfe may be able to sue you for compensation for his labor. Although Mr. Wolfe might have a claim against you, you may be able to counterclaim or sue Mr. Wolfe for breach of contract. If you provide me with authorization, I would be happy to look into the breach of contract theory.

At this point I will take no further action until I hear from you. Please telephone me with any concerns you may have and with your instructions as to what actions, if any, I should take.

Sincerely,

Paul Levenson

Sample Demand Letter

March 4, 2012

Old Navy, LLC
c/o Roger Rabbit, Esq.
500 Hilton Universal Way, Suite 1250
Universal City, CA 91602

    RE: <u>Old Navy, LLC</u>

Dear Mr. Rabbit:

    This firm represents Kim Kardashian. On behalf of Ms. Kardashian, we request that Old Navy, LLC immediately cease and desist from the current or future use of our client's likeness in any form, including the "Super C-U-T-E" video advertisement and related campaign featuring Melissa Molinaro, which first aired in February, 2011.

    Our client asserts that Old Navy intended to capitalize on the recognizable likeness and persona of Kim Kardashian by using a Kim Kardashian look-alike. We believe this use constitutes an unlawful appropriation of Ms. Kardashian's likeness under California law.

    At no time did Ms. Kardashian grant her permission, authorization, or consent to Old Navy in any form or manner. Old Navy's unauthorized use of Ms. Kardashian's likeness for its commercial gain has caused a diminution in the value that is tied to her image, which she has developed over the years, which she currently contractually capitalizes upon, and which is rightfully hers.

    Pursuant to California Civil Code § 3344,[6] Ms. Kardashian is entitled to bring an action to enjoin Old Navy's misappropriation of her likeness and to recover for her damages. Civil Code § 3344 provides, in part, that one who uses the likeness of another in any manner, without that person's consent, for the purpose of selling merchandise, shall be liable to that person for actual damages. This statute has been interpreted

---

  [6] Cal. Civ. Code Ann. § 3344(a) (West, Westlaw Current with urgency legislation through Ch. 745 of 2011 Reg.Sess. and 2011-2012 1st Ex.Sess. laws).

by the courts to include an image of the person that either suggests imitation of the person by being sufficiently reminiscent of, or readily identifiable as, that person as a result of distinctive or unique characteristics of both physical appearance and personality.[7]

In <u>Kirby v. Sega of Am., Inc.</u>, the court reasoned that though an electronic game character was not an exact replica of the person in question, the similarities, such as facial features, dress, hair color, hairstyle, and use of certain catch-phrases, were enough to survive a motion for summary judgment.[8] While Ms. Molinaro is not an exact replica of Ms. Kardashian, her appearance is similar in many respects, including hair color and style, eye color and shape, a wide smile, and a trendy persona. Slight differences in in skin tone and fashion-trendiness notwithstanding, the similarities are notable. Because the Kirby court found there was sufficient similarity, despite some differences, to survive a motion for summary judgment, the court in our case will likely find that there are sufficient material issues of fact for Ms. Kardashian's case to survive any motion Old Navy might make for summary judgment and to allow her case to be heard by a jury.

While we acknowledge that Old Navy may take some passing comfort in the notion that case law on similar matters might support a motion for summary judgment in Old Navy's favor, this is probably not the case. For instance, the court in White v. Samsung Electronics Am., Inc.,[9] held that the law protects a celebrity's right to exploit and benefit from her own celebrity. While White ultimately failed on the statutory cause of action, Ms. Kardashian's case would be more likely to survive a motion for summary judgment, given that the subject of the comparison is an actress who arguably bears resemblance to Ms. Kardashian, not a robot as inWhite.

Additionally, the court in <u>Newcombe v. Adolf Coors Co.</u>,[10] held that whether the plaintiff was readily identifiable raised a triable issue of fact

---

[7] *Kirby v. Sega of Am., Inc.*, 144 Cal. App. 4th 47 (2d Dist. 2006); *Newcombe v. Adolf Coors Co.*, 157 F.3d 686 (9th Cir. 1998).

[8] *Kirby*, 144 Cal. App. 4th at 57.

[9] *White v. Samsung Electronics Am., Inc.*, 971 F.2d 1395 (9th Cir. 1992).

[10] *Newcombe v. Adolf Coors Co.*, 157 F.3d 686 (9th Cir. 1998).

based on a primary, unique and distinctive characteristic. While identification of a primary, unique, and distinctive characteristic may be harder to find in the present comparison, it is likely that, because reasonable minds may differ on the nature of the similarity, the "sufficiently reminiscent" standard of Kirby will be enough to allow Ms. Kardashian's claim to survive any such motion.

As a result of Old Navy's unauthorized use of Ms. Kardashian's likeness, her intangible losses are significant, inasmuch as continued use of her likeness causes confusion to her fans and worse, a presumption in the advertising and entertainment community that this type of advertising is somehow permissible. Additionally, Ms. Kardashian has suffered a tangible and significant economic loss from the diminution in her commercial advertising value as a result of Old Navy's advertisement. According to the calculations of our entertainment actuary, the current amount of that damage is in the range of $5-7 million dollars, exclusive of attorney's fees and costs. Those damages continue to increase.

Therefore, we respectfully request that Old Navy immediately:

1. Cease and desist from any further use of our client's likeness in any form, including without limitation the use of the "Super C-U-T-E" video advertisement and related campaign featuring Melissa Molinaro.
2. Remove from any web page or other media any active or archived versions of the advertisement.
3. Issue a public apology to Ms. Kardashian, by way of press release and written communication to our office, which communication may be further used or published by Ms. Kardashian or her authorized representatives.
4. Refrain from any present or future advertising and related campaigns that feature Melissa Molinaro or another actress with characteristics similar to Ms. Kardashian.

Ms. Kardashian wishes to resolve this matter as expeditiously as possible. Despite the damages that Ms. Kardashian has suffered and continues to suffer, you will note that at this time she has not requested any monetary recovery for the economic losses attributed to Old Navy's misuse, nor has she requested reimbursement for attorney's fees, court costs, or related expenses borne by her to date.

Accordingly, we have included a draft settlement agreement for your consideration. While we are willing to further discuss the specifics of this agreement, resolution of this matter without further litigation would be subject to the agreement of the parties on the above terms, finalization of the agreement, and execution thereof. Alternately, if Old Navy is not amenable to the suggested terms, we are willing to participate in some form of alternative dispute resolution, either mediation or arbitration, to resolve this short of commencing litigation.

In the regrettable circumstance that Old Navy is unwilling to meet these very modest terms or participate in a mutually agreeable form of alternative dispute resolution, Ms. Kardashian intends to commence an action against Old Navy to permanently enjoin Old Navy from its use of the advertisement, and also for recovery of monetary damages, including punitive damages, costs, and attorney's fees. We hope the time and expense of such an action can be avoided by an earlier resolution of this matter.

Kindly discuss this matter and respond to our office. Your response will be considered timely if received by me by 5:00 p.m. on March 15, 2012, after which we will pursue other legal remedies.

Sincerely,

Marlyn Levenson
Attorney at Law

Enclosures
ML/jep

cc: Kim Kardashian

CHAPTER 14

PERSUASIVE LEGAL WRITING

■ ■ ■

By Mary–Beth Moylan and Adrienne Brungess

The purpose of this chapter is help students transition from objective to persuasive writing. Chapter 14 highlights the main differences between the objective and persuasive paradigms and illustrates the importance of having a solid, objectively-created foundation when beginning persuasive argument. This chapter can be used at the end of a 1L course or semester and/or at the beginning of a 2L course or second semester that focuses on persuasive writing.

Example slides are included at the end of this chapter to help illustrate the transition from objective writing to persuasive writing. Additionally, an example objective memorandum and persuasive mediation brief are included to further illustrate the process of objective analysis of a client's problem to a persuasive analysis of that same problem. The problem assumes that although the objective memo predicted an unfavorable outcome for the client, the student was instructed to make and support the client's position in a mediation brief. The same client problem referenced here is also the basis for the demand letter example included with Chapter 13.

When teaching the persuasive CRAC paradigm, you can assign a single limited topic and have students draft a single CRAC to start working with the persuasive paradigm in steps – working up to a complete persuasive argument in, e.g., a trial or appellate brief. An example "CRAC" is included; it was created for a 2L research and writing class. Students submitted a single CRAC in a memo to an assigning partner to show understanding of the new paradigm. Student can exchange their work and edit one another's CRAC structure. A Peer Edit Checklist is included for that purpose.

PRACTICE EXERCISE

Students may have a wide range of answers to the Practice Exercise on page 140 of the text. Since they have been directed to represent Goldilocks, any persuasively written rule should focus on the exception to the rule, rather than the general rule. For example, they might initially articulate the rule as follows.

Persuasive Rule: Young princesses may sleep in the bed of another person or animal when they have been left in the forest to die, despite the general rule ordinarily prohibiting such activity. Snow White v. Seven Dwarves, 357 FT.2d 468, 470 (1986).

However, since Goldilocks is not a princess, they might have to make the rule more general and focus on the exception in order to adapt the rule to fit their client's situation. An expanded rule that focuses on the exception might look like this:

Persuasive Rule: Young girls in dangerous situations may sleep in the bed of another without express permission under the exigency exception to the private bed rule. Snow White v. Seven Dwarves, 357 FT.2d 468, 470 (1986).

Their application of the rule can then focus on the similarities of Goldilocks to Snow White and urge a similar application of the rule to Goldilocks' case.

Persuasive Analysis Paragraph: The exigency exception to the rule prohibiting sleeping in another person's bed should be applied to Goldilocks. The youth and vulnerability of a lost eight year old, Goldilocks, is similar to the precarious position faced by Snow White when she was left in the forest to die. The court in Snow White reasoned that where there is an emergency, a young girl should be allowed to find protection in the bed of another. 357 FT.2d at 470. That same rationale should apply here since Goldilocks was hungry, tired, and lost. Like Snow White, she had no opportunity to seek permission for the shelter and comfort of the bed she found. And, like the princess in Snow White, she was frightened and alone. Therefore, the same exigency exception from Snow White should extend to the Goldilocks case.

Example Slides

Introduction to Persuasive Writing

Persuasive Writing Generally

- New Purpose
  - Argument and persuasion
- New Reader
  - Court/Mediator, Opposing Counsel
- New Presentation
  - Favorable rules and one-sided analysis

The Persuasive Paradigm

- What happened to the "E"?

The purpose of the document is different.
- The purpose of your objective memo was to educate and predict.
- The purpose of your persuasive brief is to persuade.

The information you need to "explain" the synth R comes by way of parenthetical explanation or supplemented case comparison using analogical reasoning.

The Persuasive First Conclusion

The first Conclusion
- It is a thesis sentence
- It needs to direct the reader and the paragraph
- It needs to assert, with conviction, that the client's position is the right result
  - Do not use probably, likely, etc.

The Persuasive Rule

- Substance of the rule must contain:
  - Language of governing statutes or case law.
  - Controlling case authority.
  - The best rules or legal authorities for your client.
  - Exceptions or defenses, if applicable
  - Unfavorable *controlling* authority -- do not assume opposing counsel won't find controlling authority and it is unethical to leave it out.

The Persuasive Rule

- Use strategic phrasing and organization of the rule to make it persuasive
  - A broad or narrow phrasing of rule can extend or restrict its persuasive effect
  - Begin the rule with the outcome you want for your client; that is, if you want an injunction to be granted begin by stating "An injunction will be granted when …"
  - Begin the rule with your client's role in the litigation; that is, Plaintiff or Defendant. For example, "A plaintiff is entitled to an injunction when …"
  - Include the favorable part of the rule at the beginning to provide emphasis.
  - Include unfavorable parts of the rule in the middle to bury them.
  - Emphasize the opposing party's requirements of proof (burdens, elements, evidence, etc.). For example, "For a defendant to prevail on his motion, he must prove five elements with substantial evidence." Or, "Defendant has the burden of proof."

The Persuasive Rule

- **EXAMPLE OBJECTIVE RULE:**
  California Civil Code Section 3344(a) provides that the knowing use of another's photograph for commercial purposes without the person's pri-or consent is a violation of that person's right of publicity. Section 3344(d) provides an exception to the consent requirement contained in § 3344(a), which states that the use of a photograph in connection with "any news, public affairs, or sports broadcast or account, or any politi-cal campaign" does not require consent

- **EXAMPLE PERSUASIVE RULE FOR PLAINTIFF:**
  The knowing use of another's photograph for commercial purposes without the person's consent violates California Civil Code Section 3344(a). The only exception to the statutory consent requirement is if the defendant can prove that the use of a photograph was in connection with a matter in the public interest. Cal. Civ. Code § 3344(d).

The Persuasive Analysis

- It shows that the application of the rules to your client's case compels the result you seek.
- Anticipates and refutes counter-arguments.

The Persuasive Analysis

- Types of reasoning are the same as objective:
  - Directly apply a rule the facts of your case
  - Analogize cases to show how your case is parallel to those cases as support for the result you seek
  - Distinguish cases to show how your case does not fit within a particular rule or approach
  - Argue policies to show that your case satisfies both the rule and the underlying purpose of the rule

The Persuasive Last Conclusion

- Restate persuasively the conclusion provided in the first C
- Clearly state the relief requested
- Assert, with conviction, that the client's position is the right result
  - Do not use probably, likely, etc.

Large-Scale Organization

- Some similarities to objective writing large-scale organizational principles:
  - Complete CRAC for each individual issue
    - No blending of issues
    - Argue each issue one at a time
  - Roadmaps
  - Point Headings
  - Thesis sentences

Large-Scale Organization

- New organizational strategies specific to persuasive writing:
  - Provide your best argument first
  - Select issues based on strength of the law
  - Anticipate and refute opponent's best arguments
  - Include policy-based arguments
  - Make assertive conclusions
  - Keep your arguments concise

Develop a Theme

- Persuasive writing must have a theme that weaves through the arguments.

- To determine your theme, ask yourself:
    - What moves you about this case?
    - What might move a judge or a jury?
    - How would you argue your case to a jury?
    - What sympathies would you play upon, etc.?

Developing a Theme

- Plaintiff's Theme
    - Plaintiffs usually develop a theme around the facts, the emotional side of the case, the injury, etc.
- Defendant's Theme
    - Defendants usually develop a theme around the law, their compliance with the law, and generally avoid the emotional side of a case.

Example "CRAC"

OFFICE MEMORANDUM

To: Clarence W. Bryant, Sr. Partner
From: John Smith, Student
Re: Argument in Opposition to Defendants' Motion for Disqualification
Date: August 28, 2013

ARGUMENT

Defendants' Motion for Disqualification of Judge Henry should be denied. The Honorable Wilhelmina Henry and Vivek Bhambra, as a judge and law clerk, respectively, are entitled to the presumption of impartiality. Further, despite the fact that Bhambra was in the process of securing employment with Bryant & Bryant while the firm was litigating a matter before Judge Henry, Bhambra's lack of involvement with the case quells any reasonable concerns of Judge Henry's partiality. Also, any duty on Judge Henry's part to avoid the appearance of partiality was fulfilled when she instructed Bhambra that he would be shielded from work on any matter before the judge being litigated by a firm with whom Bhambra had secured employment.

Judges and law clerks are entitled to the presumption that they will maintain impartiality in performance of their duties. First Interstate Bank of Ariz. v. Murphy, 210 F.3d 983, 989 (9th Cir. 2000). And, mere proof of a law clerk's relationship with one of the litigants does not in and of itself overcome this presumption. Barksdale v. Emerick, 853 F.2d 1359, 1360 (6th Cir. 1988) (determining that the fact that one of the members of a judge's small staff chambers was the son of one of the litigants was not a per se basis for disqualification).

A federal judge need disqualify herself only from when a reasonable person with knowledge of all the facts would conclude that the judge's impartiality might reasonably be questioned. 28 U.S.C. § 455 (2006); Hamid v. Price Waterhouse, 51 F.3d 1411, 1417 (9th Cir. 1995) (holding that even when a judge's clerk secures employment with a law firm representing one of the parties to a case before the judge, no reasonable person would conclude that the judge is partial where the clerk has had minimal involvement with the case). Additionally, a judge fulfills her duty to avoid the appearance of partiality in such a situation when she instructs her clerk not do any work on the matter. First Interstate, 210 F.3d at 989 (holding that a judge's instruction to a clerk to refrain from any work on a case being litigated by a firm with which the clerk had secured employment was consistent with the judge's duty to avoid the appearance of partiality).

As a judge and law clerk, the Honorable Wilhelmina Henry and Vivek Bhambra, respectively, are entitled to a presumption of impartiality. First Interstate, 210 F.3d at 989. The mere fact that Vivek Bhambra had an informal professional relationship with the firm of Bryant & Bryant is insufficient to overcome the presumption of impartiality. Decl. Bhambra ¶¶ 6-8; Barksdale, 853 F.2d at 1360. Further, Mr. Bhambra's affiliation with Bryant & Bryant and the Scheidl-Jones case are insignificant in that Mr. Bhambra has only received a verbal offer of employment from Bryant & Bryant and has had no contact with the case at bar. Decl. Bhambra ¶¶ 12-13. Therefore, no reasonable person would conclude that the impartiality of the Judge Henry's decisions in this case should be questioned. See Hamid, 51 F.3d at 1416.

Finally, because Judge Henry indicated that Mr. Bhambra would be shielded from any cases involving a law firm where she had received an offer of employment or was in serious negotiations for employment Judge Henry fulfilled her duty of avoiding the appearance of partiality. Decl. Bhambra ¶ 12; First Interstate, 210 F.3d at 989.

Both Judge Henry and Clerk Vivek Bhambra are entitled to a presumption of impartiality and no reasonable person would conclude that Judge Henry's decision making was tainted by Bhambra's employment prospects. Judge Henry fulfilled her duty of avoiding the appearance of partiality and Defendants' Motion for Disqualification of Judge Henry should be denied.

CRAC Peer Review Handout

Use this Handout to Review your colleague's CRAC assignment. Please provide comments both on this sheet and make marginal notations of areas that are confusing or grammatically challenging.

Conclusion

- ☐ Does it state the overall conclusion on the legal issue? Was it complete and does it match the rest of the CRAC?

Rule

- ☐ Does it include a statement of the rule on the legal issue?
    - ☐ Does it identify the case or cases to be used to create the rule? Does it identify specific cases to be used by name, provide a citation, or both?
    - ☐ Does it consider and identify any adverse legal authority?
    - ☐ Does it make the best use of the cases identified or does it miss an opportunity to add depth?
    - ☐ Does it include an explanation of the rule (not in the objective memo sense) but in a manner to provide enough information for the reader to understand the rule and how it operates?
    - ☐ Is the Rule crafted in a manner that favors the represented party?

Analysis

- ☐ Does it include the factual conclusion you want the judge to reach on the issue (this would be the thesis sentence to begin the A section of the CRAC)?
    - ☐ Is it more specific than the initial conclusion (the C in the CRAC)?
- ☐ Does it include analysis on the issue or just conclusions?
    - ☐ Does it use analogical reasoning?
    - ☐ Does it create clear comparisons between the facts of the precedent and your client?

- ☐ Does it connect those factual comparisons to the law to show the legal significance of the comparisons?
- ☐ Does it use policy-based reasoning?
- ☐ Does it identify the policy and provide citations to where the policy came from (rather than just a personal opinion of society)?
☐ Does it refute any adverse legal authority or rebut any anticipated arguments likely to be made by opposing counsel?

☐ Does the analysis persuade you to see the case the way the reader wants you to? Does it make sense?

Conclusion

☐ Does it restate the overall conclusion?

☐ Does it summarize the arguments made in this CRAC?

☐ Does the final conclusion tell you what the reader wants?

☐ Is it just a cut-and-paste of the first C? If so, how can you fix it so it is not exactly the same sentence?

EXAMPLE OBJECTIVE MEMORANDUM
OFFICE MEMORANDUM

TO: Supervising Attorney
FROM: Marianne Regretit
DATE: November 20, 2012
RE: Kardashian v. Old Navy

QUESTION PRESENTED

Under the California Civil Code on right of publicity, can Kim Kardashian's claim that Old Navy used her likeness survive a motion for summary judgment when an actress with similar hair color, skin color, and body type appears in an Old Navy commercial advertising the store's clothing?

BRIEF ANSWER

Probably yes. A person's likeness is appropriated when she is readily identifiable in a visual image that contains features so unique to and distinctive of her that the image calls her to mind, or at least that the image is sufficiently reminiscent enough of her to suggest imitation. The actress in Old Navy's Super C-U-T-E commercial has a distinctive feature of Kim Kardashian to make her readily identifiable within it. Kardashian is often featured for her famously large rear end. The Old Navy commercial uses an actress with a similar body shape and complexion; the actress is similar enough that a person could think it is Kardashian. Even if the court finds that Kardashian's shape, hair color, and style are not collectively unique to her, the actress in the commercial is still sufficiently reminiscent of Kardashian to call her to mind and constitute a likeness.

FACTS

Our client is Old Navy, an American brand of clothing and chain of stores targeted towards fashion-oriented but price conscious young adults. Kim Kardashian brings a statutory cause of action, alleging that Old Navy has misappropriated her likeness by using a lookalike in its Super C-U-T-E commercial, released February 2011. Old Navy has been sued in District Court in Los Angeles, and the case will be pursued in Federal Court due to diversity. We need to advise our client whether Kardashian's claim will survive a motion for summary judgment under the California statute on right of publicity, which allows persons to control the commercial use of their identities.

Kim Kardashian is an American celebrity and reality television star. She and her family are featured in their own television show on E!, Keeping Up With the Kardashians. Additionally, Kim is a model and spokeswoman for a wide variety of products including clothing, swimsuits, perfume, shoes, fast food, diet pills, jewelry, and tanning products.

Kardashian is one of the most famous Armenian-American women. Her dramatic, yet elegant makeup and long, dark hair are frequently featured on television and in magazines, including ELLE Magazine's article "Best Hair in America 2011" in which she was voted to have the best wave hairstyle. Kardashian is perhaps best known for her curvaceous body type. Many commercials of Kardashian feature her famously large rear-end and her seductive persona.

In the Old Navy commercial at issue, the actress is similarly proportioned to Kardashian. In many of the scenes, she poses and dances to accentuate her round shape. Approximately one minute long, the commercial shows the dark-haired actress from many angles and distances. The actress' hair is similar color and length and they share a similar complexion.

The following Discussion will evaluate whether Old Navy used Kardashian's "likeness" contrary to the California Civil Code provision protecting celebrities from use of their likeness without consent.

DISCUSSION

Kim Kardashian's likeness appropriation claim against Old Navy can likely survive a motion for summary judgment because there is sufficient evidence to support a finding of likeness. Under the California statute on right of publicity, a person violates another's right to publicity if she knowingly uses another's likeness for advertising purposes without that person's consent. Cal. Civ. Code Ann. § 3344(a) (West, Westlaw Current with urgency legislation and all 2011-2012 1st Ex.Sess. laws). The threshold issue is that of likeness, so this analysis will address only whether the actress in the Old Navy commercial constituted a likeness of Kardashian.

A court will most likely conclude that Old Navy could have appropriated Kardashian's likeness; the claim could therefore survive a motion for summary judgment. A person's "likeness" is appropriated when she is readily identifiable in a visual image that contains features so unique to and distinctive of her that the image calls her to mind, or at least that the image is sufficiently reminiscent enough of her to suggest imitation. Newcombe v. Adolf Coors Company, 157 F.3d 686 (9th Cir. 1998); Kirby v. Sega of Am., Inc., 144 Cal. App. 4th 47 (2d Dist. 2006); Motschenbacher v. R.J. Reynolds Tobacco Company, 498 F.2d 821 (9th Cir. 1974) (finding that a photograph of a professional driver of racing cars could constitute a likeness of him even though his face was not visible because the distinctive details on his car were associated only with him and a viewer would assume it was him because he sat in his unique car in the image).

A person's likeness is appropriated when she is readily identifiable within an image that contains features so unique to and distinctive of that person that the image calls her to mind. Newcombe, 157 F.3d 686. In Newcombe v. Adolf Coors Company, the court considered whether a magazine advertisement for beer used unique features of renowned baseball player Donald Newcombe that could constitute his likeness. Id. at 693. The image featured a pitcher in a windup stance, and his stance, shape, and skin color – Newcombe was one of the first African-American baseball players in the major leagues – were identical to Newcombe's. Id. The court held that there was a genuine issue of material fact as to whether Newcombe was readily identifiable as the pitcher in the advertisement. Id. It reasoned that Newcombe's stance was not generic but was "so distinctive that the defendants [could have] used his likeness by using a picture of Newcombe's stance." Id. Additionally, the pitcher's skin color could further a person to believe that it was Newcombe in the advertisement. Id. For these reasons, the court concluded that a jury could find that Newcombe's unique windup pitching stance made him readily identifiable in the image, even though his face was not visible. Id. Therefore, one feature of a person, such as his stance, can be so unique as to make him readily identifiable within an image that uses that feature.

Even if a visual image does not contain a unique feature of a person, it may still constitute a likeness if the image is sufficiently reminiscent of the person who claims her likeness was misappropriated. Kirby, 144 Cal. App. 4th 47. In Kirby v. Sega of Am., Inc., the court determined whether a video game avatar with physical features associated with singer Keirin Kirby could constitute a likeness of her, even though the avatar had clothing and a hairstyle that Kirby only sometimes donned. Id. at 56. Kirby herself, and the avatar in the video game "Space Channel 5," were both thin, had red lips, red or pink hair, and eyes and faces of the same shape. Id. The avatar's outfit was also something Kirby would wear:

a brightly-colored short skirt and 1960's platform shoes. Id. However, the avatar was most often pictured wearing an orange crop top, orange miniskirt, boots, and high pigtails in her hair. Id. Kirby claimed she often wore similar outfits, but was most associated with a different outfit and hairstyle, a page-boy flip. Id. The court held that despite the differences in the avatar's appearance, and the fact that Kirby only sometimes resembled it, there were enough issues of material fact to question the use of Kirby's likeness. Id. The court reasoned that the avatar's hair, clothing, shape, and makeup were "sufficiently reminiscent enough of Kirby's features and personal style to suggest imitation." Id. Therefore, even if an image does not contain a distinctive feature of a person, it may still constitute a likeness if enough similarities call to mind the person claiming misappropriation.

It is possible the court could find that the actress in Old Navy's Super C-U-T-E commercial mimics one of Kardashian's distinctive features, sufficient to make Kardashian readily identifiable. This case is similar to Newcombe where Newcombe's body position was determined to be unique to him. Newcombe, 157 F.3d at 692. Kardashian is known for her curvaceous body type and is marketed largely for that reason. She is a model and spokeswoman for a wide variety of products, and is arguably the most famous Armenian-American woman. Many advertisements with Kardashian feature her famously large rear-end and her seductive persona. In the Old Navy commercial at issue, the actress is similarly proportioned to Kardashian, and many of the scenes focus on her backside. She poses and dances to accentuate her round shape. Similarly, in Newcombe, an advertisement for beer featured a pitcher on the mound in a windup pitching stance that was solely attributable to Newcombe. Id. Newcombe was one of the first African-American men in the league, and was known for his distinctive pitching stance. Id. at 659, 692. This could make the similar-looking and acting actress readily identifiable as Kardashian.

The court could, however, find that Kardashian's shape is not a readily identifiable feature because it is common and not distinctive. In Newcombe, the image featured Newcombe in a specific pitching stance, associated with a specific sport. Id. at 692. The court in Newcombe reasoned that Newcombe was the only one to have such a pitching stance, and it was therefore distinctive enough to make him readily identifiable. Id. at 693. In Kardashian's case, the court may find that a person's shape alone could not make her readily identifiable, as opposed to an action that puts the body in a unique stance, as Newcombe's pitching stance did. Id.

Kardashian's shape may therefore not be a unique enough feature to make her readily identifiable in the commercial.

Even if the court finds that Kardashian's shape is not a uniquely distinguishing feature that makes her readily identifiable, the actress in the Old Navy commercial is still sufficiently reminiscent of Kardashian to constitute a likeness. This case is similar to <u>Kirby</u>, where Sega used several of her unique figures or styles in creating its similar avatar. <u>Kirby</u>, 144 Cal. App. 4th at 55. Kardashian is known for her beautiful face, complexion, and her long, dark hair. The actress in the Old Navy commercial has voluminous, long, dark hair, and the shape of her complexion is similar to Kardashian's. Likewise, in <u>Kirby</u> the avatar had a similarly shaped face as <u>Kirby</u>, and wore a similar hairstyle and clothing. <u>Kirby</u>, 144 Cal. App. 4th at 56.

Here, the court will likely find that the actress in the Old Navy commercial highlights enough of Kardashian's features to suggest imitation. In <u>Kirby</u>, the court held that even though Kirby more frequently wore another hairstyle than the one pictured in the video game, an issue of material fact existed as to whether Sega misappropriated Kirby's likeness. Id. The <u>Kirby</u> court reasoned that the avatar's facial features, hair color and style were sufficiently reminiscent enough of Kirby. <u>Id.</u> This reasoning applies to the instant case because even if the court decides that Kardashian's shape, hair color and style are not unique to her, it will likely find that their use together created an image that was sufficiently reminiscent of Kardashian.

Therefore, the court is likely to conclude that the actress in the Old Navy commercial is at least sufficiently reminiscent enough of Kim Kardashian's well-known physical appearance to warrant a finding that the image is her likeness.

<u>CONCLUSION</u>

Kardashian's claim will likely survive a motion for summary judgment because there is enough factual dispute about the use of Kardashian's likeness to proceed. A person's likeness is appropriated when she is readily identifiable in a visual image that contains features so unique to and distinctive of her that the image calls her to mind, or at least that the image is sufficiently reminiscent enough of her to suggest imitation. Kardashian is probably readily identifiable within the Old Navy commercial because her body shape and silhouette are her most well-known and sought-after features. She would even more likely satisfy the requirement that the image be sufficiently reminiscent of her because the collective look of the actress in the commercial is similar to Kardashian and suggests imitation. Old Navy should therefore consider alternative methods of dispute resolution.

Example Mediation Brief

OLD NAVY'S MEDIATION BRIEF

INTRODUCTION

Old Navy did not misappropriate Kim Kardashian's likeness in its commercial and Ms. Kardashian's claim is unlikely to survive a motion for summary judgment. Ms. Kardashian alleges Old Navy misappropriated her likeness under the California statute on right of publicity, which allows a person to control the commercial use of her identity. However, the actress in Old Navy's commercial does not use any unique or distinctive feature attributable only to the Plaintiff. Therefore, Ms. Kardashian does not have a valid right of publicity claim, and Old Navy will likely be granted a motion for summary judgment if litigation proceeds. However, Old Navy would prefer to have the matter resolved expeditiously and is willing to discuss possible solutions in mediation.

ANALYSIS

Old Navy's commercial did not use Ms. Kardashian's likeness. California Civil Code section 3344(a) prohibits use of another's likeness for advertising purposes without that person's consent. Cal. Civ. Code Ann. § 3344(a) (West, Westlaw Current with urgency legislation through all 2011-2012 1st Ex.Sess. laws). This discussion need not extend to a finding of consent because the Old Navy commercial at issue did not use Ms. Kardashian's likeness under either of the traditional tests for finding likeness. Ms. Kardashian is not readily identifiable in the Old Navy commercial, nor is the actress sufficiently reminiscent of her to suggest imitation.

I. OLD NAVY DID NOT USE MS. KARDASHIAN'S LIKENESS IN ITS COMMERCIAL BECAUSE SHE IS NOT READILY IDENTIFIABLE WITHIN THE COMMERCIAL, AS IT CONTAINS NO UNIQUE OR DISTINCTIVE CHARACTERISTICS OF HER.

Old Navy did not misappropriate Ms. Kardashian's likeness because she is not readily identifiable within the Super C-U-T-E commercial at issue. A person's likeness is not appropriated if a visual image uses no unique or distinctive features of the person complaining of misappropriation such that she would not be readily identifiable within the image. Newcombe v. Adolf Coors Company, 157 F.3d 686 (9th Cir. 1998). In Newcombe v. Adolf Coors Company, the court held that there was a genuine issue of material fact as to whether baseball player Donald Newcombe was readily identifiable as the pitcher in a magazine advertisement. Newcombe, 157 F.3d at 693. Since Newcombe had a unique and recognizable windup pitching stance, the court reasoned that the stance was not generic but was "so distinctive that the defendants [could have] used his likeness by using a picture of Newcombe's stance." Id.

Ms. Kardashian does not possess individual features unique to and distinctive of her that would warrant finding her likeness present in Old Navy's commercial. While Kardashian may assert that her shape is such a distinctive feature of her that any use of it would make her readily identifiable within an image, it is in fact more generic than distinctive, as supported by the court's conclusion in Newcombe. See Id. The court in Newcombe reasoned that Newcombe was the only baseball pitcher it found to use that exact windup pitching stance, and it was therefore distinctive enough to make him readily identifiable. Id.

Using this analysis, the Court in the present case is likely to find that Kardashian's shape alone could not make her readily identifiable, and that it is distinguishable from Newcombe's unique pitching stance. See Id. Ms. Kardashian's shape is not unique enough to be associated only with her as Newcombe's pitching stance was with him; a body shape cannot be claimed by one person, and as such, cannot be unique or distinctive as considered in Newcombe. Ms. Kardashian was therefore not readily identifiable in Old Navy's commercial.

Therefore, since Old Navy did not misappropriate a unique or distinctive feature of Ms. Kardashian, Old Navy believes the matter will not proceed to trial.

II. OLD NAVY DID NOT USE MS. KARDASHIAN'S LIKENESS IN ITS COMMERCIAL BECAUSE THE ACTRESS IN THE COMMERCIAL IS NOT EVEN SUFFICIENTLY REMINISCENT ENOUGH OF MS. KARDASHIAN TO SUGGEST IMITATION.

Old Navy's commercial does not use an image that is sufficiently reminiscent of Kardashian. A person's likeness is not appropriated if an image is less than sufficiently reminiscent of the person such that the image suggests no imitation. Kirby v. Sega of Am., Inc., 144 Cal. App. 4th 47 (2d Dist. 2006) (finding an image of singer Keirin Kirby could have been misappropriated where a video game avatar had similar clothing, face, hairstyle, and catch phrases to make the avatar sufficiently reminiscent of her to suggest imitation).

Ms. Kardashian does not have a valid claim under the California statute on right of publicity because the actress in the Old Navy commercial will not be found to be sufficiently reminiscent of Ms. Kardashian. Ms. Kardashian has asserted that the actress in the Old Navy commercial, Melissa Molinaro, resembles Ms. Kardashian's clothing, makeup, hairstyle, and facial features. In Kirby v. Sega of Am., Inc., entertainer Keirin Kirby alleged a video game company used her likeness in its creation of an avatar that featured similar clothing, makeup, hairstyle and facial features as her. Id. at 56. Although that court did confirm that there could be issues of fact as to whether her likeness had been misappropriated, it too made no assurance that it had been, and noted the many reasons why it may not have been. Id. at 56. This includes the court's finding that the avatar's "limited and consistently short and choppy dance movement and style differ markedly from Kirby's." Id. at 57. The similarities between Ms. Kardashian and the actress in the commercial are limited to general hair color and shape and are outweighed by the dissimilarities. The commonalities are not reminiscent of Kardashian in particular.

Old Navy did not misappropriate Ms. Kardashian's likeness because Old Navy's actress will not ultimately be found to be sufficiently reminiscent of the plaintiff. While Ms. Kardashian may have a similar hair color and skin color to the actress, it is not similar enough to be considered Ms. Kardashian's likeness. The extensive differences between the two women support the finding that Old Navy's commercial does not suggest imitation.

CONCLUSION

Old Navy has not violated Ms. Kardashian's statutory rights to control her publicity, and therefore she should withdraw her claim. Old Navy has neither created a commercial in which Ms. Kardashian is readily identifiable, nor has it employed an actress who is sufficiently reminiscent of her. None of Ms. Kardashian's features would qualify as unique and distinctive enough to make her readily identifiable in a commercial featuring another actress. Old Navy intends to participate in the mediation in good faith and will consider reasonable settlement proposals in effort to avoid additional litigation of this matter.

Date: March 18, 2013   *Lauren Order*
                                   Lauren Order
                                   Attorney for Old Navy

CHAPTER 15

PRE-TRIAL MOTIONS

■ ■ ■

By Gretchen Franz

The purpose of this chapter is to introduce students to one type of persuasive writing - Pre-Trial Motions. Chapter 15 explains the basic components of a Pre-Trial Motion: the Motion itself, the Memorandum of Points and Authorities in Support of and in Opposition to the Motion, Reply, Proof or Certificate of Service, and a draft Order. Although referenced in this chapter, evidence submitted in support of, or in opposition to, a Pre-Trial Motion (for example, affidavits and declarations) is not the focus of the Chapter.

Preparation for Writing Pre-Trial Motions

Prior to assigning this Chapter, students should have read Chapter 4 "An Overview of Statutory Interpretation and Synthesis," Chapter 5 "Legal Reasoning & Analysis Toolkit," Chapter 6 "The Process of Legal Writing," Chapter 7 "Knowing Your Audience," Chapter 14 "Persuasive Legal Writing," Chapter 22 "Research Strategies," and Chapter 24 "The Citation Requirement."

Teaching Methods for Pre-Trial Motions

1. Introduction to Pre-Trial Motions

Introduce students to Pre-Trial Motions by leading a class wide discussion about the purpose and audience of a Pre-Trial motion. It is important for students to understand why they would write a Pre-Trial Motion and who would read it.

2. Get Students Thinking Persuasively

Get students thinking about both sides of an argument through the "Jim and the Luxury Car Exercise" included at the end of Chapter 9, "The Formal Memorandum." Follow the instructions in the memorandum for using the exercise for persuasive writing.

3. <u>Samples</u>

Provide samples to the students. Chapter 15 includes a sample motion, proof of service and proposed order. It also includes an outline of the components of a memorandum of points and authorities. Sample memoranda of points and authorities in support of a motion are included **at the end of this chapter**. Professors may wish to copy or post these samples for students, and also to show the outlines of the various Pre-Trial Motion documents on an overhead.

The sample memoranda are useful for students to see and understand the CRAC paradigm "in action." Students can be asked to review a sample Memorandum of Points and Authorities and to identify the C, R, A, and C for each issue.

It is also helpful to show, and have students critique, different examples of the various components of a Memorandum of Points and Authorities. For example, a Professor can provide students with three or four examples of an Issue – one that is too general, one that is too specific, and one that is well-written. The students can evaluate and discuss the strengths and weaknesses of each example.

4. Pre-Trial Motion Editing Checklist

The Pre-Trial Motion Checklist provided at the end of this chapter is a great resource and teaching tool for three reasons:

a. It provides students with a condensed outline of the format and substance expected in a Pre-Trial Motion Memorandum of Points and Authorities;

b. It can be used for classroom exercises. Professors can have students evaluate sample Memoranda of Points and Authorities, or individual components such as Issues, Facts, etc., and discuss whether the motions comply with the guidelines set forth in the checklist as follows:

<u>Introduction Exercise:</u> Have students turn to a sample Memorandum of Points and Authorities. Students should critique the Introduction using the checklist to determine whether it includes the requisite substance.

The Introduction Exercise can be adapted to critique a Statement of Facts, Issues, Point Headings, etc.

c. Students can use the checklist to proof their own Memorandum of Points and Authorities to ensure it complies with formatting and substantive requirements.

5. <u>An Initial CRAC Assignment</u>

Professors may want to assign a simple Pass/Fail CRAC assignment prior to assigning a graded Pre-Trial Motion. Professors critique the pass/fail assignment and provide detailed comments as to how the student can improve his/her persuasive paradigm. This process has worked well for the second year Global Lawyering Skills class at Pacific McGeorge.

6. <u>Peer-Edits</u>

Instruct students to bring in a draft section of the Memorandum of Points and Authorities (this could be a few pages of the Argument for one issue, the issue itself, persuasive rules, etc.) Either assign students to exchange their work, or have students do so randomly. Students should provide written comments for each other's work, using the Editing Checklist as a guide. Give the students ample time to review each other's work. Set the time according to the length and complexity of the draft. After, have students discuss their comments with each other. This provides students an opportunity to (1) see how other colleagues wrote the assignment, (2) receive feedback from colleagues, and (3) become more comfortable with the fact that Pre-Trial Motions are generally available to the public – and that other's will be reading their written work product.

7. <u>The "'White Glove' Inspection" - Read, Edit, Re-Write ...</u>

It is important to continue to stress that good writing requires a lot of time, effort and attention to detail. Students should be encouraged to write, re-read, edit, re-read, edit, re-read again, and again.

As with The Formal Memorandum, students should allow plenty of time to "White Glove" their written work (Chapter 22, The Last Critical Task: The 'White-Glove' Inspection) to ensure that they are submitting the most professional product possible.

Pretrial-Motion Excerise:

Facts for Students

Consider the following:

Jim, a 17-year-old high school junior, wants to borrow his parent's luxury car to take his girlfriend to the junior prom. He is normally allowed to use only the family's "second" car, a beat up old Chevy.

Jim has asked his parents if they will allow him to make his case, and they have agreed to have an open discussion, even though they are not initially disposed to grant his request.

Here is the factual background that exists regarding Jim's request:

o Jim has an older sister and a younger brother. From the time his sister was fifteen, the parents have made it clear to all three children that the only car they would be allowed to drive (unless the parents were present) was the "second" car.

o Jim's sister was allowed to use the luxury car for her senior prom. At the time, she had been driving for two years and had a spotless record (no accidents or citations).

o Jim has been driving for fifteen months. In the first six months, he had four accidents, two of which were clearly his fault. (The other two probably could have been avoided if Jim had been more careful, but the other driver was also negligent.) Jim also received two citations (one for speeding, the other for running a red light) in the first three months. Since those incidents, Jim has had a clean driving record.

o At the time of Jim's last accident, his father told him that he was responsible for his own actions and that the increase in his insurance rates would come out of his allowance. Jim's father stressed that Jim should expect to be "punished" for bad performance in life, just as he should expect to "rewarded" for good performance.

o Since that discussion with his father, Jim has come back under the insurance company's "Good Driver Discount." (The company is especially lenient with new drivers.) In addition, Jim now qualifies for a "Good Student Discount," by virtue of his excellent grades in the last year.

- o   When Jim first received his license, he asked his mother if he could use the family's luxury car to take his girlfriend on a date. At that time, his mother told him that she did not consider a simple date important enough to justify a departure from the family's rules about use of the family cars.

- o   Both of the parent's closest friends have children who are Jim's age. These parents are allowing their children to use the nicer cars that they own. In one family, the child was recently cited for speeding. That child is a marginal student, but is the captain of the football team and is active in the local church. In the other, the child has a clean driving record and is a top student.

- o   Jim's parents would concede that they are thrilled with the growth and maturity that Jim has displayed in the last year or so. They are also very fond of his girlfriend.

Professor Instructions for Pre-Trial Motions

1. Divide the class into small groups. Groups are assigned to represent Jim or the parents. Since working in small groups provides individual students a better opportunity to participate in the exercise, there can be more than one group representing each side.

2. Distribute the fact pattern.

3. Give students 20-30 minutes to "brainstorm" how precedent in the family, family policy, and custom and practice of family friends support the side the students are assigned to represent.

4. Students should write a short persuasive statement of facts.

5. Students can formulate rules regarding precedent, policy, and custom and practice. See sample rules under The Formal Memorandum instructions above.

6. Students should use the facts to support each rule to craft arguments.

7. The class then reconvenes as a whole, and the professor leads a discussion by calling on each group to present their arguments.

Student Instructions when using exercise for Pre-Trial Motions

1. You will be divided into teams of three students each. The other teams will be assigned to represent Jim or the parents. If your team represents Jim, you will argue in favor of Jim taking the luxury car to the prom. If you represent the parents, you will argue that Jim should not be allowed to take the luxury car to the prom.

2. Please prepare a short:

   a. Persuasive Statement of Facts

   b. Argument. Your argument should focus on three main points and follow the CRAC paradigm:

      i. Precedent

      ii. Policy

      iii. Custom and Practice

   Make sure to use the facts to support your argument.

   Try to consider and counter how the "other" side will argue.

Sample Pre-Trial Motions

The sample pre-trial motions below are from state and federal court. Since local rules will govern the format and procedure for pre-trial motions in your jurisdiction, you may wish to find a sample that comports with the local practice in your area. These samples are annotated to show students important features of pre-trial motions across jurisdictions.

Wood, Bishop & Hardin
Laurel Hunter; State Bar No. 000000
456 Main Street
Santa Rosa, California 95403
Phone: 707.000.0000

Attorneys for Defendant,
Kinsella Winery, Inc.

SUPERIOR COURT OF CALIFORNIA

COUNTY OF SONOMA

Thomas Ford,
 	
    Plaintiff,
 	
v.
 	
Kinsella Winery, Inc.,
 	
    Defendant.
	Case No. Q32840
	
	DEFENDANT'S MEMORANDUM OF POINTS AND AUTHORITIES IN SUPPORT OF MOTION FOR PROTECTIVE ORDER AND SANCTIONS
	
	Hearing: May 15, 2006
	
	Time: 9:00 a.m.
	
	Judge: Joseph X. Quinn

INTRODUCTION

    This is an action for breach of an employment contract. [←the nature of the case] Defendant Kinsella Winery, Inc. (KWI) requests that the Court grant its Motion for Protective Order and Monetary Sanctions against Plaintiff Thomas Ford and his counsel, Sophie Parker. [←the parties, the motion, and the relief requested by the party filing the brief] During the production of documents in response to Plaintiff's Inspection Demand, KWI's attorney inadvertently disclosed an attorney-client privileged document. This document was identified in the privilege log that accompanied the document. [←facts supporting legal point justifying relief on Motion for Protective Order] Ms. Parker never told KWI that she had received the document through its counsel's inadvertence. Instead, she attempted to introduce it as an exhibit at a deposition and twice refused to return it. [←facts supporting legal point justifying relief on Motion for Monetary Sanctions]

Ms. Parker concedes that the document is protected by the attorney-client privilege, but argues that KWI waived the privilege. However, the privilege holder, KWI, did not itself disclose the document and did not consent to waiver by another. [←legal points justifying protective order] Moreover, sanctions are justified because Ms. Parker failed to satisfy her ethical obligation to immediately notify KWI that she may have received a privileged document its counsel had produced inadvertently. [←legal point justifying monetary sanctions]

STATEMENT OF FACTS

On February 13, 2006, attorneys for KWI inadvertently provided a memo (Memo) protected by the attorney-client privilege to Plaintiff, who is suing his former employer for breach of contract stemming from Plaintiff's release as KWI's Director of Winemaking. Decl. Olivia Dailey ¶¶ 4-5 (Apr. 17, 2006). Michael Chu, KWI's in-house counsel, wrote the Memo to KWI's president, Robert Kinsella, setting out his preliminary legal conclusions on the enforceability of KWI's employment contract with Plaintiff. Mr. Chu's opinion was based solely on the contract and applicable legal authorities, not interviews with potential witnesses. Decl. Michael Chu ¶ 3 (Apr. 17, 2006). Mr. Chu provided the Memo to counsel hired to represent KWI in this litigation, the law firm of Wood, Bishop & Hardin (WB&H). Mr. Chu intended that WB&H would withhold the document from discovery because it was a privileged attorney-client communication. Mr. Chu did not authorize disclosure of the Memo. Neither did any other representative of KWI. *Id.* at ¶ 4.

In response to Plaintiff's Inspection Demand, a junior associate at WB&H prepared a privilege log listing documents to be withheld, including the Memo. The associate described the Memo in the privilege log, listed the Bates number that was stamped on each page, and indicated the privilege claimed was the attorney-client privilege. Decl. Wood ¶ 3. Subsequently, the associate inadvertently included the Memo in the pages to be produced. *Id.* at ¶ 4. Those documents, along with a copy of the privilege log, were served on Plaintiff's attorney, Sophie Parker, on February 13, 2006. *Id.* at ¶ 5. No other documents between Kinsella and

Chu were identified in the privilege log or included with the documents produced. *Id.* at ¶¶ 6-7.

Ms. Parker did not inform WB&H that she had received the Memo, and on February 27, 2006, she marked the Memo as an exhibit at Mr. Kinsella's deposition. Decl. Jessica S. Wood ¶¶ 4, 8 (Apr. 17, 2006). Jessica Wood of WB&H immediately objected on the grounds that the Memo was protected by the attorney-client privilege and asked Ms. Parker to return the Memo and any copies of it. *Id.* at ¶ 5. Ms. Parker agreed that the Memo was protected by the attorney-client privilege. However, she refused to return the Memo, claiming the privilege was waived when the Memo was produced even though KWI did not intend to disclose the Memo. *Id.* at ¶ 6.

The very next day, Ms. Wood wrote to Ms. Parker in an effort to resolve the dispute and again requested that she return the Memo. *Id.* at ¶ 9. Ms. Parker wrote back and again agreed that the Memo is protected by the attorney-client privilege. But Ms. Parker again refused to return the Memo and insisted that the privilege was waived when the Memo was inadvertently produced. *Id.* at ¶ 10. As a result, KWI requires the Court's involvement in order to regain possession of the Memo and prevent Plaintiff from using it to his advantage.

ARGUMENT

I. THE COURT SHOULD GRANT THE MOTION FOR A PROTECTIVE ORDER AND MONETARY SANCTIONS. [←point heading – overall "C" (Primary Assertion)]

Under Code of Civil Procedure § 2031.060(b), the Court is authorized to grant a protective order to shield a party from "oppression, or undue burden and expense." [←**procedural rule on Motion for Protective Order with cite to controlling authority**] To obtain a protective order, the moving party need only show by a preponderance of the evidence that the order is proper. *Stadish v. Super. Ct. of L.A. County,* 71 Cal. App. 4th 1130 (2d Dist. 1999). [←**burden of proof on this motion, stated persuasively**]

Section 2031.060(d) authorizes the Court to impose monetary sanctions against the unsuccessful party or that party's attorney in the motion proceedings unless the party's position was substantially justified or the award would otherwise be unjust. [←**procedural rule on Motion for Monetary Sanctions with cite to controlling authority**] The

Legislature intended for discovery to proceed without involving the court, and as a penalty for disturbing the process, the losing party should "presumptively pay a monetary sanction to the one who prevails." **[←favorable principle affecting the application of the rule – policy leaning]** The opposing party bears the burden of demonstrating why sanctions should not be imposed. *Mattco Forge, Inc. v. Arthur Young & Co.*, 223 Cal. App. 3d 1429 (2d Dist. 1990). **[←burden of proof on this motion, stated persuasively]**

Plaintiff's counsel, Ms. Parker, has twice conceded that the Memo is protected by the attorney-client privilege. Decl. Wood ¶¶ 6, 10. **[←explaining that whether the privilege applies is not at issue]** Therefore, on the Motion for a Protective Order, the only issue is whether an inadvertent production of such a document by an attorney during discovery constitutes a waiver of the attorney-client privilege. **[←clarifying what is at issue]** The Court should grant this Motion because an attorney's inadvertent disclosure is not the equivalent of a waiver. *State Compen. Ins. Fund v. WPS, Inc.*, 70 Cal. App. 4th 644, 653 (2d Dist. 1999). **[←one-sentence summary of the argument on the substantive law supporting a protective order]**

The Court should also grant the Motion for Monetary Sanctions because Ms. Parker violated her ethical obligations when she examined the Memo more than was necessary to determine privilege and failed to immediately notify KWI that she had received a privileged document through its attorney's inadvertent production. *See id.* at 657. **[←one-sentence summary of the argument on the substantive law supporting an order for monetary sanctions]]**

> A. <u>The Court should grant the Motion for a Protective Order because KWI, the privilege holder, did not waive the attorney-client privilege when its legal counsel inadvertently disclosed the Memo during discovery.</u> **[←subheading – opening "C" (Secondary Assertion)]**

[R→] California Evidence Code § 912(a) states that the attorney-client privilege can be waived only "if any holder of the privilege, without coercion, has disclosed a significant part of the communication or has consented to disclosure." Section 912(a) also specifies that consent can be manifested by the holder's statement or conduct. As defined by Evidence Code § 953, the client is the holder of the attorney-client privilege. To determine whether the conduct of a client was sufficient to constitute waiver, courts examine the "subjective intent and the relevant surrounding circumstances for any manifestation of the holder's consent to disclose the information." *State Fund*, 70 Cal. App. 4th at 653. **[policy leaning→]** The attorney-client privilege seeks to maintain confidential communications and, therefore, should be given generous protection. *Benge v. Super. Ct. of Tulare County*, 131 Cal. App. 3d 336, 344 (5th Dist. 1982).

[E→] Outside counsel's inadvertent disclosure of privileged information is not a waiver of the attorney-client privilege. *State Fund*, 70 Cal. App. 4th at 654. In *State Fund*, in-house counsel prepared claim summary forms in order to determine the strengths and weaknesses of insurance claim cases. The attorney marked the forms as "Confidential" and "Attorney-Client Communication," and the forms were Bates stamped. *Id.* at 648, 650. State Funded forwarded to its outside trial counsel for its own use these forms along with other documents already disclosed to WPS. *Id.* at 650. State Fund's outside counsel did not identify and remove the privileged claim summary forms from the other documents when forwarding them to WPS's counsel for use at trial. Further, the documents were not listed on the privilege log. *Id.* at 651.

When it is not the privilege holder who discloses the document, a trial court will consider whether the privilege holder manifested consent to disclosure by another person. Since State Fund's outside counsel disclosed the document, not State Fund itself, the court focused on whether any statement or conduct by State Fund indicated that it consented to outside counsel's disclosure. *Id.* at 652. State Fund's in-house counsel testified she never intended to disclose the documents and marked them as confidential. Outside counsel testified that the disclosure was unintentional. In addition, outside counsel carefully reviewed the documents and maintained a privilege log to ensure privileged documents would not be produced. And outside counsel immediately attempted to regain possession of the documents after realizing that they had been disclosed. *Id.* at 653. Based on this evidence, the court found that State Fund never intended to waive the privilege and held that waiver "does not include accidental, inadvertent disclosure of privileged information by the attorney." *Id.* at 654.

A paralegal or junior associate's slip-up is not the equivalent of the privilege holder's actual consent. *O'Mary v. Mistsubishi Elecs. Am. Inc.*, 59 Cal. App. 4th 563, 577 (4th Dist. 1997). In *O'Mary*, in-house counsel for Mitsubishi requested a list of employees facing termination in order to give his legal opinion about upcoming layoffs. During discovery, this list was inadvertently disclosed. After learning about the error, counsel for

Mitsubishi immediately demanded that O'Mary return the list. In holding that Mitsubishi did not waive the attorney-client privilege, the court rejected O'Mary's argument that any uncoerced disclosure waives the privilege. The court noted that the discovery process is inherently coercive and declined to adopt O'Mary's "gotcha" theory of waiver. *Id.*

The attorney-client privilege protects communications between the attorney and the client, not the disclosure of underlying facts. *Aerojet-General Corp. v. Transport Indem. Ins.,* 18 Cal. App. 4th 996, 1004 (1st Dist. 1993). In *Aerojet,* plaintiff's attorney received a memo to the file that defense counsel had written. This memo contained privileged information and identified a potential witness. *Id.* at 1000. The memo was on plain paper and did not indicate that it was privileged or otherwise confidential. *Id.* at 1001. The memo did not come from defendant or its counsel. Instead, the memo came from one of the plaintiff's employees; the employee received the documents from the plaintiff's insurance broker. *Id.* at 1000. Plaintiff's attorney acknowledged that he had no reason to believe Aerojet had consented to the disclosure and did not immediately inform defense counsel that he received the memo. *Id.* at 1001.

The court reversed a sanctions order because the identification of potential witnesses is not privileged information. *Id.* at 1004. While the court stated in passing that the attorney-client privilege is not an insurer against inadvertent disclosure, *id.* at 1004, the court emphasized that plaintiff's attorney used only the information about the identity of the witness from the memo and did not try to introduce any of the memo's contents that were subject to the attorney-client privilege. *Id.* at 1002. The court reasoned that plaintiff's attorney had done nothing wrong when he used the information because the opposing party is entitled to this type of non-privileged information anyway. *Id.* at 1004.

[A→ ("A" section starts with the conclusion that KWI wants the court to reach)] KWI did not waive the attorney-client privilege. Here, KWI itself did not disclose the Memo, and KWI's conduct did not manifest intent to waive the attorney-client privilege. Under Evidence Code § 953, as the client, KWI is the holder of the privilege. [←rule-based reasoning] Since KWI did not disclose the Memo, the focus of the analysis is whether KWI manifested consent to disclosure by another. *State Fund*, 70 Cal. App. 4th at 652. [←rule-based reasoning] KWI did not subjectively intend to disclose the Memo. No representative of KWI authorized the Memo's disclosure. Similar to State Fund's in-house counsel, who testified that she never intended to disclose the claim summary forms, *id.* at 653, KWI's in-house counsel declared that neither he nor any other representative of KWI authorized WB&H to disclose the Memo. Instead, KWI's in-house counsel intended that WB&H would withhold all privileged documents, including the Memo. Decl. Chu ¶ 4. [←analogical and rule-based reasoning]

WB&H's inadvertent disclosure of privileged information is not a waiver of the attorney-client privilege. *See State Fund*, 70 Cal. App. 4th at 654. The surrounding circumstances demonstrate the WB&H intended to maintain the privilege. The junior associate who prepared the documents testified that she intended to withhold the Memo. Decl. Dailey at ¶ 4. The junior associate identified the Memo as privileged, initially segregated it, and identified the Memo on the privilege log. *Id.* at ¶¶ 1-3. These actions are consistent with an attempt to retain the attorney-client privilege and are analogous to use of "Confidential" and "Attorney-Client Communication" on the claim forms in *State Fund*, 70 Cal. App. 4th at 648. While the Memo itself was unmarked, here the privilege log provides even stronger evidence of intent not to disclose than in *State Fund* where the court found no waiver even though the claim forms were not listed on the privilege log. *Id.* at 654. [←analogical and rule-based reasoning]

Efforts to secure a privileged document's return are additional evidence that the privilege holder did not consent to waiver. *O'Mary*, 59 Cal. App. 4th at 577; *State Farm*, 70 Cal. App. 4th at 653-54. In *State Farm*, counsel immediately attempted to regain possession of the forms after learning they had been disclosed. 70 Cal. App. 4th at 653. Likewise, KWI's outside counsel immediately objected to Plaintiff's attempt to admit the Memo as evidence at the deposition and then wrote Plaintiff's counsel, requesting that she return the Memo. Decl. Wood ¶¶ 5-6, 9. [←analogical reasoning]

The contents of the Memo are not the type of underlying facts that a party is required to disclose during discovery. The court in *Aerojet* emphasized that the opposing party is entitled to non-privileged information such as the identity of a witness. 18 Cal. App. 4th at 1004. In contrast, Plaintiff's counsel received a document which contained an attorney's analysis of the strengths and weaknesses of Plaintiff's case. The Memo did not contain any summaries of interviews with potential witnesses. Decl. Chu ¶¶ 3, 4. [←analogical reasoning]

[closing C (longer conclusion summarizing key points)→] The Court should grant KWI's Motion for a Protective Order. KWI, as the holder of the privilege, did not itself disclose the Memo or manifest its consent to disclosure, and the slip-up by KWI's outside counsel is not the equivalent of KWI's consent to disclosure. **[policy reasoning included in this C→]** Like the court in *O'Mary*, 59 Cal. App. 4th at 577, this Court should also reject the "gotcha" theory of waiver.

> B. <u>The Court should grant the Motion for Monetary Sanctions because Ms. Parker did not comply with her ethical obligation after she received the obviously privileged Memo through the inadvertence of KWI's counsel.</u> **[←subheading – opening "C" (Secondary Assertion)]**

[R→] An attorney who receives what appear to be privileged documents due to opposing counsel's inadvertence has an ethical obligation to examine the documents no further than necessary to determine whether they are privileged, and if they are, to then immediately notify the sender. A court is justified in awarding sanctions when a party fails to satisfy this obligation. *State Fund,* 70 Cal. App. 4th at 657. **[burden of proof→]** An attorney who seeks to hold another attorney accountable for misusing privileged information has the burden of demonstrating inadvertence. *Id.* at 656.

[E→] To protect the sanctity of the attorney-client privilege and to discourage unprofessional conduct, the *State Fund* court set this standard of conduct for California attorneys faced with receipt of privileged documents. *Id.* at 657. In *State Fund*, the court found that the claim summary forms were clearly identifiable as containing confidential attorney-client communications that State Farm's outside counsel had forwarded inadvertently. *Id.* at 655. Nonetheless, defense counsel did not inform State Farm's in-house counsel about the disclosure but instead further circulated the forms and, once State Farm discovered that it had disclosed the forms, defense counsel refused to return them. *Id.* at 647. However, the court reversed an award of sanctions because the lower court relied on American Bar Association ethics materials, which it considered to be binding, to award sanctions. *Id.* at 655. On appeal, the court noted that California had not adopted the ABA materials, and although defense counsel's conduct was discouraged, it was not prohibited at that time by any official authority in the State. *Id.* at 656.

To further two policy concerns, the court established the standard for future application. First, the court acknowledged the value of full disclosure by clients to their counsel and that a client should not enter the attorney-client relationship fearful that an error by the client's attorney would result in waiver of the privilege. Second, the court noted that "[a]n attorney has an obligation not only to protect his client's interests but also to respect the legitimate interests of fellow members of the bar, the judiciary, and the administration of justice." *Id.* at 657.

[A→ ("A" section starts with the conclusion that KWI wants the court to reach)] Ms. Parker's conduct is sanctionable under the *State Fund* standard, and if Plaintiff approved her conduct, the Court should sanction him as well. Ms. Parker almost certainly had knowledge that that WB&H inadvertently produced the Memo and that the Memo was privileged. Ms. Parker acknowledged that KWI did not intend to disclose the Memo, Decl. Wood ¶ 6, which indicates she was aware that WB&H produced the Memo in error. Just as the claim summary forms in *State Fund* were clearly identifiable as containing confidential attorney-client communications, 70 Cal. App. 4th at 655, the Memo was easily identifiable at protected by the attorney-client privilege. The Memo was the only document between Mr. Chu and Mr. Kinsella identified in the privilege log, and the Memo was the only document between Mr. Chu and Mr. Kinsella that WB&H produced. Moreover, the Memo was Bates stamped; the privilege log included those same Bates numbers. Decl. Dailey ¶¶ 3, 6-7. [←analogical and rule-based reasoning]

Ms. Parker did not read the Memo only to the extent necessary to determine if it were privileged as required under *State Fund*. 70 Cal. App. 4th at 656. She seemed to have thoroughly reviewed the Memo since she identified it as sufficiently relevant to admit into evidence during a deposition. Decl. Wood ¶ 3. [←rule-based reasoning]

Like defense counsel in *State Fund* who failed to notify State Fund about the inadvertent disclosure, 70 Cal. App. 4th at 655, Ms. Parker did not notify KWI and its counsel that she had received the Memo inadvertently. Decl. Wood ¶ 8. KWI and its counsel did not learn that she had the Memo until two weeks later at a formal discovery proceeding when Ms. Parker attempted to use it as an exhibit. *Id.* at ¶ 4. KWI's counsel twice asked Ms. Parker to return the Memo, but Ms. Parker twice refused. *Id.* at ¶¶ 9, 10. [←analogical and rule-based reasoning]

[closing C→] The Court should grant the Motion for Monetary Sanctions. [policy reasoning (no, it is not necessary to include policy reasoning in the closing C; it's just the way it worked out for the two closing Cs in this Memorandum)→] While Ms. Parker has an obligation to protect her client's interests, like all attorneys, she also had a duty to respect the legitimate interests of fellow members of the bar, the judiciary, and the administration of justice. *See State Farm*, 70 Cal. App. 4th at 657.

CONCLUSION

The Court should grant KWI's Motion for a Protective Order and Monetary Sanctions. WB&H's accidental disclosure of the Memo during discovery is not the equivalent of a waiver of the attorney-client privilege. Additionally, Ms. Parker's conduct is sanctionable, and if Plaintiff approved her conduct, the Court should sanction him as well. Ms. Parker thoroughly read the Memo, failed to immediately notify KWI's counsel that she had received the Memo, and twice refused to return the Memo though she acknowledged it was privileged.

Date: April 17, 2006

                                                            Laurel Hunter
                                                            Attorneys for Defendant

Sample Brief, Illinois State Bar No. 246810
Student Written
Student and Associates
250 Oak Boulevard
Chicago, Illinois 60601
Telephone: 312-222-2222

Attorneys for Defendant,
Get Fixed County General Hospital

UNITED STATES DISTRICT COURT

FOR THE NORTHERN DISTRICT OF ILLINOIS, EASTERN DIVISION

SHEILA SMART, an individual Plaintiff, v. GET FIXED COUNTY GENERAL HOSPITAL, A municipal corporation Defendant.	Case No. CVF12345 Memorandum of Points and Authorities in Support of Motion to Dismiss Complaint Against Defendant Get Fixed County General Hospital [Fed. R. Civ. P. 12(b)(6)]

INTRODUCTION

Plaintiff, Sheila Smart ("Plaintiff"), seeks compensatory and punitive damages against defendant ("Defendant"), Get Fixed County General Hospital ("Hospital") claiming that it failed to reasonably accommodate Plaintiff's known disability as required by the Americans with Disabilities Act ("ADA"). Defendant files this Memorandum of Points and Authorities in support of its motion to dismiss Plaintiff's complaint ("Complaint").

This motion is made pursuant to Rule 12(b)(6) of the Federal Rules of Civil Procedure ("Rule 12(b)(6)"), based upon a failure of the Complaint to allege facts from which this Court could find there is any claim upon which relief could be granted. The Complaint fails to allege that the Plaintiff suffers from a recognized disability under the ADA, and even if the Plaintiff does have a recognized disability, the Complaint fails to allege that the Defendant did not reasonably accommodate her disability. Therefore, the Court cannot grant the requested relief and should dismiss the Complaint.

STATEMENT OF FACTS

Defendant employed Plaintiff as the Chief of Emergency Medicine ("COEM") from June 1, 1991 through November 11, 2002. As COEM, Plaintiff worked as the manager of the Emergency Room ("ER"). Since 1993, Defendant has employed Plaintiff's supervisor, Dr. Sexist as Chief of Surgery ("COS"). As COS, Dr. Sexist supervises the Surgery Department. Since 1996, Dr. Sexist began working as Chief of Staff for Critical Services ("CSCS") and has been acting as administrator. As CSCS, Dr. Sexist acts as supervisor of the ER and Intensive Care Unit ("ICU") department chiefs. The Hospital's other departments are supervised by the Chief of Staff for General Services ("CSGS"). Pl.'s Compl. ¶¶ 5-9, 11 (Jan. 3, 2003).

Plaintiff alleges that in February 2000, Dr. Sexist began a pattern of abusive behavior towards Plaintiff and her ER staff. As a result of Dr. Sexist's abusive behavior, she experienced extreme stress from February 2000 until she resigned on November 11, 2002. In May 2000, a licensed psychologist diagnosed Plaintiff as having depression caused by conflicts with Dr. Sexist. The psychologist recommended that she transfer to a position that was not supervised by Dr. Sexist. Plaintiff alleges that her extreme stress and anxiety constitute a disability that limited her ability to work. *Id.* at ¶¶ 14, 24-25.

Plaintiff states that Defendant was aware of her alleged disability caused by Dr. Sexist's behavior, but failed to provide her reasonable accommodation. Plaintiff submitted verbal grievances to the Defendant's Human Resources Department ("HR") describing Dr. Sexist's behavior. Each grievance requested that either Plaintiff or Dr. Sexist be transferred. She specifically requested that Defendant do one of the following: (1) transfer her to a department chief position in one of the departments supervised by the CSGS; (2) transfer her to the position of CSGS; or (3) transfer Dr. Sexist to the position of CSGS. *Id.* at ¶¶ 26-27.

After each grievance, the Director of Human Resources ("Director") met with Plaintiff. As to Plaintiff's requests for a transfer, the Director stated that there were currently no vacant positions for department chiefs. The Director also advised the Plaintiff that she could transfer to the position of the CSGS after she submits an application and followed Defendant's other standard procedures for promotions within. In addition, the Director repeatedly stated that Dr. Sexist would not be transferred from his position as CSCS. *Id.* at ¶ 28.

Plaintiff alleges that even though the positions of department chief of the Ob-Gyn Department, Pediatrics Department and Psychiatric Department were all filled by others, Defendant should have transferred her to one of those positions and then transferred the displaced person to the position of COEM. Since the position of CSGS was vacant at the time of her grievances, Plaintiff states that she should have been transferred so, she would have been at the same level as Dr. Sexist and he would no longer be her supervisor. Plaintiff also alleges that the Defendant should have transferred Dr. Sexist to the position of CSGS. *Id.* at ¶¶ 29-32.

Plaintiff's Complaint was filed to this court on January 3, 2003. In lieu of an answer, the Defendant has moved, pursuant to Rule 12(b)(6), to dismiss the Plaintiff's Complaint for failure to state a claim upon which relief could be granted.

ARGUMENT

I. **PLAINTIFF'S COMPLAINT SHOULD BE DISMISSED FOR FAILURE TO STATE A CLAIM UNDER THE ADA.**

A court may grant a motion to dismiss a complaint for failure to state a claim if it appears beyond doubt that the plaintiff could prove no set of facts entitling her to relief. *Triad Assoc. v. Chi. Hous. Auth.*, 892 F.2d 583, 586 (7th Cir. 1989). The court must test the sufficiency of the claim based on the facts alleged in the Complaint and properly grant the motion if the facts alleged do not entitle the Plaintiff to relief. *Id.* The Court takes the plaintiff's allegations as true when ruling on a motion to dismiss. *Id.* Applying these standards to the Complaint, the facts alleged do not demonstrate that the Plaintiff is entitled to relief under the ADA. Therefore, the Court should dismiss the Complaint.

The ADA exists to "provide clear, strong, consistent, enforceable standards addressing discrimination against individuals with disabilities." 42 U.S.C.A §12101(b)(2) (West 1995). The ADA defines a disability as "a physical or mental impairment that substantially limits one or more of the major life activities of [the] individual." *Id.* at §12102(2)(a). An employer is obligated under the ADA to reasonably accommodate the disability, unless the "accommodation would impose an undue hardship" on the employer. *Id.* at §12112(B)(5)(a).

Plaintiff's Complaint should be dismissed for failure to state a cause of action because it fails to allege that the Plaintiff suffers from a recognized disability under the ADA, and even if the Plaintiff alleges that she suffers from a recognized disability, she fails to allege that the Defendant failed to reasonably accommodate her disability.

A. Plaintiff's Complaint should be dismissed for failure to state a claim in that it fails to allege that the Plaintiff suffers from a recognized disability under the ADA.

A plaintiff who merely cannot work under a certain supervisor, because of anxiety and stress, does not suffer from a disability within the meaning of the ADA since the major life activity of working is not substantially limited. *Weiler v. Household Fin. Corp.*, 101 F.3d 519, 524 (7th Cir. 1996); *Palmer v. Cir. Ct. of Cook County, Soc. Services Dept.*, 905 F.Supp. 499, 507 (N.D. Ill. 1995). The plaintiffs in *Weiler* and *Palmer* sued their employers claiming that the stress and anxiety caused by their inability to work with their supervisor constituted a disability recognized under the ADA and that the employers failed to reasonably accommodate their disabilities. *Weiler*, 101 F.3d at 522; *Palmer*, 905 F.Supp. at 501. Because the plaintiffs could perform the same job for another supervisor, the courts held that the plaintiffs' anxiety and stress, caused by their inability to work under a certain supervisor, did not substantially limit the major life activity of working and did not constitute a disability under the ADA. *Weiler*, 101 F.3d at 525; *Palmer*, 905 F.Supp. at 508.

Like Weiler and Palmer, Plaintiff does not suffer from a disability recognized under the ADA. Plaintiff alleges that she could continue working if either she or her supervisor would be transferred so that she would no longer be under Dr. Sexist's supervision. Thus, Plaintiff's stress and anxiety, caused by her inability to work with Dr. Sexist, do not substantially limit her ability to work in general. Based upon *Weiler* and *Palmer*, plaintiff does not suffer from a recognized disability. Therefore, the Complaint should be dismissed because it fails to allege that the Plaintiff suffers from a recognized disability under the ADA.

B. The Plaintiff's Complaint should be dismissed for failure to state a claim in that even if the Plaintiff has a recognized disability under the ADA, the Plaintiff fails to allege facts that the Defendant failed to reasonably accommodate her disability.

The ADA does not obligate the employer to "bump" other employees to create a vacancy to reassign a disabled employee nor does it require an employee to accommodate a disabled employee if such accommodation imposes an undue hardship on the employer. *Weiler*, 101 F.3d at 526. The plaintiff in *Weiler* refused to come back to work after her disability leave unless she was transferred to another supervisor or the employer transferred her current supervisor. *Id*. She argued that because her inability to work with her current supervisor caused her disability, the ADA required the employer to transfer her to work for another supervisor or transfer her supervisor in order to reasonably accommodate her disability. *Id*. The court rejected this argument and found that an employer was not required to shift the authority to make decisions about supervisory assignments to the employee in order to reasonably accommodate an employee's disability. *Id*.

Although the ADA does not require the employer to change its policies regarding job transfers, an employer is required to take further actions to reassign a disabled employee to a vacant position for which the employee is otherwise qualified. *Gile v. United Airlines, Inc.*, 213 F.3d 365, 374 (7th Cir. 2000). In *Gile*, the plaintiff, who suffered from a disability, caused by her working the night shift, requested to be transferred to the day shift. *Id*. at 369. Even though Gile was otherwise qualified, the employer refused to transfer her unless she first followed established procedures of bidding for a vacant position. *Id*. at 370. The *Gile* court held that the employer failed to reasonably accommodate by refusing the plaintiff's request and by assuming it had no further duty to accommodate because its shift bidding process was in place. *Id*. at 373. The Court determined that even though the ADA did not require Gile's employer to abandon its bidding procedures in order to transfer Gile as a reasonable accommodation for her disability, it was obligated to take further actions to reassign Gile to a vacant position for which she was otherwise qualified. *Id*.

The Defendant in this case did not fail to reasonably accommodate Plaintiff's disability. Like Weiler, Plaintiff alleges that, because her inability to work with Dr. Sexist caused her disability, the employer was required to either transfer her to the position of department chief of the Ob-Gyn, Pediatrics or Psychiatric Department or transfer Dr. Sexist to the position of CSGS to accommodate her disability. However, as stated in *Weiler*, an employer is not required to "bump" other employees to create a vacancy to reassign a disabled employee nor does it require an employer to accommodate a disabled employee if it imposes an undue hardship.

The Plaintiff, in essence, requested the Defendant transfer her to one of the filled positions of department chief of the Ob-Gyn, Pediatrics or Psychiatric Department, and then "bump" the employee in that position to the position of CSGS. In addition, the Plaintiff's requirement to reasonably accommodate her disability by transferring Dr. Sexist to the position of CSGS imposes an undue hardship to the Defendant. It would require the Defendant to remove Dr. Sexist from a position in which he is already familiar with the quality of work of his current supervisees, and move him to a position in which he has to be acquainted with new supervisees. Thus, as in *Weiler*, Defendant was not required to shift the decision-making authority regarding supervisory assignments to the Plaintiff in order to reasonably accommodate her disability.

As in *Gile*, the Plaintiff here requested to be transferred to accommodate her disability. However, Gile requested to be transferred to a position for which she was otherwise qualified. Here, the Plaintiff requested to be transferred to a position for which she failed to allege in her Complaint that she is otherwise qualified. When the Plaintiff requested to be transferred to the position of CSGS, the Director advised her that she could be transferred to the position of CSGS after submitting an application and following the Hospital's standard procedures for promotions. Unlike the employer in *Gile*, the Defendant here did not fail to reasonably accommodate Plaintiff's disability because the ADA does not require the Defendant to abandon its procedures for promotions, nor does it obligate the Defendant to take further actions to transfer the Plaintiff to a vacant position for which she may or may not be qualified. Therefore, the Complaint should be dismissed because it fails to allege that even if the Plaintiff suffers from a recognized disability, the Defendant failed to reasonably accommodate her disability.

CONCLUSION

The Complaint fails to allege that the Plaintiff suffers from a recognized disability under the ADA. Even if the Complaint alleges that the Plaintiff has a recognized disability, it fails to allege that the Defendant did not reasonably accommodate the Plaintiff's disability. Defendant respectfully requests that this Court grant its motion to dismiss the Complaint because it fails to allege facts to support a claim under the ADA.

Date: March 27, 2003

                                           Student Written
                                           Student and Associates

                                           Attorneys for Defendant
                                           Get Fixed County General Hospital

Student
Law Offices of Manning & Gorman
111 Capital Mall, Suite 520
Sacramento, CA 95814
Telephone: (916) 555-1212

Attorneys for Plaintiff,
Susan Scheidl-Jones

UNITED STATES DISTRICT COURT
FOR THE MIDDLE DISTRICT OF CALIFORNIA

SUSAN SCHEIDL-JONES Plaintiff vs. MARIANNE GORDON, M.D. and THOMAS NORTON Defendants.	Civil Action No. 2008-863 WHH Judge: Wilhelmina H. Henry MEMORANDUM OF POINTS AND AUTHORITIES IN SUPPORT OF PLAINTIFF'S MOTION FOR PARTIAL SUMMARY JUDGMENT AND IN OPPOSITION TO DEFENDANTS' CROSS-MOTION FOR SUMMARY JUDGMENT

INTRODUCTION

Privacy and confidentiality in medical settings is a right that people have come to rely on. The privacy that is supposed to exist when an individual bears her intimate thoughts and fears to her therapist encourages and fosters the psychological healing process. It was Susan Scheidl-Jones' right to this privacy that was breached by Dr. Marianne Gordon and invaded by Tomas Norton. The Defendants have taken legally recognized confidential information, shared it with each other, and broken the promise of confidentiality that Ms. Scheidl-Jones reasonably expected. Based on these actions Ms. Scheidl-Jones' Motion for Summary Judgment should be granted, while Defendants' cross-motion should be denied.

STATEMENT OF FACTS

While temporarily living in Austria, Ms. Scheidl-Jones began seeing Dr. Gordon, a psychotherapist, to deal with the traumatic and psychologically damaging effects that resulted after she was forced to shoot a fleeing felon during her work as a police officer in Roseville, California. Decl. Scheidl-Jones ¶¶ 7-9. Before beginning therapy, Dr. Gordon asked Ms. Scheidl-Jones if she could record the therapy sessions. Decl. Gordon ¶ 6. Ms. Scheidl-Jones was initially uneasy about this, but agreed to record the sessions only after Dr. Gordon assured her of the strict confidentiality laws in force in Austria. Id.

After a year of therapy, Ms. Scheidl-Jones felt her problems were solved and ceased her sessions with Dr. Gordon and returned to Roseville, California. Upon return she led a peaceful life for four years during which time she earned her Bachelor's degree and taught physical education. Decl. Scheidl-Jones ¶ 14.

Ultimately, Ms. Scheidl-Jones wanted to return to the police force, and sought Dr. Gordon's assistance by asking her to write a letter to the Roseville Police Department informing them of the state of her mental health. Id. at ¶ 16. Dr. Gordon, after reviewing the tapes, was unsure of whether she felt it was safe for Ms. Scheidl-Jones to return to the force. Decl. Gordon ¶ 10. Instead of expressing this to the police department, Dr. Gordon telephoned Thomas Norton, a newspaper reporter who had covered the story of Ms. Scheidl-Jones' previous shooting of the felon. Id. at ¶¶ 11-12. She disclosed to Mr. Norton the existence of the tapes, at which time Mr. Norton expressed interest in their contents, and while Dr. Gordon told Mr. Norton they were confidential, Mr. Norton felt as if she wanted to disclose the contents of them to him. Depo. Norton 11:2-6.

Shortly after this conversation, Mr. Norton made a previously arranged trip to Austria, during which he met with Dr. Gordon in her office to discuss Ms. Scheidl-Jones' situation. Id. at 11:21-25. During this visit, Dr. Gordon stepped out of her office for a few moments leaving Mr. Norton alone with the tapes in his plain view. Id. at 12:10-14. Knowing that she knew of his interest in the tapes, Mr. Norton took this as an indication that Dr. Gordon wanted him to listen to their contents. Id. He, therefore, took them and made copies, and returned them to her before he left to return to the United States. Id. at 12:16-23.

Mr. Norton plans to make public the contents of the tapes to expose allegedly wrongful police practices. Decl. Norton ¶ 4. The contents of the tapes disclose the troubling thoughts of a woman who was suffering great emotional distress five years ago, and who confided her feelings in the privacy of a therapy session with her psychotherapist. Partial Transcr. Psychotherapy Sess. 3. The breach of this confidential understanding by Dr. Gordon, and the invasion into this legally recognized privacy interest by Mr. Norton is what Ms. Scheidl-Jones seeks redress for in her Motion for Summary Judgment.

ARGUMENT

Both Ms. Scheidl-Jones and the Defendants have filed for partial summary judgment in this case. A court will enter summary judgment when there is no triable issue as to any material fact, so that the moving party is "entitled to a judgment as a matter of law." Celotex Corp. v. Catrett, 477 U.S. 317, 322. The party filing for summary judgment will succeed when the non-moving party fails to "make a sufficient showing on an essential element of [their] case." Id. at 323. In this case, the court should grant the Plaintiff's Motion for Summary Judgment, as there is no genuine issue of material fact surrounding Dr. Gordon's breach. Additionally, the Defendant's Motion for Summary Judgment should be denied because elements of the dangerous patient justification have not been met. Finally, Plaintiff's Motion for Summary Judgment regarding Mr. Norton's invasion of privacy should be granted.

I. The substantive law of Austria should be applied to the breach of confidentiality claim because its provisions best serve the interest of the injured party and offer her the best protections and compensation.

Austrian law should be applied to the breach of confidentiality claim in this case. While there is no dispute over applying California law to the invasion of privacy claim filed against Mr. Norton, the elements of Austrian law are specifically applicable to the breach of confidentiality claim filed against Dr. Gordon. The choice of law rules within the forum must first be determined to decide which law to apply. When in federal court under diversity subject matter jurisdiction, the federal court is to apply the substantive law of the forum. Eerie R.R. Co. v. Tompkins, 304 U.S. 64 (1938).

California's choice of law rule, therefore, determines whether California substantive law or Austrian substantive law will apply. To make such a determination California courts rely on a three step governmental interest test. Wash. Mutual Bank v. Super. Ct. of Orange Co., 24 Cal. 4th 906, 919 (2001). Using this test courts must determine how the foreign law differs from California law, whether each state has an interest in having its own law applied, and finally which state's interest would be more impaired if not applied. Id. at 919-920. California's interest in applying its law rests on its desire to protect its citizens and offer them the most effective means of relief. Kasel v. Remington Arms Co., 24 Cal. App. 3d 711, 734 (1972).

Austrian law applies to this case if there is a material difference between Austrian law and California law relating to the claim. Wash. Mutual Bank, 24 Cal. 4th at 919. Confidentiality laws in Austria and California do materially differ. Kenworthy, Dana J., The Austrian Psychotherapy Act: No Legal Duty to Warn, 11 Ind. Intl. and Comp. L. Rev. 469 (2001). The two differ regarding disclosure of therapy records of allegedly dangerous patients. Id. at 490. To address this, the United States creates a duty within the therapist to disclose the information to the party who may be potentially harmed. Id. Austria, however, gives the therapist discretion to determine whether or not to take action. Id. Austria, therefore, imposes guidelines that more substantially protect the privacy of the individual patient. By allowing, but not mandating, a therapist to disclose such information patients enjoy a greater sense of confidentiality in Austria. Id. at 474.

Next, the court must determine whether both the foreign country and California have an interest in having their law applied. Wash. Mutual Bank Co., 24 Cal. 4th at 920. Austria is known as the home of modern psychology, and the Austrian Psychotherapy Act "seeks to protect its creation." Kenworthy, 11 Ind. Intl. and Comp. L. Rev. at 473. Being the only law that provides for strict confidentiality makes it have its own distinct interest. Id. at 474. The Act furthers a patient's right to privacy and in doing so further protects people seeking the psychotherapeutic treatment. Id. Protecting these interests is its goal, and in doing so it "contributes to a clearly defined psychotherapeutic relationship, thus acknowledging the importance of confidentiality for psychotherapy to be effective." Id. at 475.

Finally, Austrian law should be applied because its interests will be more impaired if it is not applied. Austria's as an interest in protecting the privacy and confidentiality of patients in the psychotherapy sessions. Kenworthy, 11 Ind. Intl. and Comp. L. Rev. at 474-475. If Austrian law is not applied Dr. Gordon will be allowed to transcend its laws and violate the strict confidentiality that the country seeks to protect. Id. Even though Austria allows disclosure under certain circumstances, these circumstances were not met in this case. The result would be a complete breach of the country's laws without a proper justification.

Additionally, California's interest will not be substantially impaired by applying Austrian law to the case. California's interest in compensating

Ms. Scheidl-Jones, a California domiciliary, is best accomplished by applying Austrian law as it more thoroughly protects her privacy. California has an interest in protecting its citizens and providing effective relief. Kasel, 24 Cal. App. 3d at 734. In cases that courts have found California law to apply, the injured party has been the one advocating for the application of Californian law. Id.; Hurtado v. Super. Ct. of Sacramento Co., 11 Cal. 3d 574 (1974). California's interest in applying the law that best compensates the injured party was best served in these situations by applying California law. Kasel, 24 Cal. App. 3d at 734. In this case, however, the law that best serves the interest of the injured party and the states involved is Austrian law. Ms. Scheidl-Jones, the injured party, and a California domiciliary, will be best protected and compensated by applying Austrian law.

Austrian law should, therefore, be applied to the breach of confidentiality claim against Dr. Gordon. Austrian law materially differs from California law, it serves an important interest, and it would be greatly impaired if it were not applied.

II. **Ms. Scheidl-Jones' motion for summary judgment against Dr. Gordon should be allowed because there is no genuine issue of material fact regarding her breach of Ms. Scheidl-Jones' confidentiality.**

There is no question that by disclosing the contents of Ms. Scheidl-Jones' therapy session, Dr. Gordon breached Ms. Scheidl-Jones' psychotherapist-patient confidentiality privilege. Whether Austrian law or California law applies, the breach is clear.

A. Under Austrian law, Dr. Gordon unjustifiably breached the psychotherapist-patient confidentiality because she allowed Mr. Norton to take the therapy session tapes without being sure of any threat or harm that Ms. Scheidl-Jones posed to others.

Applying the stricter standards of Austrian confidentiality laws, there is no genuine issue of any material fact surrounding the breach. The Austrian Psychotherapy Act "provides no exceptions to patient confidentiality." Kenworthy, 11 Ind. Intl. and Comp. L. Rev. at 469. More specifically, the act states that "psychotherapists . . . shall be obliged to keep confidential all secrets shared with them or becoming known to them in the exercise of their profession." Id. at 473. The only exception provided by the statute is that in "case of the imminent threat of a criminal act involving the life, physical integrity, or freedom of the victim, the possible disadvantages as a result of the criminal act will generally have precedence over the breach of confidentiality." Id. at 474. The statute provides, however, that these threats must be direct or imminent, and certain or highly probable. Id. Additionally, this exception is allowed, not mandated. Id.

The breach in this case occurred when Dr. Gordon allowed the tapes to be taken by Mr. Norton, an act that was not justified by any allowed exception under the law. It is undisputed that Dr. Gordon left the tapes, which she had control over at the time, alone in her office, in plain view of Mr. Norton. Depo. Norton 12: 10-14. Whether this act was negligent or intentional, Dr. Gordon broke her obligation of keeping confidential "all secrets shared with [her] or becoming known to [her] in the exercise of [her] profession." Kenworthy, 11 Ind. Intl. and Comp. L. Rev. at 473.

Additionally, Defendant's Partial Motion for Summary Judgment does not survive under Austrian law because the material facts surrounding this argument do not indicate that the imminently dangerous patient exception elements have been met. The contents of Ms. Scheidl-Jones' therapy tapes do not indicate any direct, imminent, or highly probable danger. Id. at 474. While the contents may indicate that five years ago, at the time of her therapy sessions, Ms. Scheidl-Jones possessed some potentially dangerous thoughts, there was no indication that these internal thoughts would ever surface, no indication that their occurrence was imminent, and no concrete threat. Partial Transcr. Psychotherapy Sess. 3. The fact that in the five years since the therapy session took place these thoughts never came to pass additionally indicates that Ms. Scheidl-Jones posed no imminent or concrete threat to any member of society.

Defendants' motion for summary judgment based on the Austrian imminent threat exception is unsupported by any facts of imminent or concrete threats, and therefore should fail.

B.   Under Californian law Ms. Scheidl-Jones' motion for summary judgment should be granted because Dr. Gordon breached Ms. Scheidl-Jones' right to confidentiality, and was not justified in doing so.

Applying California law, there again is no genuine issue of any material fact in finding that Dr. Gordon breached Ms. Scheidl-Jones' right to doctor patient confidentiality. California Evidence Code §1014 creates a duty for psychotherapists to keep the contents of therapy sessions confidential. It states that the patient has the privilege "to refuse to disclose, and to prevent another from disclosing, a confidential communication between patient and psychotherapist." Cal. Evid. Code Ann. § 1014 (West 2008). Breach of this promise of confidentiality is a recognized tort in California. To determine whether a breach has occurred, California courts must demonstrate that:

> "the plaintiff conveyed confidential and novel information to the defendant, the defendant had knowledge that the information was being disclosed in confidence, there was an understanding between the defendant and the plaintiff that the confidence be maintained, and there was a disclosure or use in violation of the understanding."

Berkla v. Corel Corp., 302 F.3d 909 (9th Cir. 2002).

A therapist, however, may justify a breach by relying on a duty to disclose that is present under California law when they feel a patient is a danger to themselves or society. Tarasoff v. Regents of the University of California, 17 Cal. 3d 425 (1976). Under the Tarasoff rule, "[w]hen a therapist determines, or pursuant to the standards of his profession should determine, that his patient presents a serious danger of violence to another, he incurs an obligation to use reasonable care to protect the intended victim." Id. at 431. This obligation involves warning "the intended victim or others likely to apprise the victim of the danger, to notify the police, or to take whatever other steps are reasonably necessary under the circumstances." Id. The intended victim, however, has to be readily identifiable; a blanket threat is insufficient to trigger the duty to warn. Thompson v. County of Alameda, 27 Cal. 3d 741, 752-753 (1980).

Ms. Scheidl-Jones conveyed confidential and novel information to the Defendant. As the transcript of the therapy session indicates, she told Dr. Gordon information that she had not previously told any other individual, and which she only felt secure in telling Dr. Gordon because of the confidential nature of the therapy session. Partial Transcr. Psychotherapy Sess. 2. Having never told anyone her thoughts before, the information was surely novel and as they were in the setting of a therapy session, the intent of it remaining confidential was clear. Id.

Additionally, Dr. Gordon was aware that the information was being told to her in confidence and that this confidence should be maintained.

Dr. Gordon repeatedly assured Ms. Scheidl-Jones' that she could trust her with her story and information. Id.; Decl. Scheidl-Jones ¶ 9. Ms. Scheidl-Jones only agreed to have the therapy sessions taped after relying on Dr. Gordon's promise of confidentiality. Decl. Scheidl-Jones ¶ 9. Additionally, the importance of keeping therapy sessions confidential has even been recognized by the United States Supreme Court. Jaffee v. Redmond, 518 U.S. 1, 11 (1996). Based on these beliefs and understandings it is clear that Dr. Gordon should have been aware that Ms. Scheidl-Jones was revealing her thoughts to her in confidence under a belief that her thoughts would remain private.

Finally, there was a disclosure or use of the tapes that violated this confidence. The ambiguous language of this rule does not indicate whether such a disclosure or use must be intentional or negligent. Berkla, 302 F.3d at 917. Therefore, even if Dr. Gordon was negligent when she left the tapes alone with Mr. Norton, her actions still resulted in a disclosure to a third party, and violated Ms. Scheidl-Jones' confidence.

The Defendants' Motion for Summary Judgment relies on the dangerous patient exception under the Tarasoff rule. This Motion, however, fails as it is disputed whether Ms. Scheidl-Jones was truly a threat to society. Ms. Scheidl-Jones made no threats to any "identifiable victim." Thompson, 27 Cal. 3d at 752-753. Although the open and confidential character of therapy sessions "encourages patient to express threats of violence," this does not mean that therapists should be "encouraged to routinely reveal such threats." Tarasoff, 17 Cal. 3d at 441. In Thompson, a patient's threat to kill a child in a specific neighborhood was considered too vague as to create a duty to disclose. 27 Cal. 3d at 746. If a threat as specific as that in Thompson does not create a duty to warn, the mere thoughts of violence that Ms. Scheidl-Jones enunciated are surely not specific enough.

There was no substantiated threat that Ms. Scheidl-Jones was a threat. In Tarasoff, the Court stated that therapists should take *reasonable* steps to inform the intended victim, or those who are likely to tell the victim of the threat, or to notify the police when they feel there is an imminent threat to the individual. 17 Cal. 3d at 431. Dr. Gordon did not tell the identifiable victim, as there was none, or the police, she told a newspaper reporter who she knew covered stories relating to Ms. Scheidl-Jones. Decl. Gordon ¶¶ 11-12. In addition to this, she took this unreasonable step without even being sure of Ms. Scheidl-Jones' current mental state. Id. at ¶ ¶ 10-11. As there was no identifiable victim, and because Dr. Gordon did not take reasonable measures to warn, the argument that Ms. Scheidl-Jones was a threat to society is unsubstantiated.

As a result of her actions, Dr. Gordon breached Ms. Scheidl-Jones' right to confidentiality under both Austrian and Californian law. She did so unjustifiably, as the requirements for a dangerous patient exception have not been met. The summary judgment motion in favor of a breach should therefore be granted, while the Defendants' summary judgment motion on the basis of the justification should be denied.

III. <u>The summary judgment motion in favor of Ms. Scheidl-Jones' claim of invasion of privacy against Mr. Norton should be granted because Mr. Norton invaded a legally recognized privacy right in a highly offensive manner.</u>

Mr. Norton's taking of Ms. Scheidl-Jones' tapes and his subsequent threat of publishing those tapes constitute an offensive invasion of Ms. Scheidl-Jones' privacy rights. Under California law, an invasion of privacy claim can be shown by proving that there was an intrusion into a private matter, "in a manner highly offensive to a reasonable person." <u>Shulman v. Group W. Prods.</u>, 18 Cal. 4th 200, 231 (1998). This is proven only if the plaintiff "had an objectively reasonable expectation of [privacy] in the [information]." <u>Id.</u> at 232. The reasonable expectation of privacy is an "objective entitlement" based on accepted community norms. <u>Susan S. v. Philip D. Israels</u>, 55 Cal. App. 4th 1290, 1295 (1997). Determining offensiveness requires "consideration of all the circumstances of the intrusion," including the potential motive of gathering news. <u>Shulman</u>, 18 Cal. 4th at 236-237. The importance of gathering news, however, cannot be an affront to breaking laws that protect an individual's privacy. <u>Id.</u> at 236.

Ms. Scheidl-Jones possessed a legally recognized, and reasonable, expectation of privacy in her confidential medical records. The law recognizes Ms. Scheidl-Jones' right to keep private the contents of her therapy session. Cal. Evid. Code § 1014. Mr. Norton, however, took the tapes, listened to them, and intends to publish them all without the permission of Ms. Scheidl-Jones. Depo. Norton 12:16-23.

The reasonableness of Ms. Scheidl-Jones' privacy expectation is evidenced by the fact that Dr. Gordon promised her complete privacy, and Ms. Scheidl-Jones relied on this when agreeing to record the therapy sessions. Depo. Scheidl-Jones 8:19-25. Additionally, the doctor-patient environment "carries a traditional and legally well-established expectation of privacy." <u>Shulman</u>, 18 Cal. 4th at 234. This belief in privacy is further accepted and supported by the United States Supreme Court, which recognizes that the right to privacy is integral in the success of therapy and the continued mental health of our society. Jaffee, 518 U.S. at 11. Because this understanding is so thoroughly understood by our society, Ms. Scheidl-Jones' reliance on Dr. Gordon's promise of confidentiality was completely reasonable, and Mr. Norton should have understood the degree of privacy that surrounded and protected the tapes.

Mr. Norton's invasion of Ms. Scheidl-Jones' privacy constituted a highly offensive and serious invasion of her privacy right. Just as the court in Susan S. found, the reading and dissemination of Ms. Scheidl-Jones' medical records, "knowing the information contained in them could be highly sensitive and embarrassing to her," constitutes a serious invasion of an individual's privacy. 55 Cal. App. 4th at 1299. The argument that the contents of the tapes are important for news purposes is not applicable because of the illegal method used to gather this information. The California Supreme Court recognizes that "the mere fact the intruder was in pursuit of a 'story' does not . . . justify an otherwise offensive intrusion." Shulman, 18 Cal. 4th at 237. Based on the importance of privacy in therapy sessions, Norton's invasion into Ms. Scheidl-Jones' legally recognized privacy right should be considered a highly offensive intrusion.

By taking, Ms. Scheidl-Jones' private medical record, Norton seriously invaded her legally recognized and objectively reasonable privacy right. The motion for summary judgment for invasion of privacy against Mr. Norton should therefore be granted.

CONCLUSION

Under either Austrian or Californian law, the Defendants in this case have breached Ms. Scheidl-Jones' right to confidentiality, and invaded her legally recognized privacy rights. There are no genuine issues of material fact surrounding the breach or the invasion of privacy. Dr. Gordon did not uphold her obligation to keep the contents of the tapes private, and even if she felt disclosure was necessary, she did not warn the proper parties in a reasonable way. Additionally, there is no genuine issue of material fact surrounding Mr. Norton's invasion of privacy. He invaded a legally recognized privacy right in an offensive manner. Ms. Scheidl-

Jones' Motion for Partial Summary Judgment should, therefore, be granted and the Defendants' cross-motion should be denied.

Dated: November 5, 2008

Respectfully submitted,

_____

Student
Law Offices of Manning & Gorman
111 Capital Mall, Suite 520
Sacramento, CA 95814
Telephone: (916) 555-1212

Attorney for Plaintiff
Susan Scheidl-Jones

MEMORANDUM OF POINTS AND AUTHORITIES IN SUPPORT OF MOTION CHECKLIST

1. **<u>Entire Memorandum</u>**

    ☐ Locate the following section headings and put a check next to them

    - ☐ Introduction
    - ☐ Statement of Facts
    - ☐ Argument
    - ☐ Conclusion

    ☐ Are all of the section headings:

    - ☐ In ALL CAPS?
    - ☐ Centered on the page?
    - ☐ <u>Underlined</u>?

2. **<u>Introduction</u>**

    For the Introduction, confirm that it:

    - ☐ Introduces the parties involved in the litigation

    - ☐ Provides context to the motion and the relevant procedural background

    - ☐ Clearly states the relief the client desires

    - ☐ Introduces a theme

    - ☐ Includes the primary legal points that justify the relief requested

3. **Statement of Facts**

Locate the <u>first paragraph</u>. Locate and CIRCLE the following information:

- ☐ The parties and the client

- ☐ The client's problem or goal

- ☐ The general time and location of events

- ☐ Any procedural history or status of the case [this could be in the last paragraph instead]

Confirm that the Facts:

- ☐ Use a persuasive tone highlighting good facts and deemphasizing bad facts

- ☐ Tell a "story" and develop a theme

- ☐ Include all of the facts relied upon in the Argument

- ☐ Include all relevant facts from the case file

- ☐ Includes background facts so that the Facts are focused on the motion

- ☐ Accurately describe the facts

- ☐ Are effectively organized to tell a cohesive story with a logical flow

- ☐ Provide closure at the end rather than ending abruptly

- ☐ Includes a citation after every Fact in compliance with the citation manual required by the court

4. **<u>Argument</u>**

For the Argument, confirm that it:

- ☐ Includes an Umbrella section where appropriate (if there are multiple point headings, consider using an umbrella section that provides the overall conclusion, the general legal concepts the Argument will address, and a directional roadmap).

If there is an Umbrella section, read it and identify the following (if any of these are missing, make a note to fix it):

- ☐ The statutory rule or rules or synthesized common law rule or rules

- ☐ The purpose or policy of those rules

- ☐ A quick definition of those rules

- ☐ Any part of the rules that will not be discussed and a quick explanation as to why it will not be discussed

- ☐ An organization sentence describing how the Argument is structured

- ☐ A statement of the overall conclusion of the section the roadmap precedes

- ☐ A brief statement of the reasons for that conclusion (only if it can be done succinctly)

Following the Umbrella paragraph, look for the following in the Argument section:

- ☐ Presents arguments with the big rules or legal concepts first working down to the specific legal issues the memo is addressing.

- ☐ Provides a separate CRAC for each legal Argument. Please write C, R, A, C in the margin for each persuasive paradigm to make sure that it is in the proper C-R-A-C order

☐ Begins each CRAC with the overall <u>conclusion</u> on the legal issue, which matches the rest of the CRAC.

☐ Each CRAC includes a complete, synthesized statement of the <u>rule</u> on the legal issue and:

☐ The <u>rule</u> identifies specific cases to be used by name and includes a citation

☐ The <u>rule</u> considers and identifies any adverse legal authority

☐ The <u>rule</u> makes the best use of the cases identified

☐ The <u>rule</u> includes an explanation of the rule (not in the Formal Memorandum sense, but provides enough information for the reader to understand the rule and how it operates).

☐ The <u>rule</u> is crafted favorably and persuasively for the client, while still being accurate

☐ Each CRAC includes <u>analysis</u> on the issue not just conclusions

☐ Each analysis paragraph beings with a thesis sentence that asserts a position regarding how the law or policy applies to the client's facts

☐ The analysis clearly connects the argument and the client's facts to law, rather than relying upon factual narrative or conjecture (NOTE: the argument should cite to the Facts and law frequently)

☐ If the analysis employs analogical reasoning, it should establish clear comparisons/distinctions between the facts of the precedent and the client's facts. There should be a connection between the

☐   factual comparisons/distinctions to the law to show their legal significance and how they support the client's argument.

☐   If the analysis is policy based, it should clearly connect the policy to the facts of the client's case to show how it supports the client's argument.

☐   If the analysis utilizes rule-based reasoning, it should connect the rule to the client's facts and show how it supports the client's argument.

☐   Each analysis should refute any adverse legal authority or rebut any anticipated arguments by opposing counsel without emphasizing or highlighting them

☐   The analysis is organized to highlight the client's strongest argument(s) first

☐   The CRAC ends with a final <u>conclusion</u> that summarizes the arguments made in the CRAC. (NOTE: this does not apply to a single CRAC memo; only multi-CRAC issues)

☐   Locate the last sentence at the end of each section (it should be the last sentence prior to the heading for the next section or the big CONCLUSION at the end of a memo)

☐   Read the last sentence of the section. Is it the last C in a CRAC? If there is only 1 CRAC, this is okay

☐   If there is more than one CRAC, then there needs to be a separate conclusion sentence to sum up the multiple CRACs before moving onto the next section

5. **<u>Persuasive Point Headings and Sub-Headings</u>**

Locate each heading and sub-heading and highlight it. For <u>each</u> heading, check the <u>technical</u> compliance:

- ☐ Is it only one (1) sentence?

- ☐ Do the lines of text wrap under each other so the left margin of the heading is even?

- ☐ Does it use emphasizers (bold, italic, underline, etc.) appropriately to allow the headings to stand out from the text of the memo but not scream at the reader?

- ☐ Are the emphasizers used consistent with the other headings and sub-headings?

- ☐ Evaluate the consistency of all of the headings:

    - Do the headings or sub-headings begin with the same phrasing?

    - If not, why not?

- ☐ For <u>each</u> heading and sub-heading, check the <u>substantive</u> compliance:

    - Read the section the heading or sub-heading represents and CIRCLE key legal terms

    - Check to see that those legal terms are included in the heading or sub-heading.

    - Read the section the heading or sub-heading represents and <u>underline</u> the key facts used in that section

    - Check to see that those key facts are included in the heading or sub-heading.

- ☐ Read the heading and <u>label</u> each part of the heading formula:

- The legal conclusion
- Because or because equivalent
- The part of the rule justifying the legal c conclusion
- The key relevant fact(s)

6. **Conclusion**

   Read the overall CONCLUSION at the end of the memo. It should:

   ☐ Provide a conclusion for each issue raised in the brief

   ☐ Restate the conclusion the client wants the judge to reach

   ☐ Track the organization of the Argument section

7. **Citations**

   Review the memo to ensure:

   ☐ Each legal principle or rule stated in the brief has a citation

   ☐ The first time a case or other authority is cited, that it is in the proper full citation form

   ☐ Citations that have already been fully cited are in the proper short citation format

   ☐ When required, each citation has a proper pinpoint cite

   ☐ That all Facts, in the Facts section and in the Argument section are cited

CHAPTER 16

THE APPELLATE PROCESS AND STANDARD OF REVIEW

■ ■ ■

By Jennifer A. Gibson

A. THE APPELLATE PROCESS

This chapter introduces students to the appellate court systems in the United States and the appellate process in general. As part of that introduction, the chapter also examines the various considerations that affect the decision to initiate an appeal. Therefore, in addition to an overview of the appellate process, this chapter also provides an in-depth discussion of stare decisis and standards of review. Because this chapter provides an overview of the appellate process, typically it would be assigned as a general introduction to the material covered in Chapter 17 and Chapter 18.

B. OVERVIEW OF THE APPELLATE COURT SYSTEMS

This part of the chapter describes the three-tiered court systems in most states and in the federal system. It also covers stare decisis across systems.

1. STARE DECISIS

Most students struggle with the concept of mandatory and persuasive authority. Two important concepts to emphasize with this topic are the differences between published and unpublished decisions and the binding impact of published court of appeal decisions on lower courts.

Unpublished decisions in state courts may not be cited as authority in any subsequent unrelated case. Students must understand that even if an unpublished decision can be found online, it may not be cited as authority in another unrelated case. Even so, the rules in some jurisdictions may allow use of unpublished decisions for a particular purpose. Therefore, students should consult each jurisdiction's local rules on citing to unpublished decisions.

Whether published decisions are binding on subsequent cases also presents difficulty for students when the decision is issued by an intermediate court of appeal. Specifically, in states in which the intermediate appellate court is divided into multiple districts or divisions, the published decision of one division is generally not binding on another. In those states, if there are conflicting court of appeal decisions, lower courts can generally decide which decision to follow. Once the state's highest court resolves the conflict, however, all courts within the state must follow that decision, however.

2. STARE DECISIS ACROSS SYSTEMS

The chapter also examines the implications of stare decisis across court systems. In this section, the most important concepts to emphasize for students are first, federal courts must follow the decision of the highest state court on an issue of state law, but are not required to follow a state court's decision on federal issues.[11] Second, students must understand that state courts are only required to follow decisions of the United States Supreme Court on federal and constitutional issues.[12]

C. TAKING THE APPEAL: GENERAL CONSIDERATIONS

One important skill of appellate practice covered in this chapter is assessing the merits of appealing a lower court's decision. A discussion of this section should highlight the key considerations that factor into that decision, such as appealability of the order or decision, party's standing to bring the appeal, justiciability, timeliness of the appeal, and the standard of review the court of appeal will use to determine if the lower court erred.

---

[11] "Although state courts have the authority to decide issues of federal constitutional law, state court decisions are not binding upon the federal courts." Sys. Contractors Corp. v. Orleans Parish Sch. Bd., 148 F.3d 571, 575 (5th Cir. 1998).

[12] "We are not bound by decisions of the lower federal courts, even on federal questions; they are persuasive and entitled to great weight." Barrett v. Rosenthal, 146 P.3d 510, 526 (Cal. 2006).

1.   IS IT APPEALABLE?

On the issue of appealability, one area of emphasis is the idea that not every order is appealable.

As a rule, final judgments, judgments that completely resolve the matter between the parties, are appealable. But there are exceptions. And students should come away with an understanding that there are orders, such as collateral orders and post-judgment orders, that are not final judgments and must be appealed in a timely fashion or appellate review is lost.

In addition, students should also glean from a discussion of this chapter an understanding that appellate review of orders that are not final judgments is possible through special procedures, like certification, which is available in all jurisdictions.

2.   DOES THE PARTY HAVE THE RIGHT TO APPEAL?

The next consideration in deciding to bring an appeal is justiciability, which refers to whether the court is being asked to decide an actual controversy between actual parties aggrieved by the lower court's decision. This justiciability requirement exists to prevent appellate courts from rendering advisory opinions that do not affect actual parties.

Students should take away from a discussion of this section that three considerations primarily determine whether an appeal presents a justiciable issue: an aggrieved party, an issue that is not moot, and an issue that is ripe, meaning there is a present need for the appellate court to act.

One means of reinforcing this concept is to create an assignment that presents a fact pattern where the injury is resolved before the appeal can be decided or where the injury is complete and the court of appeal's decision cannot undo the harm. An area of law that provides a rich resource for creating the assignment is the law arising out of challenges to contempt actions.

3.   WAS THE APPEAL TIMELY FILED IN THE RIGHT COURT?

Perfecting the appeal means timely filing the notice of appeal in the lower court along with the appropriate filing fee. Subject to very limited exceptions for criminal appeals filed by incarcerated defendants, the appellate courts must dismiss any appeal in which the notice of appeal was not filed timely.

In both federal and state courts of appeal, the time limit for filing the notice of appeal is triggered by the entry of the final judgment. Most states have time limits ranging from thirty days to 180 days from the entry of judgment.

One assignment I have used to reinforce this concept is to create a series of exercises using filed notices of appeal. Students must determine which one is untimely, timely, and which one appeals an order that is not appealable. In creating the exercises, I incorporate common issues that can affect the deadline for filing a notice of appeal, such as whether the time to appeal was triggered by the clerk's service of notice of entry of the judgment or by entry of the judgment itself. In addition, in the series of exercises, a seemingly late notice of appeal can be saved by the unanticipated extensions of the deadline because the last day to file the notice of appeal fell on a weekend or court holiday.

4. WRIT IT?

The discussion for this part of the chapter should focus on the availability of the writ process as a rare alternative to appellate review. As discussed in the chapter, there are generally three kinds of writs: mandate, prohibition, or certiorari. A reviewing court issues a writ of mandate to correct an abuse of discretion or compel the performance of a ministerial duty. Appellate courts issue writs of prohibition to prevent a judicial act that exceeds the jurisdiction or power of the particular judge or court. Writs of certiorari are issued to correct a judicial act that has already been completed, and which is in excess of the court or judge's jurisdiction or power. While not encouraged as a substitute for an appeal, the writ petition is one means by which appellate courts can expeditiously exercise their reviewing power.

One potential assignment to reinforce the concepts in this section is an exercise that requires students to determine the type of writ that should be filed to challenge a lower court's decision or conduct, specifically, whether a writ of mandate, prohibition, or certiorari is required.

5. STAYING ENFORCEMENT OF THE JUDGMENT WHILE THE APPEAL IS PENDING

Intuitively, students understand that there is a need to maintain the status quo while an appeal is pending. Thus, a discussion of this part of the chapter can allow students to explore that intuitive understanding and provide information about the means of staying the enforcement of the judgment while an appeal is pending. Specifically, there are three traditional ways of obtaining a stay of enforcement of a judgment that is not automatically stayed: posting a bond or undertaking, requesting a discretionary stay from the lower court, or filing a petition for a writ of supersedeas or stay in the appellate court.

D. TAKING THE APPEAL: SPECIFIC CONSIDERATIONS

Even if the order is one that is appealable, four additional considerations affect the decision to initiate an appeal: standard of review that applies to the issue, preservation of the error, the error's impact on the decision (prejudice), and finally, appropriateness of the appeal.

1. STANDARD OF REVIEW

In truth, the touchstone of appellate decision-making is the concept of standard of review. Students must understand that the standard of review governs not only how the court will view the lower court's decision, but also fundamentally determines whether the court of appeal will consider the lower court's decision erroneous. If a very deferential standard of review applies, the court of appeal likely will not find that the lower court's decision was erroneous. If reasonable minds can disagree, there is no error. Thus, students should understand that even if the court of appeal disagrees with the lower court's decision, if a deferential standard of review applies, the lower court's decision does not constitute appealable error.

Students should also understand that the standards of review are rooted in the traditional functions of the lower and the appellate courts. As discussed in this chapter, lower courts are charged with determining the facts of the particular case and applying the correct law to those facts. It is the "first-hand observer" of the happenings at a trial, and serves as the fact-finder and litigation manager who is familiar with the litigants and their counsel.[13]

In its proper role, the appellate court provides predictability for litigants by ensuring that the legal principles governing trials are sound, uniform, and correct. Thus, for decisions that raise legal issues, the court of appeal has the power to reverse a trial court's erroneous interpretation or application of the law.

The discussion should also emphasize the five primary standards that apply to issues on appeal: (1) de novo, (2) abuse of discretion, (3) clear error, (4) substantial evidence, and (5) mixed question. Students should ultimately comprehend that having familiarity with the standards of review allows the appellate practitioner to select the arguments or issues to be raised in the appeal by weeding out weaker issues in favor of those subject to the appellate court's independent review. Furthermore, even if the issue is one that could be reviewed under a deferential standard, experienced appellate practitioners will seek ways to transform the issue into one of law so that the court will apply an independent standard of review.

a. De Novo

From this section, students should understand that de novo review applies to legal issues and that in deciding whether the lower court erred, the court of appeal does not have to grant any deference to the lower court's decision. Thus, for issues subject to de novo review, the appellant stands a better chance of prevailing on appeal because the appellate court can reach a different decision from the lower court. Students should also be able to identify that whenever the issue involves correcting legal errors or articulating the correct rule that should be applied to settled facts, the standard is likely to be de novo.

b. Substantial Evidence

From a discussion of this topic, students should understand that the court of appeal grants great deference to the lower court's factual findings. Even if the reviewing justices would have ruled differently or

---

[13] Amanda Peters, The Meaning, Measure, and Misuse of Standards of Review, 13 LEWIS & CLARK L. Rev 233, 259 (2009).

drawn different inferences from the facts, if there is evidence to support the lower court's decision, the appellate court is without power to reverse.

The exercise in this section is designed to show, first, that the testimony of a single witness could constitute sufficient evidence to support a factual finding. Second, it is designed to show that credibility determinations are left to the lower court, and the court of appeal cannot second-guess those credibility determinations.

The standard of review that applies is of course substantial evidence because this is a factual determination or factual finding. A discussion of the exercise should emphasize that courts of appeal as a general matter do not reverse factual findings unless there is no substantial evidence in the entire record to support the finding. In this exercise, the finding would not be reversed because there is actual evidence to support it. Even though James Frey is known for fabricating a story about his life, the fact-finder assesses credibility, and the court of appeal will not second-guess that assessment.

PRACTICE EXERCISE

Consider the following hypothetical: A plaintiff sued the defendant for injuries sustained in a car accident. The plaintiff's theory of the case states that the accident occurred because the defendant ran a red light while the plaintiff had the green light. Four witnesses—the Pope, Nelson Mandela, Warren Buffet, and Oprah Winfrey—all testify that at the time of the accident the plaintiff had a red light. Another witness, James Frey,[14] testifies he had a clear view of the intersection and the plaintiff had the green light and the defendant's light was red.

If the jury finds the defendant's light was red and the plaintiff's light was green, what standard of review applies? Would the appellate court be able to reverse that finding?

---

[14] James Frey is the author of the best-selling book, A MILLION LITTLE PIECES (Anchor Books 2003). He offered the book as a memoir of his life. He later admitted that parts of the book were fiction.

c. Clearly Erroneous

This standard is as deferential as substantial evidence. It applies to factual findings by district courts in the federal system.[15] As long as the district court's decision is plausible in light of the entire record, the appellate court may not reverse it even if it would have reached a different result.[16]

The practice exercise below is designed to highlight that the lower court's factual finding power is not without limit. Its factual determinations must still be based on evidence that is ponderable and of solid value. Here, the court of appeal might reverse because an authenticated photo may leave the court of appeal with a definite and firm conviction that the district court made a mistake when it disregarded an authenticated photograph.

PRACTICE EXERCISE

In the previous practice exercise, the plaintiff sued the defendant for injuries sustained in a car accident. Recall that the plaintiff's theory of the case is that the accident occurred because the defendant ran a red light while the plaintiff had the green light. This time, five witnesses, the Pope, Nelson Mandela, Warren Buffet, Queen Elizabeth of England, and Oprah Winfrey testify that at the time of the accident the plaintiff had a green light. The defense produces an authenticated traffic camera photo showing that at the exact time the plaintiff entered the intersection, he was speeding and the light was red. If the court finds the plaintiff had a green light and the defendant had a red light, what standard of review applies?

Clear error applies because this is a factual finding by the district court. And what is the likely result on appeal?

d. Mixed Question

A discussion of this topic should emphasize that a mixed question of law and fact is an issue that requires the lower court or jury

---

[15] Concrete Pipe & Products of Calif., Inc. v. Construction Laborers Pension Trust for So. Calif., 508 U.S. 602, 622 (1993); FONTHAM ET AL., *supra*, at 288.
[16] Hovey v. Ayers, 458 F.3d 892, 900 (9th Cir. 2006).

to first make findings of historical or ultimate facts and then apply a legal standard to those factual determinations to arrive at a conclusion. The discussion should also emphasize that whether an independent standard of review or a more deferential one applies to a mixed question is determined by whether the legal issues or the factual issues predominate. If deciding the issue primarily requires the lower court's fact-finding expertise, then the factual nature of the inquiry predominates and the appellate court reviews the issue for clear error or under the substantial evidence standard. If the issue requires "the exercise of judgment about legal principles," de novo review applies.[17]

e. Abuse of Discretion

Students should glean from a discussion of this topic that there is no consensus on what it means to say that a lower court has abused its discretion. At times, courts have defined this standard as permitting reversal only if the appellate court has determined that the lower court's decision "lies beyond the pale of reasonable justification under the circumstances."[18]

Students should also realize from this section of the chapter that it is possible to obtain a reversal of a decision subject to abuse of discretion because courts can abuse their discretion even if their decisions are not "irrational" or "wacky." If the lower court's decision falls outside the legal principles granting the court its discretion, the appellate court may reverse. But an appellate court may not reverse a lower court's ruling subject to abuse of discretion standard of review merely because the reviewing court disagrees with the decision.[19] If the lower court's action falls within the permissible range of options set by the governing legal criteria, then the appellate court cannot reverse.[20]

2. WAS THE ISSUE PRESERVED?

Students should also take away from this chapter the concept that errors must be preserved, that means that the error being challenged was

---

[17] Tolbert v. Page, 182 F. 3d 677, 682 (9th Cir. 1999).
[18] Harman v. Apfel, 211 F.3d 1172, 1175 (9th Cir. 2000).
[19] Debra Lyn Bassett, *"I Lost at Trial-in the Court of Appeals!": The Expanding Power of the Federal Appellate Courts to Reexamine Facts* 38 HOUS. L. REV. 1129, 1152 (2001).
[20] Myers v. Hertz Corp., 624 F.3d 537, 547 (2d Cir. 2010), *cert. denied,* 132 S.Ct. 368 (2011).

raised before the lower court, and actually considered and decided by the lower court. If an issue is not adequately preserved, it is waived. Whereas a "waiver is a positive act the defendant makes—the intentional relinquishment of a known right, a forfeiture is an act of omission—the failure to make the timely assertion of a right."[21] Both can foreclose an appeal of the issue.

Even so, students must also understand that a court of appeal still has discretion to hear an issue that was waived. In addition, appellate courts may address plain errors on appeal even if the errors were not preserved.[22]

3. WAS THE ERROR PREJUDICIAL?

The concept of prejudice is critical to assessing the potential success of an appeal. From this topic, students should have an understanding of the concept of prejudice as well as the prejudicial error standard that applies depending on the type of error alleged. Prejudicial analysis of an error can prove frustrating for appellate practitioners because even if the error is preserved, the appeal may lack merit because the error did not affect or "prejudice" the outcome of the proceedings in the lower court.

To reinforce the concept of prejudice, I have given students a series of exercises that require them to assess the type of error and the type of prejudicial error standard applicable. The types of errors included in the exercises are structural errors, such as, failure to appoint counsel, denial of right to retained counsel, and failure to provide notice of a hearing, and constitutional errors subject to the *Chapman* standard. In addition to identifying the type of error and the standard applicable to it, for these exercises, students have to apply the appropriate standard of prejudice, and predict whether the court of appeal is likely to reverse the error.

4. IS THE APPEAL RIGHT FOR THE CLIENT?

Students should have an understanding that even if the issue is appealable, can be reviewed de novo, and raises prejudicial error, it still may not be in the client's best interest to pursue the appeal. This is

---

[21] MICHAEL E. TIGAR & JANE B. TIGAR, FEDERAL APPEALS JURISDICTION AND PRACTICE § 5:3 (3d ed., West 2012).
[22] FED. R. CRIM. P. 52.

because in some cases, there are potential adverse consequences that militate against filing an appeal.

Many adverse consequences arise in the criminal context, such as a defendant being exposed to the risk of a lengthier sentence or additional charges on retrial. In the civil context, one major potential adverse consequence is the payment of attorney fees and costs to the respondent if the appeal is unsuccessful. In some cases, that could amount to tens of thousands or even hundreds of thousands of dollars.

E. THE APPELLATE PROCESS

This section of the chapter provides a brief overview of what can be expected once the appeal is filed, and it introduces material covered in depth in Chapter 17 and Chapter 18.

1. THE RECORD

Once the notice of appeal is filed, the appellant has to designate the record and request that the record is prepared. The record consists of the reporter's transcript and clerk's transcript.

The reporter's transcript is the transcript of the oral proceedings before the trial court. If a reporter was not present at the proceedings, the parties may file an agreed or settled statement that accurately summarizes the testimony at the trial or hearing.

The clerk's transcript consists of the original pleadings, exhibits, and other papers filed with the lower court clerk. The appellant requests the clerk's record or transcript and the clerk prepares it and files it with the appellate court.

2. THE BRIEFS

There are primarily three briefs filed over the course of an appeal. The first brief is the appellant's opening brief. Next, is the respondent's brief. Finally, the appellant has the option of filing a reply brief, which addresses arguments raised in the respondent's brief.

Of the three, the appellant's opening brief is considered the most important because it defines which issues the appellate court will review. Thus, if the opening brief fails to raise an issue and the respondent's brief does not raise the issue, the appellant cannot raise it in the reply brief. Sometimes the appellate court may ask the parties to file a supplemental brief on an issue not raised in any of the briefs. The request for supplemental briefing is usually a signal to the parties regarding the issue the appellate court considers determinative in the appeal.

3. ORAL ARGUMENT

Once the briefing is complete, the court may schedule oral argument. In the federal courts, the parties do not have a right to oral argument.[23] Rather, if the panel that examined the briefs unanimously decides that oral argument is unnecessary, oral argument will not be granted. Even so, some circuits, like the United States Court of Appeal for the Sixth Circuit, allow oral argument for all litigants.

Usually, the appellate court will grant oral argument unless, the appeal is considered frivolous, the dispositive issue was decided recently and authoritatively, or the brief adequately presents the issues to be decided and oral argument would not aid that process.[24]

4. THE DECISION

When the district court's decision is reversed, the reversal effectively annuls or sets aside the lower court's decision for all purposes. If a decision is reversed, both state and federal courts of appeal usually remand the case for further proceedings or with instructions for the lower court. Sometimes, the appellate court remands with instructions for the lower court or district court to enter a different judgment than the original one.

In the federal system, the party who lost on appeal can consider whether to seek en banc review of the decision.[25] A simple majority of the active judges on the circuit can grant en banc review.[26] Another option is to seek review in the United States Supreme Court. Any party to any case in the "federal courts of appeal" can petition the Supreme Court to review the

---

[23] FED. R. APP. PROC. 34.
[24] FED. R. APP. PROC. 34 (A)(2).
[25] FED. R. APP. P. 35 (B).
[26] FED. R. APP. P. 35 (A).

case via a writ of certiorari before or after the federal appellate court has rendered a decision.[27]

Students should understand that the Supreme Court will only exercise its discretion to grant certiorari for compelling reasons, like those identified in this section of the chapter: conflicts among circuit courts of appeal on an important federal question, conflicts among state high courts on important federal questions, and important federal questions decided by a state court or a circuit court of appeal that the Supreme Court has not previously addressed, but should.[28]

In state court systems, if the lower court's decision is affirmed, the appellant must consider whether to file a petition for rehearing. If that is unsuccessful, the appellant can seek discretionary review in the state's highest court. Generally, a state's high court grants review for issues that are necessary to secure uniformity of decision or to settle an important question of law that affects more than just the parties of that particular case.[29] Students should understand that even if the lower court's decision was ostensibly wrong, that *is not* sufficient reason for a state's high court to grant review.

---

[27] 28 U.S.C. § 1254 (1) (2006).
[28] ROBERT L. STERN, EUGENE GRESSMAN, STEPHEN M. SHAPIRO & KENNETH S. GELLAR, SUPREME COURT PRACTICE 222 (8th ed., BNA 2002).
[29] See California, for example, CAL. R. CT. R. 8.500.

Chapter 17

The Appellate Brief

■ ■ ■

By Mary-Beth Moylan

The purpose of this chapter is to give students the nuts and bolts of an appellate brief. While the chapter is generally tailored to most federal appellate courts, the sections of the brief discussed are most often required in state appellate courts as well.

When teaching the components of an appellate brief, it is useful to go through each one separately. While the students generally have already had experience with a Statement of Facts, Argument, and Conclusion, many of the sections are new to them. You can refer the students back to Chapter 14 Persuasive Legal Writing for a more detailed discussion of a persuasive statement of facts and argument section.

The components in most appeals courts are:

1. Jurisdictional Statement
2. Statement of Oral Argument
3. Issue Question
4. Statement of the Case
5. Statement of Facts
6. Summary of Argument
7. Argument
8. Conclusion

Students also usually need to be reminded that they need a Table of Contents, Table of Authorities, counsel signature, word count certification, certificate of service, and unless they are in a jurisdiction that allows electronic filing, they will need a front and back cover. In our class, we direct the students to the Federal Rules of Appellate Procedure for finding the proper color cover for an Appellant or Appellee brief. This is a great chance to discuss the importance of following the local rules of practice in the jurisdiction where the appeal has been filed.

The following sections are broken down into highlights that can be included in a power point presentation or slide show focused on the components.

Jurisdictional Statement

1. District court's subject matter jurisdiction (28 U.S.C. 1331)
   a. Facts
   b. Applicable statute
2. Court of Appeals' jurisdiction (28 U.S.C. 1291)
   a. Facts
      i. Final judgment or order
      ii. Other type of order that may be appealed
   b. Applicable statute
3. Dates to show timeliness (FRAP Rule 4(a))
   a. Judgment/order appealed from
   b. Filing of notice of appeal

Oral Argument Statement

Advocate for oral argument by illustrating novel and complex issues presented, if possible.

Cite to the FRAP (hint: 34) that governs oral argument and apply the criteria listed in that section.

Full dockets mean that more cases will be decided without the benefit of a hearing. Give reasons why your case should have the benefit.

Is there a reason you might argue against oral argument?

Issue Question

Components of the Issue Question or Question Presented:

1. A question that can be answered "yes" or "no."

2. A reference to the relevant law.

3. A reference to legally significant facts.

Statement of the Case

    Sometimes separated out from the Statement of Facts, and sometimes subsumed within it.

    What do the local rules say?

    Should present all relevant procedural history and give the court a clear picture of the procedural life of the case prior to the appeal.

Statement of Facts

    Same function as the Statement of Facts in the Persuasive Brief to the trial court. Include all facts used in legal Argument.

    To ensure you do this, either:

A. Write the Argument section first and then Statement of Facts; or

B. Go back through Statement of Facts and amend after the Argument section is written.

    Persuasive Facts

    Do not argue in the fact section. Let the facts argue for you. Three techniques:

    (1) Use selective detail or quotes to emphasize facts that support your case;

    (2) Use punctuation to slow the reader in places where you want to draw emphasis;

    (3) Make careful use of rhetorical devices (repetition, parallel construction or cadence) to build momentum through strong facts.

Summary of Argument

    1. Provide Road Map for the Argument

        a. Succinctly state all major arguments.

        b. Provide reader with context and order for the section that follows.

2. Focus on the Forest

    a. Give policy insights into the law.

    b. Take a broad brush to explain why your side should prevail.

<u>Argument</u>

Follow CRAC formula for each major issue.

CRAC = Conclusion, Rule, Analysis, Conclusion

Separate major issues with Point Headings and use sub-heading to indicate component parts of major issues.

Argument Outline – Approach One

ARGUMENT

Brief umbrella paragraph setting up the order of the issues.

Point Heading Issue #1

Thesis/Conclusion/What You Will Show

Standard of Review

Substantive Rule

Sub-Heading #1

Application

Conclusion

Sub-Heading #2

Application

Conclusion

Point Heading Issue #2

REPEAT if subheadings or CRAC if no subheadings

Point Heading Issue #3

REPEAT

Argument Outline – Approach Two

ARGUMENT

Umbrella

Standard of Review

Point Heading #1

Umbrella

Subheading #1 CRAC

Subheading #2 CRAC

Point Heading #2

REPEAT or just CRAC if no subheadings

<u>Conclusion</u>

1. Summarize the main points you have presented.

2. Restate the relief requested.

<u>What to Argue</u>

Think about your theory of the case:

1. Adapt it from your trial theory to meet your strategy on appeal;

2. Weave it through your argument;

3. Select your theory/theme carefully.

The theory and theme can be the glue that holds it all together or it can be a distraction. Try to use a theme to reinforce your theory strategically, rather than just including a theme because it is a requirement.

Structure Argument for Your Side

Appellants' Counsel: look for legal error. Did the District Court apply the wrong standard? Did the District Court apply the standard incorrectly?

Appellee's Counsel: District Court opinion is correct. Do not stop there. Are there alternative grounds? Does the District Court's opinion need shoring up? Be careful of focusing too much on the opinion in your brief.

Outline of Argument Should Contain

1. Order of Argument

2. Thesis for Each Section

3. Cases you plan to use to support your thesis

4. List of comparisons and distinctions between your case and these cases.

5. Legal significance of these comparisons and distinctions.

Roadmaps

Draft Roadmaps for Each Section in Your Argument Section after Outline is Complete.

Each should contain the standard of review that you believe should be applied to the issue and an indication of the order in which you will address your arguments, including any major sub-issues.

Sample Appellate Brief

A Sample Appellate Brief from an anonymous student author follows. The problem involves a same gender couple and their adopted daughter. The marriage of the couple and the adoption of the child took place in the Netherlands. The family challenges a Mississippi state law, which the Department of Human Services is relying on to deny recognition of the parent-child relationship between one of the women and the child. This brief is an Appellee's Brief written on behalf of the State of Mississippi, which is defending the law.

No. 2012-02235

In the
United States Court of Appeals
For the Thirteenth Circuit

B.A., et al.,

Plaintiffs-Appellants

vs.

Mitch Lanham,

Defendant-Appellee

Appeal from the United States District Court
For the Middle District of Mississippi

APPELLEE'S BRIEF

1051
Mississippi Dept. of Justice
345 Main Street
Lofborough, MS 38706
Attorney for Mitch Lanham,
Defendant-Appellee

TABLE OF CONTENTS

TABLE OF CONTENTS i

TABLE OF AUTHORITIES iii

JURISDICTIONAL STATEMENT 1

STATEMENT OF ORAL ARGUMENT 2

STATEMENT OF THE ISSUES PRESENTED 2

STATEMENT OF THE CASE 3

STATEMENT OF FACTS 4

SUMMARY OF THE ARGUMENT 6

ARGUMENT 8

I. THE DISTRICT COURT PROPERLY DISMISSED COUNT III FOR FAILURE TO STATE A CLAIM BECAUSE INTERNATIONAL COMITY IS DISCRETIONARY AND THE NETHERLANDS JUDGMENT IS REPUGNANT TO MISSISSIPPI LAW AND MISSISSIPPI PUBLIC POLICY. 8

II. THE DISTRICT COURT PROPERLY GRANTED SUMMARY JUDGMENT IN FAVOR OF MITCH LANHAM FOR COUNT I BECAUSE THE MISSISSIPPI CODE DOES NOT BURDEN A FUNDAMENTAL RIGHT AND IT IS RATIONALLY RELATED TO A LEGITIMATE GOVERNMENT INTEREST 14

III. THE DISTRICT COURT PROPERLY GRANTED SUMMARY JUDGMENT IN FAVOR OF MITCH LANHAM FOR COUNT II BECAUSE THE MISSISSIPPI CODE IS VALID UNDER BOTH A RATIONAL BASIS REVIEW AND A HEIGHTENED LEVEL OF SCRUTINY 19

    A.   Mitch Lanham was Entitled to Judgment as a Matter of Law Under a Rational Basis Review Because the Mississippi Code is Rationally Related to a Legitimate Government Interest. . . 21

    B.   Mitch Lanham was Entitled to Judgment as a Matter of Law Under a Heightened Scrutiny Test Because the Mississippi Code is Substantially Related to an Important Government Interest 23

CONCLUSION 25

CERTIFICATE OF SERVICE 26

WORD COUNT CERTIFICATION 27

TABLE OF AUTHORITIES

CASES

United States Supreme Court Cases

Anderson v. Liberty Lobby,

477 U.S. 242 (1986) 15, 22

Ashcroft v. Iqbal,

556 U.S. 662 (2010) 8–9, 11

Bell Atlantic Corp. v. Twombly,

550 U.S. 544 (2007) 8

Carey v. Population Services,

431 U.S. 678 (1977) 16–17

Celotex Corp v. Catrett,

477 U.S. 317 (1986) 15, 19

City of Cleburne v. Cleburn Living Center,

473, U.S. 432 (1985) 20

Collins v. City of Harker Heights,

503 U.S. 115 (1992) 17

FCC v. Beach Communications,

508 U.S. 307 (1993) 15, 18, 20, 22–23

Griswold v. Connecticut,

381 U.S. 479 (1965) 17

Heller v. Doe,

509 U.S. 312 (1993) 23

Hilton v. Guyot,

159 U.S. 113 (1895) 9–10, 14

Lawrence v. Texas,

539 U.S. 558 (2003) 21, 24

Meyer v. Nebraska,

262 U.S. 390 (1923) 16

Moore v. City of East Cleveland,

431 U.S. 494 (1977) .... 16 –17

Planned Parenthood of Southeastern Pennsylvania v. Casey,

505 U.S. 833 (1992) 15

Romer v. Evans,

517 U.S. 620 (1996) 20–22, 24

Troxel v. Granville,

530 U.S. 57 (2000) 16–17

United States v. Virginia,

518 U.S. 515 (1996) 20

United States Court of Appeals Cases

Adar v. Smith,

639 F.3d 146 (5th Cir. 2011) 13–14

Finstuen v. Crutcher,

496 F.3d 1130 (10th Cir. 2007) 12, 14

JP Morgan Chase Bank v. Altos Hornos de Mexico,

412 F.3d 418 (2d Cir. 2005). 8

Lofton v. Secretary of Dept. of Children and Family Services,

358 F.3d 804 (11th Cir. 2004) 16–18, 22–23

McCauley v. City of Chicago,

671 F.3d 611 (7th Cir. 2011) 19

Seegmiller v. LaVerkin City,

528 F.3d 762 (10th Cir. 2008) 14–15

Windsor v. United States,

699 F.3d 169 (2d Cir. 2012) 23–24

Other Federal Cases

De la Mata v. American Life Insurance Co.,

771 F. Supp. 1375 (D. Del. 1991) 10

In re Kandu,

315 B.R. 123 (W.D. Wash. 2004) 10

State Court Cases

Hosain v. Malik,

108 Md. App. 284 (1996) 12–13

Laskosky v. Laskosky,

504 So.2d 726 (Miss. 1987) 10, 12

Loucks v. Standard Oil,

120 N.E. 198 (N.Y. 1918) 12

Tsilidis v. Pedakis,

132 So.2d 9 (Fla. Dist. App. 1961) 10–11

STATUTES

Federal Statutes

28 U.S.C. § 1291 (2006) 1

28 U.S.C. § 1331 (2006) 1, 3

28 U.S.C. § 1343(3) (2006) 1, 3

28 U.S.C. § 1367 (2006) 1

Federal Rules

Fed. R. App. P. 4(a)(1)(A) 1

Fed. R. App. P. 34(a)(2) 2

Fed. R. Civ. P. 8(a) 9

Fed. R. Civ. P. 12(b)(6) 3, 6, 8–9

Fed. R. Civ. P. 26(f) 3

Fed. R. Civ. P. 56 .... 4, 8, 15, 19

State Statutes

Miss. Code Ann. § 93-17-3(5) (West 2012) .... *passim*

OTHER AUTHORITIES

U.S. Const. amend. XIV § 1 .... 15, 19–20

Article 30, Title 5, Book I of the Dutch Civil Code 5

Article 227, Title 12, Book I of the Dutch Civil Code 5

JURISDICTIONAL STATEMENT

Plaintiffs-Appellants, B.A., C.J., and M.S.-J. ("Claimants"), brought suit against the Defendant-Appellee, Mitch Lanham, in his official capacity as Director of the Mississippi Department of Human Services ("Mitch Lanham"). The District Court for the Middle District of Mississippi has subject matter jurisdiction over Counts I, II, and III of the Claimants' complaint. See 28 U.S.C. §§ 1331, 1343(3) (2006). Counts I and II are based on the Due Process Clause and Equal Protection Clause in the Fourteenth Amendment of the U.S. Constitution. (R. at 6). Counts I and II are therefore "civil actions arising under the Constitution . . . of the United States" pursuant to 28 U.S.C. § 1331 and they claim to "redress the deprivation" of a Constitutional rights under 28 U.S.C. 1343(3). The district court has jurisdiction for Count III pursuant to 28 U.S.C. § 1331 because the principles of international comity arise under the "laws [and] treaties of the United States." 28 U.S.C. § 1331. In addition, Count III satisfies the requirements for supplemental jurisdiction pursuant to 28 U.S.C. § 1367(a) because Count III is part of the "same case or controversy" as Counts I and II. (R. at 3).

The Court of Appeals has jurisdiction over the final order issued by the Middle District of Mississippi pursuant to 28 U.S.C. § 1291. On October 5, 2012, the District Court issued a final order on Mitch Lanham's motion to dismiss and on November 30, 2012, the District Court issued a final order and judgment on Mitch Lanham's Motion for Summary Judgment. (R. at 202). Furthermore, the Claimants gave Notice of Appeal on December 15, 2012. (R. at 213). The Claimants' Notice of Appeal was timely filed within thirty days of the district court order. See Fed. R. App. P. 4(a)(1)(A).

STATEMENT OF ORAL ARGUMENT

Mitch Lanham requests oral argument. Under the Federal Rules of Appellate Procedure, oral argument is allowed unless "the appeal is frivolous," "the dispositive issue or issues have been authoritatively decided," or the facts are "adequately presented in the briefs and record, and the decisional process would not be significantly aided by oral argument." Fed. R. App. P. 34(a)(2). While the District Court order was correctly decided, Mitch Lanham still requests oral argument in order to clarify any questions this Court may have. (R. at 209). The complexity and emotions involved in this appeal are not frivolous. For this reason, Mitch Lanham and the State of Mississippi request oral argument to aid the court's interpretation of Mississippi Code § 93-17-3(5) and to explain the rationale of the Mississippi Legislature. Oral argument is necessary to clearly represent the established laws and policy of Mississippi and to show that, as a Mississippi public servant, Mitch Lanham was required to adhere to the laws of the State.

STATEMENT OF THE ISSUES PRESENTED

1. Under the principles of international Comity cited in Count III of the Claimants' complaint, did the District Court properly find that Mitch Lanham is not required to violate the public policy and law of Mississippi by enforcing an adoption by a same-sex couple that occurred in the Netherlands when Comity is not a mandatory doctrine and Comity is not required when the foreign judgment is repugnant to the public policy or the affirmative laws of the forum?

2. Under the Due Process Clause of the U.S. Constitution cited in Count I of the Claimants' complaint, did the District Court properly grant Mitch Lanham's motion for summary judgment when there is no dispute of material fact, the right to adopt or be adopted is not a "fundamental right," and deference was given to the Mississippi Legislature under rational-basis review?

3. Under the Equal Protection Clause of the U.S. Constitution cited in Count II of the Claimants' complaint, did the District Court properly grant summary judgment in favor of Mitch Lanham when the Supreme Court uses rational-basis scrutiny for classification of same-gender couples and the record shows that Mississippi Code § 93-17-3(5) was rationally related to the government interest of protecting the child's best interest?

STATEMENT OF THE CASE

On July 24, 2012, the Claimants filed their complaint for declaratory and injunctive relief against Mitch Lanham and the State of Mississippi in the United States District Court for the Middle District of Mississippi. (R. at 1–8). The District Court has jurisdiction pursuant to 28 U.S.C. §§ 1331 and 1343(3). Counts I and II of the Claimants' complaint allege that Mississippi Code § 93-17-3(5) violates the Substantive Due Process and Equal Protection rights guaranteed by the United States Constitution. (R. at 6–7). Count III alleges that the principles if international Comity require the State of Mississippi to recognize a Netherlands adoption. (R. at 7).

On September 1, 2012, Mitch Lanham filed a motion to dismiss Count III for failure to state a claim upon which relief can be granted pursuant to Fed. R. Civ. P. 12(b)(6). (R. at 26–27). The parties met to discuss a discovery plan pursuant to Fed. R. Civ. P. 26(f) on September 10, 2012, where the parties stipulated that "The Hague Convention does not form a basis for a claim by the plaintiffs . . . ." (R. at 39). Mitch Lanham's motion to dismiss Count III was granted by the District Court on October 5, 2012. (R. at 41–47). The District Court dismissed Count III for failure to state a claim because "nothing in the law mandates recognition of a foreign adoption decree," and the Netherlands adoption policy is "repugnant to the policy of Mississippi." (R. at 47).

Mitch Lanham answered the complaint on October 8, 2012. (R. at 48–50.) On October 15, Mitch Lanham filed a motion to for summary judgment on Counts I and II of the Claimants' complaint pursuant to Fed. R. Civ. P. 56. (R. at 59–60). The District Court granted Mitch Lanham's motion for summary judgment on Counts I and II of the Claimants' complaint on November 30, 2012. (R. at 202–212). Summary judgment was granted because adoption is not a fundamental right, sexual orientation is not a suspect class, and Mississippi Code § 93-17-3(5) satisfies rational-basis scrutiny. (R. at 206, 210, 212). The Claimants appealed the District Court's final order. (R. at 213).

STATEMENT OF FACTS

In the year 2000, Mississippi lawmakers enacted Mississippi Code § 93-17-3(5), prohibiting same-gender couples from adopting children. (R. at 37). The bill nearly died in the legislature but was revived "amid public pressure" after lawmakers were "deluged with phone calls" in support of the legislation. (R. at 35). Statements after the enactment of Mississippi Code § 93-17-3(5) indicate that the primary reasons behind the law included preventing "future harms" suffered by children adopted by homosexual partners, "preserv[ing] traditional family values," and preempting a "homosexual agenda" that would "not be healthy for a child" in the future. (R. at 67–70). Representative Rita Martinson, for example, stated that "adopted children should go to parents with stable relationships" and she did not believe that homosexual couples would provide this needed stability. (R. at 71). Senator Tim Johnson explained "when you look at adoptions, you want a child to go into a house with a father and a mother, in a traditional home setting." (R. at 68). Eleven years after Mississippi Code § 93-17-3(5) became law, the Claimants moved to Mississippi. (R. at 4).

Before moving to Mississippi, the Claimants lived in the Netherlands. (R. at 4). In 2005, C.J. moved to the Netherlands and was appointed the legal guardian of M.S.-J. after M.S.-J's parents were killed in an automobile accident. (R. at 4). C.J. is the biological aunt of M.S.-J. (R. at 4). In November 2006, C.J. met B.A. and in February 2007, B.A. and her biological daughter, P.A., moved into the same residence as C.J. and M.S.-J. (R. at 22). In August 2007, C.J. and B.A. were married in a same-gender civil union pursuant to Article 30, Title 5, Book I of the Dutch Civil Code. (R. at 4). Before moving to Mississippi in 2011, B.A. and C.J. adopted M.S.-J. in a co-parent adoption pursuant to Article 227, Title 12, Book I of the Dutch Civil Code. (R. at 4). On April 15, 2011, the Dutch Council for the Protection of Children approved the adoption. (R. at 18–25).

In June, 2011, B.A., P.A., C.J., and M.S.-J moved to Bristol, Mississippi. (R. at 4). After the move, B.A. began working for the Mississippi Department of Human Services ("MDHS") and sought to add both her biological daughter and M.S.-J. to her employee benefits package. (R. at 4–5). P.A. was added to the benefits plan, but M.S.-J. was not because B.A.'s adoption of M.S.-J. was inconsistent with Mississippi law. (R. at 5). Defendant Mitch Lanham, a public servant working for the MDHS, issued the denial of benefits because the Netherlands adoption "violates the public policy of the state as expressed in Mississippi Code § 93-17-3(5)." (R. at 10).

SUMMARY OF THE ARGUMENT

The District Court properly granted Mitch Lanham's motion to dismiss Count III and properly granted summary judgment in favor of Mitch Lanham on Counts I and II of the Claimants' complaint. As a public servant for the State of Mississippi, Mitch Lanham is required to enforce Mississippi Code § 93-17-3(5). In addition, the court should give deference to the Mississippi Legislature in reviewing laws enacted to promote the welfare of adopted children in Mississippi. This brief first discusses Count III of the Claimants' complaint followed by Counts I and II.

Count III of the Claimants' complaint was properly dismissed by the District Court for failure to state a claim pursuant to Fed. R. Civ. P. 12(b)(6). Count III relies on the principles of international Comity to enforce a Netherlands judgment approving an adoption by a same-sex couple. The Claimants cannot rely on international Comity for relief because Comity is not a mandatory doctrine. Furthermore, international Comity does not apply to foreign judgments that are repugnant to the affirmative laws or the public policy of the forum. The Netherlands adoption is repugnant to both Mississippi public policy and Mississippi

Code § 93-17-3(5), which explicitly prohibits adoption by same-gender couples. As a result, international Comity does require Mitch Lanham to enforce the Netherlands adoption and the District Court properly concluded that Count III of the Claimants' complaint does not state a claim upon which relief can be granted.

Count I of the complaint relies on the Due Process Clause of the U.S. Constitution. The District Court properly granted summary judgment in favor of Mitch Lanham on Count I because deference is given to the state legislature when a state action does not burden a fundamental right. The right to adopt or be adopted is not a fundamental right and the Supreme Court restrains courts from expanding the scope of fundamental rights. As a result, the District Court properly gave deference to the Mississippi legislature using a rational-basis review. Under rational-basis review, Mississippi must show that the statute rationally relates to a legitimate government interest. Statements by Mississippi officials and studies in the record show that Mississippi Code § 93-17-3(5) was enacted for the best interest of adopted children. Section 93-17-3(5) therefore passes rational-basis review and the District Court properly granted summary judgment in favor of Mitch Lanham on Count I.

Count II of the Claimants' complaint relies on the Equal Protection Clause of the U.S. Constitution. The District Court properly granted summary judgment in favor of Mitch Lanham on Count II because the Supreme Court does not classify same-gender couples as suspect class. As a result, rational-basis scrutiny of Mississippi Code § 93-17-3(5) is the appropriate standard of review. Mississippi Code § 93-17-3(5) satisfies rational-basis review because the Mississippi legislature could rationally conclude that prohibiting homosexual adoption serves the best interest of adopted children that need a stable home in Mississippi. Even under a heightened standard of scrutiny for same-gender couples, the District Court decision was proper because the best interest of the child is an important government interest and Mississippi's determination of a stable home for adopted children is substantially related to the welfare of the child.

ARGUMENT

The District Court properly dismissed Count III of the Claimants' complaint pursuant to Fed. R. Civ. P. 12(b)(6) and the District Court correctly ruled in favor of Mitch Lanham's motion for summary judgment on Counts I and II pursuant to Fed. R. Civ. P. 56.

I. THE DISTRICT COURT PROPERLY DISMISSED COUNT III FOR FAILURE TO STATE A CLAIM BECAUSE INTERNATIONAL COMITY IS DISCRETIONARY AND THE NETHERLANDS JUDGMENT IS REPUGNANT TO MISSISSIPPI LAW AND MISSISSIPPI PUBLIC POLICY.

The District Court's dismissal of Count III should be reviewed de novo because international Comity claims require the Court's "conclusions of law." *JP Morgan Chase Bank v. Altos Hornos de Mexico*, 412 F.3d 418, 423 (2d Cir. 2005). A Rule 12(b)(6) motion to dismiss for failure to state a claim upon which relief can be granted requires the court to assume everything in the complaint is true. *Bell Atlantic Corp. v. Twombly*, 550 U.S. 544, 555 (2007); Fed. R. Civ. P. 12(b)(6). However, the Court is not required to accept as true the legal conclusions stated in the complaint. *Ashcroft v. Iqbal*, 556 U.S. 662, 678 (2010). In order to survive a Rule 12(b)(6) motion to dismiss, the pleadings must be facially plausible, but also must allow "the court to draw the reasonable inference that the defendant is liable for the misconduct alleged." *Id.*; *see also* Fed. R. Civ. P. 8(a). Count III of Claimants' complaint was properly dismissed by the District Court pursuant to Rule 12(b)(6) because Mitch Lanham is not liable for any misconduct even if everything in the complaint is true. Count III of the complaint relies on the principles of international Comity, which are discretionary and do not apply to foreign adoptions that are repugnant to the laws or public policy of the forum state. As a result, Comity does not require Mitch Lanham to enforce a Netherlands judgment that is inconsistent with the laws enacted by the Mississippi State Legislature.

In 1895, the U.S. Supreme Court defined Comity as the "recognition" of foreign judgments, "having due regard both to international duty and convenience." *Hilton v. Guyot*, 159 U.S. 113, 143 (1895). Comity is discretionary and is "neither a matter of absolute obligation . . . nor of mere courtesy and good will." *Id.* Later courts have interpreted *Hilton* to find that Comity should be recognized when a foreign judgment meets the following criteria:

> (1) Opportunity for a full and Fair trial (2) Trial before a court of competent jurisdiction (3) Proceedings following due citation or voluntary appearance of adversary parties (4) Trial conducted upon regular proceedings (5) Trial under a system of jurisprudence likely to secure an impartial administration of justice between the citizens of its own country and those of other countries (6) No evidence to demonstrate (a) fraud in the procuring of the judgment (b) prejudice in the system of laws in which the court was

sitting (c) prejudice in the court (d) any other special reason why comity of the United States should not allow full effect.

De la Mata v. American Life Insurance Co., 771 F. Supp. 1375, 1381 (D. Del. 1991) (summarizing the Supreme Court criteria for international Comity in *Hilton*). Under the sixth *Hilton* consideration, courts consistently find that the principles of international Comity do not apply when judgments are "repugnant to the laws or policy of the local forum." *Tsilidis v. Pedakis*, 132 So.2d 9, 12 (Fla. Dist. App. 1961); *see also Hilton*, 159 U.S. at 145 ("A judgment affecting the status of persons, such as a decree confirming or dissolving a marriage, is recognized as valid in every country, unless contrary to the policy of its own law."); *Laskosky v. Laskosky*, 504 So.2d 726, 730 (Miss. 1987) ("Our courts may honor a foreign nation's custody decree where the foreign court exercised jurisdiction substantially in conformity with our constitutional standards and the foreign nation's ruling does not offend our positive laws").

The District Court properly dismissed Count III of the Claimants' complaint because the principles of international Comity do not require enforcement of foreign judgments. *See In re Kandu*, 315 B.R. 123, 133–134 (W.D. Wash. 2004) (holding that the "assertion that comity is mandatory is simply not supported by case law"). Even when a foreign judgment satisfies most of the *Hilton* considerations, a court may still voluntarily refuse to find the foreign judgment controlling. The *In re Kandu* court, for example, refused to recognize a same-sex marriage that took place in Canada because "Comity is voluntary" and in the case of a policy conflict, the court "must prefer its own laws." *Id.* Similarly, Mitch Lanham must prefer the laws of Mississippi when a foreign judgment conflicts with Mississippi policy. Mitch Lanham is not required by law to recognize foreign judgments and is therefore not "liable for the misconduct alleged" as required to state a proper claim. *Ashcroft*, 556 U.S. at 678.

The District Court's dismissal of Count III was also proper because the Netherlands judgment directly conflicts with Mississippi law. Mississippi Code § 93-17-3(5) establishes that "adoption by couples of the same gender is prohibited." The Netherlands judgment recognized an adoption by a same-gender couple and is therefore directly repugnant to Mississippi Code § 93-17-3(5). Mitch Lanham cannot enforce a foreign judgment contrary to Mississippi law and the principles of international Comity do not require otherwise. The Florida District Court of Appeals illustrated this limitation on Comity in a case involving a foreign adoption. *See Tsilidis*, 132 So.2d at 13. In *Tsilidis*, the Court refused to enforce a valid Greek adoption because a Florida statute implied that the adoption was repugnant to the laws of Florida. *Id.* The Florida court stated "[w]e need proceed no further than the clear limitation of the statute in holding that the appellant is not entitled under the laws of Florida to share in the estate." *Id.* Similarly, Count III of the Claimants' complaint seeks enforcement of a foreign adoption that directly conflicts with Mississippi Code § 93-17-3(5). Just as the *Tsilidis* court refused to proceed beyond the limitations of Florida law, the District Court properly dismissed Count III and refused to proceed beyond the limits of Mississippi law.

Count III of the complaint was also correctly dismissed because the public policy exception to the principles of international Comity prevents enforcement of the Netherlands judgment in Mississippi. In the New York Court of Appeals, Justice Cardozo stated that Comity should be recognized unless it "would violate some fundamental principle of justice, some prevalent conception of good morals, some deep-rooted tradition of the common weal." *Loucks v. Standard Oil*, 120 N.E. 198, 201 (N.Y. 1918). Mississippi Code § 93-17-3(5) represents the "conception of good morals" and "deep-rooted traditions" in Mississippi. When the Mississippi legislature enacted Mississippi Code § 93-17-3(5), the law reflected the "deep-rooted traditions" of the State. Lawmakers encountered "public pressure" and were "deluged with phone calls" in support of the legislation. (R. at 35). Furthermore, in the words of the Tenth Circuit, "[s]tatutes are interpreted to attain that purpose and end championing the broad public policy purposes underlying them." *Finstuen v. Crutcher*, 496 F.3d 1130, 1152 (10th Cir. 2007). Mississippi Code § 93-17-3(5) illustrates that adoption by same-gender couples is against Mississippi public policy. The Netherlands adoption by a same-gender couple is therefore repugnant to Mississippi public policy and the Claimants are not entitled to relief under principles of international Comity.

Mississippi courts also make it clear that they "must decline to honor foreign nation custody decrees when they contravene with the best interest of the child." *Laskosky*, 504 So.2d at 730. There is evidence in the record that the Netherlands judgment considered the "child's best interest." (R. at 25). Some courts have held that Comity can still be recognized in cases where there is a similar public policy interests. *See Hosain v. Malik*, 108 Md. App. 284, 315–316 (1996) (granting Comity to a Pakistani custody judgment because the best interest of the child standard was similar to the Maryland standard). However, the *Hosain* reasoning does not apply here because the determination of the child's best interest in Mississippi is directly at odds with the same determination in the Netherlands. The record shows that Mississippi Code § 93-17-3(5) was enacted with the best interest of the child in mind. (R. at 67–70). After the enactment of Mississippi Code § 93-17-3(5), statements indicated the purpose was to prevent "future harms" suffered by children adopted by homosexual partners, "preserve traditional family values," and preempt a "homosexual agenda" that would "not be healthy for a child" in the future. (R. at 67–70). The Netherlands adoption report, on the other hand, identified the Claimants as a same-gender couple but still approved the adoption as being in the best interest of the child. (R. at 20, 22–23, 25). Mississippi Code § 93-17-3(5) was enacted to prevent such a result because the State has determined same-gender adoption would not be in the child's best interest. (R. at 67–70). The best interest of the child standard in Mississippi directly conflicts with the same standard in the Netherlands therefore the policy interests are not similar enough to justify granting Comity under the *Hosain* rationale.

The District Court properly concluded that the positive law and the public policy of Mississippi prevail over the principles of international Comity. Some courts do not even enforce adoptions from other U.S. States despite the Full Faith and Credit Clause of the U.S. Constitution. *See Adar v. Smith*, 639 F.3d 146, 152 (5th Cir. 2011). In *Adar*, for example, a Louisiana Court held that the State was not required to issue amended birth certificates for a child adopted by a same-gender couple in New York. *Id.* According to the *Adar* court, "enforcement measures do not travel with the judgment." *Id.* Here, the Claimants seek enforcement of the Netherlands judgment by including M.S.-J on B.A.'s state benefit plan. (R. at 4–5). Considering *Adar*, the District Court should not enforce a foreign judgment under the principles of international Comity when other courts have held that similar judgments are not enforceable under the higher constitutional standard of the Full Faith and Credit Clause. *Compare Hilton* 159 U.S. at 143 (describing Comity as having "due regard both to international duty and convenience") *with Finstuen*, 496 F.3d at 1152 (describing the nation-building requirement of recognizing state judgments under the Full Faith and Credit Clause in the U.S. Constitution). The District Court correctly rejected the Claimants' assertion that the principles of international Comity should be recognized in contradiction to the law of the forum.

The District Court properly granted Mitch Lanham's motion to dismiss Count III for failure to state a claim upon which relief can be granted because the principles of international Comity are not mandatory. Furthermore, the Netherlands judgment is repugnant to both Mississippi law and Mississippi public policy. The principles of international Comity do not allow for enforcement of judgments that are repugnant to the policy or law of the forum. Therefore, Count III does not state a claim upon which relief can be granted.

II. THE DISTRICT COURT PROPERLY GRANTED SUMMARY JUDGMENT IN FAVOR OF MITCH LANHAM ON COUNT I BECAUSE THE MISSISSIPPI CODE DOES NOT BURDEN A FUNDAMENTAL RIGHT AND IT IS RATIONALLY RELATED TO A LEGITIMATE GOVERNMENT INTEREST.

Purely legal questions, such as substantive due process claim, are reviewed de novo by the U.S. Court of Appeals. *See Seegmiller v. LaVerkin City*, 528 F.3d 762, 766 (10th Cir. 2008). Parties are entitled to Summary Judgment when there is "no genuine dispute as to any material fact" and the defendant is "entitled to judgment as a matter of law." Fed. R. Civ. P. 56(a); *see also Celotex Corp v. Catrett*, 477 U.S. 317, 323 (1986). The "genuine dispute" of a material fact, however, cannot be simply "some alleged factual dispute between the parties" but rather a dispute material to the substantive law. *Anderson v. Liberty Lobby*, 477 U.S. 242, 247–248 (1986). The District Court properly held that, as a matter of law, Mississippi Code § 93-17-3(5) does not violate the Due Process Clause of the U.S. Constitution because adoption is not a fundamental right and prohibiting same-gender couples from adopting is rationally related to the welfare of adopted children.

The Due Process Clause of the Fourteenth Amendment provides that no state shall "deprive any person of life, liberty, or property, without due process of law." U.S. Const. amend. XIV § 1. Substantive due process limits state involvement in constitutionally protected liberties; however, the government and courts must also balance "liberty" and "the demands of organized society." *Planned Parenthood of Southeastern Pennsylvania v. Casey*, 505 U.S. 833, 846–847, 850 (1992). To achieve this balance, courts typically give deference to the state legislature by using a "rational-basis" review to determine the constitutionality of state actions that burden individual liberties. *FCC v. Beach Communications*, 508 U.S. 307, 309 (1993). "Rational-basis" review only requires a "plausible reason" for the state action and "may be based on rational speculation unsupported by evidence or empirical data." *Id.* at 314–315. State actions that burden a "fundamental right," on the other hand, are subject to "strict-scrutiny" review, which requires the state to prove that the law is narrowly tailored to a compelling government interest. *See e.g.*, *Moore v. City of East Cleveland*, 431 U.S. 494, 502 (1977) (holding a zoning ordinance unconstitutional for preventing a grandmother from living with her nuclear family); *Meyer v. Nebraska*, 262 U.S. 390, 399–400 (1923) (finding a statute that mandates using the English language in schools violated a fundamental right); *see also Carey v. Population Services*, 431 U.S. 678,

685 (1977) (listing fundamental rights that are protected from "unjustified government interference").

Count I of the Claimants' complaint alleges that Mississippi Code § 93-17-3(5), which prohibits same-gender couple adoptions, violates the Due Process Clause of the Constitution. The District Court properly held that rational-basis scrutiny of Mississippi Code § 93-17-3(5) is the proper standard of review because the right to adopt is not a fundamental right. *See Lofton v. Secretary of Dept. of Children and Family Services*, 358 F.3d 804, 811–812 (11th Cir. 2004) (noting that both parties agreed "there is no fundamental right to adopt, nor any fundamental right to be adopted" and that "adoption is a privilege created by statute and not by common law"). In *Lofton*, for example, the Eleventh Circuit upheld a Florida statute that prohibited adoption by same-sex couples because adoption is not a fundamental right and the statute satisfied rational basis review. *Id.* at 812, 815. Mississippi Code § 93-17-3(5) is nearly identical to the statute upheld in *Lofton* and was therefore properly upheld by the District Court.

The U.S. Supreme Court does protect against state actions that unconstitutionally infringe upon "fundamental parental right(s)." *See Troxel v. Granville*, 530 U.S. 57, 67 (2000) (holding that the court cannot infringe on parental rights by determining visitation that serves the best interest of the child). However, *Troxel* is distinguished from Count I of the Claimants' complaint because Mississippi Code § 93-17-3(5) does not infringe upon the Claimants visitation rights or ability to rear children. Mississippi Code § 93-17-3(5) simply restricts the right to adopt, which is not a fundamental right. *Lofton*, 358 F.3d at 811–812. While the U.S. Supreme Court's list of constitutionally protected rights extends to "decisions relating to marriage, procreation, contraception, family relationships, and child rearing and child education," adoption is not included. *Carey*, 431 U.S. at 685.

Furthermore, the U.S. Supreme Court is extremely reluctant to expand the list of fundamental rights is therefore unlikely to add adoption. *See Collins v. City of Harker Heights*, 503 U.S. 115, 125 (1992) (noting the under the "doctrine of judicial self-restraint" even the Supreme Court is required to "exercise the utmost care" when asked to classify a fundamental right). Due to the "treacherous" history of enhancing substantive due process protection, courts "counsel caution and restraint" when considering additional due process protection. *Moore*, 431 U.S. at 502. Additional fundamental rights are limited by careful review of deep-rooted societal values, history, and a "wise appreciation of the great roles that the doctrines of federalism and separation of powers have played in establishing and preserving American freedoms." *Griswold v. Connecticut*,

381 U.S. 479, 501 (1965) (Harlan, J., concurring). For these reasons, Count I of the Claimants' complaint was properly reviewed in the same way as *Lofton*, where the Eleventh Circuit Court of Appeals refused to "exceed [their] judicial mandate" and expand fundamental rights to encompass adoption. *Lofton*, 358 F.3d at 815.

Mississippi Code § 93-17-3(5) is valid under rational-basis review because limiting the right to adopt is rationally related to Mississippi's interest in protecting the best interest of the child. In *Lofton*, for example, the court found that "Florida clearly has a legitimate interest in encouraging a stable and nurturing environment for the education and socialization of its adopted children" and that the statute prohibiting homosexuals from adopting was rationally related to this interest. *Lofton*, 358 F.3d at 819. Similarly, after the enactment of Mississippi Code § 93-17-3(5), the record shows that Mississippi has a legitimate interest in placing adopted children in stable homes that are in the best interest of the child. (R. at 67–71). Senator Tim Johnson, for example, explained "when you look at adoptions, you want a child to go into a house with a father and a mother, in a traditional home setting." (R. at 68). Mississippi Code § 93-17-3(5) is also "rationally related" because it is rational that the Mississippi Legislature relied on studies to determine that traditional households will serve the government interest. (R. at 73–74).

Under rational-basis review, the burden is on the Claimants to prove that there is no conceivable basis to support the legislation. *FCC*, 508 U.S. at 315. Mississippi Code § 93-17-3(5) satisfies rational-basis review if there is any "plausible reason" or "rational speculation" that the Mississippi Legislature enacted the Code for a legitimate government interest. *FCC*, 508 U.S. at 309. The best interest of the child rationale behind Mississippi Code § 93-17-3(5) is both plausible and supported by evidence. (R. 67–74). As a result, the Claimants do not meet their burden of proof and the District Court properly held that, as a matter of law, Mississippi Code § 93-17-3(5) does not violate the Due Process Clause of the Fourteenth Amendment.

III. THE DISTRICT COURT PROPERLY GRANTED SUMMARY JUDGMENT IN FAVOR OF MITCH LANHAM FOR COUNT II BECAUSE THE MISSISSIPPI CODE IS VALID UNDER BOTH A RATIONAL BASIS REVIEW AND A HEIGHTENED LEVEL OF SCRUTINY.

Equal Protection claims that are purely legal should be reviewed de novo by the U.S. Court of Appeals. *See McCauley v. City of Chicago*, 671 F.3d 611, 615 (7th Cir. 2011). Pursuant to Rule 56, a moving party is entitled to summary judgment when there is "no genuine dispute as to any material fact" and the party is "entitled to judgment as a matter of law." Fed. R. Civ. P. 56(a); *see also Celotex Corp*, 477 U.S. at 323. The District Court properly granted summary judgment on Count II in favor of Mitch Lanham because there is no genuine issue of material fact, homosexual partners are not a suspect class, and prohibiting same gender partners from adopting children is rationally related to the welfare of adopted children. Even under an intermediate level of scrutiny, which is inappropriate in this case, Mitch Lanham would still be entitled to summary judgment because Mississippi Code § 93-17-3(5) is "substantially related" to furthering the best interest of the child in Mississippi.

The Equal Protection Clause of the Fourteenth Amendment provides that no state shall "deny to any person within its jurisdiction the equal protection of the laws." U.S. Const. amend. XIV § 1. The Equal Protection Clause, however, "must coexist with the practical necessity that most legislation classifies for one purpose or another, with resulting disadvantage to various groups or persons." *Romer v. Evans*, 517 U.S. 620, 631 (1996). As a result, when a state law "neither burdens a fundamental right nor targets a suspect class," courts will give deference to the state legislature and "uphold the legislative classification so long as it bears a rational relation to some legitimate end." *Id.; see also FCC v. Beach Communications*, 508 U.S. 307, 313 (1993). ("[E]qual protection is not a license for courts to judge the wisdom, fairness, or logic of legislative choices").

When a state legislature targets a "suspect class" or a "quasi-suspect class," however, courts review the state action using a higher level of scrutiny. State actions disadvantageous to a "suspect class", such as "race, alienage, or national origin", will be "subject to strict scrutiny and will be sustained only if they are suitably tailored to serve a compelling state interest." *City of Cleburne v. Cleburne Living Center*, 473 U.S. 432, 440 (1985). State actions that disadvantage a "quasi-suspect class," such as gender or illegitimacy, will be subject to "intermediate scrutiny," which requires the state to show "that the challenged classification serves important governmental objectives and that the discriminatory means employed are substantially related to the achievement of those objectives." *United States v. Virginia*, 518 U.S. 515, 533 (1996).

A. Mitch Lanham was Entitled to Judgment as a Matter of Law Under a Rational Basis Review Because the Mississippi Code is Rationally Related to a Legitimate Government Interest.

The District Court properly found that rational-basis scrutiny was the appropriate test to review Mississippi Code § 93-17-3(5) because the Code does not burden a fundamental right and the Claimants are not members of a suspect or quasi-suspect class. *See supra*, Part II (explaining why Mississippi Code § 93-17-3(5) does not burden a fundamental right). The U.S. Supreme Court has never classified homosexual partners as a suspect or quasi-suspect class and has therefore consistently reviewed state actions involving homosexual partners under rational-basis scrutiny. *See e.g., Romer*, 517 U.S. at 635 (finding that in a case involving homosexual persons, the "law must bear a rational relationship to a legitimate government purpose"); *Lawrence v. Texas*, 539 U.S. 558, 580 (2003) (describing the court's use of "rational basis review" in the Equal Protection Clause claims by same-gender couples). While using rational basis review, however, both *Romer* and *Lawrence* added that "a bare . . . desire to harm a politically unpopular group cannot constitute a legitimate governmental interest." *Romer*, 517 U.S. at 634; *Lawrence*, 539 U.S. at 580 (both quoting *U.S. Dept. of Agriculture v. Moreno*, 413 U.S. 528, 534 (1973)). U.S. Supreme Court precedent, therefore, dictates that rational-basis scrutiny with an additional inquiry to avoid a "bare desire to harm" is the appropriate test to review Mississippi Code § 93-17-3(5).

The District Court properly concluded that prohibiting same-gender couples from adopting under Mississippi Code § 93-17-3(5) is rationally related to the welfare of adopted children. Mitch Lanham does not dispute any material fact and stipulates that some studies suggest the effect of homosexual parenting "remains an open question." (R. at 75). However, "some alleged factual dispute between the parties" is not enough to overcome a motion for summary judgment. *Anderson*, 477 U.S. at 247–248. With the information available, Mississippi Code § 93-17-3(5) satisfies a rational basis review because other studies and the background of Mississippi Legislators could rationally lead to the conclusion that prohibiting same-gender couple adoptions is in the best interest of the child. (R. at 67–71, 73–74). The Mississippi Code, for example, is similar to the Florida statute prohibiting homosexual adoption that was contested in the Eleventh Circuit. *Lofton*, 358 F.3d at 806–807. The *Lofton* court held that "[i]t is not irrational to think that heterosexual singles have a markedly greater probability of . . . providing their adopted children with a stable, dual-gender parenting environment." *Id.* at 822. The District Court was correct in using the same rationale as *Lofton* and finding that the Mississippi Code satisfies rational-basis review.

In addition, Mississippi Code § 93-17-3(5) does not constitute "a bare . . . desire to harm a politically unpopular group" because it is motivated, in part, to promote the welfare of adopted children. *See Romer*, 517 U.S. at 634; (R. at 68, 71). Under rational basis review, state actions "must be upheld . . . if there is any reasonably conceivable state of facts that could provide a rational basis for the classification." *FCC*, 508 U.S. at 313. Furthermore, deference is given to the state legislature and a "strong presumption of validity" is given to state law such as Mississippi Code § 93-17-3(5) that does not burden a fundamental right or disadvantage a suspect class. *See Heller v. Doe*, 509 U.S. 312, 319 (1993) (giving deference to the Kentucky legislature for their procedures of involuntarily committing dangerous mentally retarded patients). Similar to the Florida statute in *Lofton*, there are "reasonably conceivable facts" to support the conclusion that Mississippi Code § 93-17-3(5) is rationally related to the purpose of protection the best interest of adopted children in Mississippi. *FCC*, 508 U.S. at 313. As a result, deference should be given to the Mississippi Legislature to enact laws that promote the welfare of adopted children in Mississippi and the District Court properly held that Mississippi Code § 93-17-3(5) satisfies rational-basis review.

  B. Mitch Lanham is Entitled to Judgment as a Matter of Law Under an Intermediate Scrutiny Test Because the Mississippi Code is Substantially Related to an Important Government Interest.

The District Court properly concluded that a heightened level of scrutiny is not the appropriate standard to review Mississippi Code § 93-17-3(5). Before 2012, classifications based on homosexuality had "never been held by the Supreme Court or any Circuit Court to involve a suspect or quasi-suspect classification." *Windsor v. United States*, 699 F.3d 169, 209 (2d Cir. 2012), cert. granted, 81 U.S.L.W. 3116 (Dec. 7, 2012) (No. 12-307). In October 2012, however, the Second Circuit Court of Appeals defied precedent by holding that homosexuals are in a "quasi-suspect" class and are subject to an "intermediate scrutiny." *Id.* at 185. *Windsor*, however, is not binding on this Court and the holding was in regard to a federal rather than a state statute. *See id.* at 179 ([O]ur heightened scrutiny analysis . . . under federal law is distinct from the analysis necessary to determine whether the marital classification of a state would survive such scrutiny."). The U.S. Supreme Court is binding precedent, however, and not a single Supreme Court case has used anything other than rational basis review. *See e.g., Romer*, 517 U.S. at 635; *Lawrence*, 539 U.S. at 580. Therefore, the

District Court properly determined that a heightened level of scrutiny is not the appropriate standard to review Mississippi Code § 93-17-3(5).

Even under a heightened standard of review, however, summary judgment should still be entered in favor of Mitch Lanham. Under *Windsor*, intermediate scrutiny requires the classification to be "substantially related to an important government interest." *Windsor*, 699 F.3d at 185. In *Windsor*, the Second Circuit found that prohibiting same gender marriage was not substantially related to the government interests of defining marriage, protecting marital benefits, preserving traditions, and responsible procreation. *Id.* at 185–188. An adopted child's best interest, however, is both an "important government interest" in Mississippi and the morality and stability of the adoptive parents are "substantially related" to the welfare of the adopted child. (R. at 67–71, 73–74). As a result, Mississippi Code § 93-17-3(5) would pass a higher level of scrutiny even if the *Windsor* court articulated the appropriate standard. Under the appropriate rational-basis standard, however, judgment was properly entered in favor of Mitch Lanham for Count II because Mississippi Code § 93-17-3(5) is rationally related to the government interest of protecting adopted children.

CONCLUSION

This Court should affirm the District Court's decision on Counts I, II, and III of the Claimants' complaint. The District Court properly dismissed Count III of the Claimants' complaint because the principles of international Comity are discretionary and do not apply to foreign judgments that are repugnant to the policy or laws of the forum. The District Court properly granted summary judgment in favor of Mitch Lanham for Counts I and II of the Claimants' complaint because rational-basis scrutiny is the appropriate standard to review a Fourteenth Amendment attack on Mississippi Code § 93-17-3(5). Rational-basis review applies because the right to adopt or be adopted is not a fundamental right and same-gender couples are not a suspect class under Supreme Court precedent. Mississippi Code § 93-17-3(5) satisfies rational-basis review because the record shows that the Code is rationally related to the welfare of adopted children in Mississippi. Under the circumstances alleged in Counts I, II, and III, Supreme Court precedent calls for giving deference to the Mississippi Legislature. Mitch Lanham is public servant who properly enforced Mississippi Code § 93-17-3(5) because it is a State law validly enacted by the Mississippi Legislature.

February 18, 2013   1051

CERTIFICATE OF SERVICE

I certify that on this 18th day of February, 2013, I served the foregoing Appellate Brief upon the plaintiffs, B.A., M.S.-J., and C.J., by causing a copy thereof to be mailed, first-class postage prepaid, to their attorney of record, Natalie Moldonado, 405 Court Street, Lofborough, MS, 38706.

Dated: February 18, 2013 _____

1051
Mississippi Dept. of Justice
345 Main Street
Lofborough, MS 38706
Telephone: (756) 922-9911
Attorney for Mitch Lanham,
Defendant-Appellee

WORD COUNT CERTIFICATION

I, 1051, certify that the attached Appellate Brief complies with the Local Rules and is no more than 7050 words. I further certify that, in preparation of this brief, the word processing program used has been specifically applied to include all text, including headings, footnotes, and quotations in the following word count.

I further certify that the attached memorandum contains 7046 words.

Dated: February 18, 2013 _____

1051
Mississippi Dept. of Justice
345 Main Street
Lofborough, MS 38706
Telephone: (756) 922-9911
Attorney for Mitch Lanham,
Defendant-Appellee

CHAPTER 18

ORAL ARGUMENT

■ ■ ■

By Mary–Beth Moylan

The purpose of this chapter is to introduce students to the basic skill of oral argument. It can be read before or after the writing and soft skills chapters, but probably should be read after Chapter 6 The Process of Legal Writing because some of the outlining advice references back to that chapter.

Practicing oral advocacy can be a lot of fun. Any written motion or brief can have a corresponding oral argument attached to it. There are numerous court websites that post audio and video recordings of oral argument that can be watched. Some of these are included in the text of the book. Others are listed in the chart at the end of this chapter. Very often live demonstrations of oral argument provided by your teaching assistant, a school moot court team, or even yourself can give the students a great idea of how an oral argument feels.

We also require students to attend a trial court law and motion hearing and an appellate court argument during our year long course. Importantly, we have a faculty member attend all sessions that the students will attend, so that there is someone to give feedback on what they have seen. Very often our students return from the court arguments with stories of attorney error that they would not have made. Sometimes too they are impressed by the quality of the arguments and the questions by the judges. These visits always drive home the value of preparation.

For a fun warm up exercise before beginning the process of preparing for an oral argument associated with a graded assignment, I often find a timely (but not too controversial) news item and ask the students to practice outlining and giving an oral presentation with some form of support. One that I used following the 2012 Summer Olympics is here.

Oral Argument Preliminary Exercise

Bob Costas (and numerous other commentators) have spent the last several weeks saying that Michael Phelps is the greatest Olympian of all time. Even his competition has been quoted saying things like "Personally, I think Michael Phelps is the best athlete on the planet, of any sport. So to be in the same race as him is a real special occasion." James Devaney, *Briton James Goddard calls Michael Phelps 'the best athlete on the planet'*, NBC Olympics, http://www.nbcolympics.com/news-blogs/blog=olympic-talk/post/briton-james-goddard-calls-michael-phelps-the-best-athlete-on-the-planet.html (accessed August 5, 2012).

Take a position on the statement "Michael Phelps is the greatest Olympian of all time." You may either choose to support or oppose this position.

Draft an outline of your argument including support for your conclusion. Your outline should not be more than one page. Be prepared to deliver an oral argument in support of your position.

Oral Argument Clips Chart

URL	Citation/Court	Case Name	Transcript Type	Topic/Comments	Location
http://www.oyez.org/cases/2000-2009/2004/2004_04_108/argument/	U.S. Supreme Court	*Kelo v. City of New London*, 545 U.S. 469 (2005).	Written	Example of good theme; example of attorney handling difficult questions.	First few minutes
http://www.oyez.org/cases/1990-1999/1999/1999_98_1101	U.S. Supreme Court	*Drye v. United States*, 528 U.S. 49 (1999).	Audio	Example of attorney going overboard on a theme.	First few minutes
http://video.google.com/videoplay?docid=542542714065823 0084	U.S. Court of Appeals, Ninth Circuit	*Hepting v. AT&T Corp.*, 539 F.3d 1157 (2008).	Video	Example of good opening and good answer to first question; example of good	0:00 to 2:38

				speed.	
http://video.google.com/videoplay?docid=542542714065823 0084	U.S. Court of Appeals, Ninth Circuit	*Hepting v. AT&T Corp.*, 539 F.3d 1157 (2008).	Video	Example of attorney conceding point and transitioning back.	57:23 to 59:45
http://www.oyez.org/cases/1990-1999/1995/1995_94_1809	U.S. Supreme Court	*Matsushita Electric Industrial Co., Ltd. v. Epstein*, 535 U.S. 1017 (2002).	Audio	Example of attorney arguing the point the court does not want to hear.	0:00 to 4:08
http://www.oyez.org/cases/2000-2009/2004/2004_04_108/argument/	U.S. Supreme Court	*Kelo v. City of New London*, 545 U.S. 469 (2005).	Written	Example of attorney stopping when time is up.	54:56 to 57:08; bottom of argument.
http://video.google.com/videoplay?docid=542542714065823 0084	U.S. Court of Appeals, Ninth Circuit	*Hepting v. AT&T*, 539 F.3d 1157 (2008).	Video	Example of good closing.	1:33:33 to 1:34:12
http://www.oyez.org/cases/2000-2009/2000/2000_00_949/argument/	U.S. Supreme Court	*Bush v. Gore*, 531 U.S. 98 (2000).	Written	Example of error in Justices name.	36:04 to 38:04
http://video.google.com/videoplay?docid=542542714065823 0084	U.S. Court of Appeals, Ninth Circuit	*Hepting v. AT&T*, 539 F.3d 1157 (2008).	Video	Example of good opening and answer.	39:40 to 41:43

URL	Court	Case	Media	Description	Time
http://www.youtube.com/watch?v=r5EdBJTD88Q	U.S. Court of Appeals, Ninth Circuit	*Al-Haramain Islamic Foundation, Inc. v. Bush*, 507 F.3d 1190 (2007).	Video	Examples of good oral argument.	First few minutes
http://www.youtube.com/watch?v=GEajn-FLm3A	Florida District Court of Appeals, Second District	*Bush v. Schiavo*, 866 So. 2d 136 (2004).	Video	Example of judge telling attorney to discuss specific topic twice.	First ten minutes
http://www.youtube.com/watch?v=c8ksvG_X4Z4	U.S. Court of Appeals, Seventh Circuit	*United States v. Johnson*, 415 F.3d 728 (2005).	Audio	Example of bad oral argument; good clip for students to watch because they cannot do much worse than this attorney.	0:00 to 3:43
http://www.youtube.com/watch?v=QdCsup3zqyA&feature=channel	U.S. Court of Appeals, Second Circuit	*Fox Television v. F.C.C.*, 489 F.3d 444 (2007).	Video	Example of attorney who could improve demeanor and deference; example of attorney who used swear words.	1:20 to 4:10
http://deimos3.apple.com/WebObjects/Core.woa/Browse/suffolk-public.1525745332 Select "Legal Writing Tips," then select "Oral Argument."	N/A	N/A	Audio	Tips/advise on how to give the best oral argument.	0:00 to 8:36

http://www.youtube.com/watch?v=BzjLlqIuVhI	N/A	N/A	Video	Bird Poops in T.V. reporter's mouth. Example of importance of avoiding distractions while speaking and anticipating things that may arise.	0:00 to 0:22
http://www.oyez.org/cases/1970-1979/1971/1971_70_18	U.S. Supreme Court	*Roe v. Wade*, 410 U.S. 113 (1973).	Audio	Example of actual argument.	First few minutes
http://www.oyez.org/cases/1960-1969/1965/1965_759	U.S. Supreme Court	*Miranda v. Arizona*, 384 U.S. 436 (1966).	Audio	Example of actual oral argument; good theme; clear issue given to court.	First few minutes
http://www.oyez.org/cases/1960-1969/1962/1962_155	U.S. Supreme Court	*Gideon v. Wainwright*, 372 U.S. 335 (1963).	Audio	Example of actual argument; example of attorney with monotone voice.	First few minutes
http://www.oyez.org/cases/1960-1969/1960/1960_236	U.S. Supreme Court	*Mapp v. Ohio*, 367 U.S. 643 (1961).	Audio	Example of actual argument.	First few minutes
http://www.courtinfo.ca.gov/courts/supreme/audio-arch.htm Click on "People v. Gay"	California Supreme Court	*People v. Gay*, 178 P.3d 422 (2008).	Audio	Example of attorney who says a lot of "um's" and "ah's."	First five minutes
http://www.courtinfo.ca.gov/courts/	California Supreme	*Ross v. Ragingwire Telecommuni*	Audio	Example of good answer to first question and	First few minutes.

supreme/audio-arch.htm Click on "Ross v. Ragingwire Telecommunication, Inc."	Court	*cations, Inc.*, 174 P.3d 200 (2008).		good deference to court.	
http://www.courtinfo.ca.gov/courts/supreme/audio-arch.htm Click on "Viva! International Voice for Animals et al. v. Adidas Promotional Retail."	California Supreme Court	*Viva! Int'l Voice for Animals et al. v. Adidas Promotional Retail*, 162 P.3d 569 (2007).	Audio	Example of weak opening; example of attorney who needs to listen to the questions the judge asks.	First few minutes
http://www.courtinfo.ca.gov/courts/supreme/audio-arch.htm Click on "People v. Sandoval"	California Supreme Court	*People v. Sandoval*, 161 P.3d 1146 (2007).	Audio	Example of attorney with passion in voice.	First few minutes.
http://www.courtinfo.ca.gov/courts/supreme/audio-arch.htm	Court of Appeals, Fourth District	*In re Jamie P.*, Not reported.	Audio	Example of use of current news article to tie together theme.	First few minutes
http://www.ca7.uscourts.gov/fdocs/docs.fwx?caseno=09-1891&subm	U.S. Court of Appeals, Seventh Circuit	*United States v. Vrdolyak*, 593 F.3d 676 (2010).	Audio	Example of fraud case; issue whether the court understood the nature and	33 minutes

URL	Court	Case	Type	Description	Length
it=showdkt&yr=09&num=1891 Click on "Oral Argument"				amount of the loss and whether the sentence was unreasonable.	
http://www.ca7.uscourts.gov/fdocs/docs.fwx?caseno=08-4241&submit=showdkt&yr=08&num=4241 Click on "Oral Argument"	U.S. Court of Appeals, Seventh Circuit	*N.R.A. v. Chicago*, 567 F.3d 856 (2009).	Audio	Good example of attorney knowing relevant case precedent; NRA challenged Chicago's handgun restrictions on Second Amendment grounds.	34 minutes
http://www.ca7.uscourts.gov/fdocs/docs.fwx?caseno=08-2527&submit=showdkt&yr=08&num=2527 Click on "Oral Argument"	U.S. Court of Appeals, Seventh Circuit	*Wiesmueller v. Kosobucki*, 571 F.3d 699 (2009).	Audio	Wisconsin admitted two students to the bar without having to take the bar exam; based on "diploma privilege." Practice is being challenged on equal protection and commerce clause grounds.	26 minutes
http://www.ca7.uscourts.gov/fdocs/docs.fwx?caseno=06-3674&submit=showdkt&yr=06&num=3674	U.S. Court of Appeals, Seventh Circuit	*Andrews v. Chevy Chase Bank*, 536 F.3d 693 (2008).	Audio	Attempt to certify a class action lawsuit against a bank for violations of the Truth in Lending Act.	33 minutes
http://www.ca7.uscourts.gov/fdocs/	U.S. Court of Appeals, Seventh	*United States v. Black*, 530 F.3d 596	Audio	Two doctors were convicted of unlawful	33 minutes

docs.fwx?caseno=07-4080&submit=showdkt&yr=07&num=4080 Click on "Oral Argument"	Circuit	(2008).		distribution of OxyCotin and sentenced to five and fifteen years.	
http://www.ca7.uscourts.gov/fdocs/docs.fwx?caseno=07-1101&submit=showdkt&yr=07&num=1101	U.S. Court of Appeals, Seventh Circuit	*Chicago Lawyers' Comm. for Civil Rights Under the Law Inc. v. Craigslist*, 519 F.3d 666 (2008).	Audio	Chicago Lawyer's Committee brought suit alleging Craigslist violated federal housing law by allowing the posting of certain ads.	40 minutes

CHAPTER 19

ALTERNATIVE DISPUTE RESOLUTION

■ ■ ■

By Mary-Beth Moylan and Stephanie Thompson

The purpose of this chapter is to introduce students to Alternative Dispute Resolution (ADR). We hope that after being introduced to arbitration and mediation, our students will be interested to take full courses on these topics with their elective units. This chapter, and Chapter 20 Negotiation, can be read together, and as a pair they cover a basic introduction to ADR.

We begin our discussion of ADR with the following PowerPoint presentation.

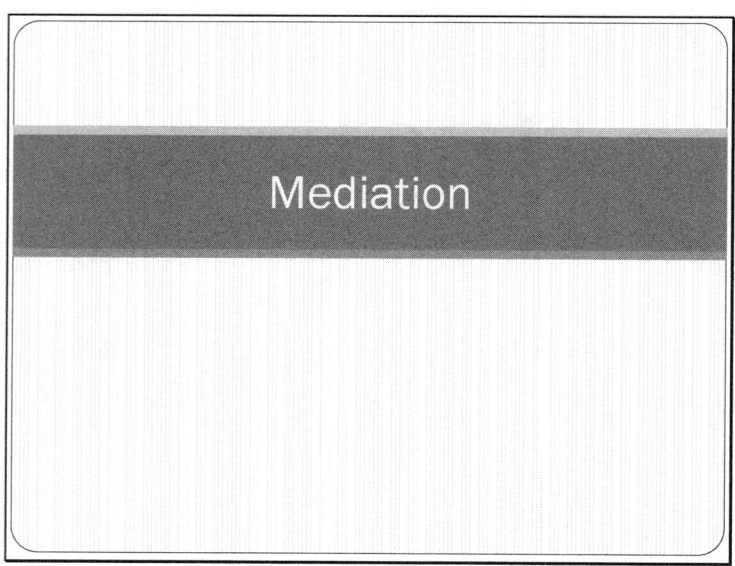

What is Mediation?

- Mediation is a voluntary process in which two or more parties involved in a dispute work with an impartial party, the mediator, to generate their own solutions in settling their conflict.
  - Assisted Negotiation
  - Advocates and the Clients retain ultimate control
  - Mediator is Facilitator

What is Mediation?

- Mediation is …
  - About finding a solution that works for both parties;
  - A forward-looking process;
  - To facilitate a problem-solving dialog; and
  - Not a debate to "win."

What is the mediator's role?

- Facilitate communication
- Promote understanding
- Assist with identifying and exploring issues, prioritize interests, and possible bases for agreement or settlement
- Help parties evaluate the likely outcome in court or arbitration if they cannot reach settlement through mediation
- Play "devil's advocate" to explore how realistic the positions of the participants are
- Assessing the relative strengths and weaknesses of positions

When to go to Mediation?

- Party Initiated
- Secondary Party Referral
- Court or Other Authority

Mediation?

- Why do you think you would want to mediate a case?
- If you think you are going to win, would you go to mediation? Why or why not?

What are the benefits of mediation?

- Psychological
- Time and money
- Focused on the underlying interests; not on winning or losing
- Creative and customized solutions
- It can be confidential

How does the Mediation work?

There are 6 steps to a formal mediation:
1) Introductory remarks by the mediator
2) Statement of the problem by the parties
3) Information gathering time
4) Identification of the problems
5) Bargaining and generating options
6) Reaching an agreement

Mediator's Approach

- Some mediators employ a more *facilitative style* that is designed to help the parties generate ideas on how to resolve their dispute for themselves.
    - Common facilitative techniques are asking the parties questions that help them see the dispute from the other side's perspective or help them question their own assumptions about their needs in the dispute.
- Other mediators employ a more *evaluative style*.
    - In an *evaluative* mediation, the mediator takes a more directive approach in the discussion that is designed to advise the parties, to a lesser or greater degree, how the dispute should be fairly resolved.
    - A common evaluative technique is to provide an opinion as to the merits of particular issue or position. Evaluative mediators often employ a kind of shuttle diplomacy, alternately meeting separately with the each participant and privately explaining weaknesses in their case and emphasizing the strengths of the other party's case.

What is a Mediation Brief?

- The mediation brief is a party's first opportunity to present the mediator with a statement of the issues, legal arguments, and goals.
- This is done outside the limitations and structure of the mediation session.

The Mediation Brief

- What is included?
  - It varies and is dependent upon the mediator.
- Typically, a mediation brief includes:
  - Introduction
  - Facts (procedural and factual)
  - Analysis of the legal issues
  - Conclusion
  - Settlement request or proposed solution
  - Confidentiality clause, if applicable

Strategies of the Mediation Brief

- The mediation brief primarily is used to educate the mediator.
- It promotes other objectives as well:
  - It shows that you are working on the case diligently and have invested time in thoughtful preparation thereby earning the respect of your adversary;
  - It helps to assure that your adversary is acutely aware of your position; and
  - It provides a useful script to follow in the oral phase of the mediation.

Styles of the Mediation Brief

- Mediation briefs can take many forms:
  - Informative – an objective style
  - Adversarial – a persuasive style
  - Letter form
  - Brief form
  - Submitted to all parties
  - Submitted to mediator only
- The style depends on the purpose of the mediation and the relationship of the parties.

Mediation Brief

- Mediation briefs are not always used
- It is up to the mediator:
  - Some mediators prefer pre-mediation conferences
  - Deeper conversations about the real issues
- Attorneys may not want to put anything in writing

Arbitration

What is Arbitration?

- Arbitration is a contact-based litigation process.
  - Parties to agree to submit to the process through contract
  - Both sides present evidence and legal arguments
  - Arbitrator is decision maker
  - Arbitration can be binding or non-binding

Mediation v. Arbitration?

- **Mediation** is the more informal process in which the parties are empowered to make their own decisions with the help of the mediator, who obtains key information from the parties and works to find solutions with the parties. There is no witness testimony and there is no cross-examination. There is a lot of talking, thinking and negotiating - a lot of back and forth and compromises from all sides. Other than rules of courtesy and respect, there are generally no set rules for mediation. This is nothing like a typical court proceeding or trial.

- **Arbitration** on the other hand is very similar to a court proceeding. The arbitrator acts very much like a judge and is there to receive evidence (documents and witness testimony) and to render a decision which may or may not be binding on the parties (depending on the case). The parties have no part in making any decisions about their own case and the parties must follow specific rules and abide by the decision made for them.

What is the arbitrator's role?

- Listen to the evidence
- Listen to legal and technical arguments
- Weigh evidence against legal arguments
- Assess the likelihood of success in a court setting
- Reach a result
- Provide a final decision for the parties

When to go to Arbitration?

- Contractually required to do so
- Party initiated
- Court dockets are full and resolution is needed more quickly than can be accommodated by the courts

> ### How does the Arbitration work?
>
> Arbitration procedure is similar to trial procedure with some exceptions:
> 1) Rules for admissible evidence may be relaxed or altered depending on the arbitration service and agreement of the parties
> 2) Level of formality may be different than a court setting
> 3) Decision may be binding or non-binding depending on the agreement of the parties
> 4) Arbitration awards are enforceable in courts of law

Mediation exercises can accompany any legal research and writing assignment that the students are working on. We always include a class period where the students are assigned roles in mediation and are required to attempt to resolve the case through mediation. All students are asked to hand in a form reflecting on their experience with the mediation. Examples of mediation exercises are below.

In-Class Exercise (Party-Initiated Mediation):

The following exercise can be done after the students write an objective memorandum and attempt to resolve a case before litigation is even initiated. This can be done either as a party-initiated mitigation or a second-party referral, such as an employment-related situation. As the instructions provide, we do this assignment with another section of our legal research and writing course.

These Instructions explain the procedure for your in-class mediation exercise which will take place on **DATE 1** and **DATE 2** during your regular class time.

Assignment for DATE 1:

For **DATE 1**, you will be acting as counsel for your client in the case of <u>Audrey Stadler v. GBS</u> and Professor Proske's students will serve as your co-mediators in the mediation. Your opponent will be pre-assigned (see below).

In preparation for your mediation, please read the attached "The Advocates Opening" to give you some insights into successful techniques for advocacy in mediation.

Please prepare a <u>2-3 minute</u> opening statement for the mediation, which you may model on the attached "Sample Attorney Mediation Opening Statement."

Your opening statement should include the following components:

- Introduce yourself and state who you are representing [your client's name]
- Briefly summarize the nature of the case and state what you think the issues are in the case
- Explain the legal support for your position
- Explain where you think the parties agree about crucial facts or legal issues
- Explain where you think the parties disagree about the facts or legal issues
- If applicable, concede facts or issues
- Make it clear that you have come to the mediation voluntarily
- Make it clear that you and your client are open to settlement

When presenting your opening statement, use an appropriate tone:

- Be sure to be diplomatic, educational, and informative
- Do not be hostile, argumentative, or adversarial

To prepare for the mediation, you need to have a solid understanding of the following:

- The law
- The facts
- The history
- The potential outcome on appeal
- Will the dispute end with the appeal
- The emotions
- The end goal of your client

Also, as an advocate, you will need to decide the following: (1) whether to encourage a settlement, and (2) whether to take a conciliatory or aggressive position in the negotiation.

Remember, that the ultimate decision about settlement is your client's decision. I will be acting as both clients during the mediation. Thus, if you have a question for your client or require authorization to settle your case, you need to find me and ask me your questions. If you are able to reach a settlement, you may model your settlement on the attached sample Settlement Agreement.

Assignment for DATE 2:

On **DATE 2** you and a partner [who will be assigned to you – see below] will act as co-mediators of a lawsuit with students from Professor Proske's class who will be representing clients on opposite sides of the dispute.

For **DATE 2**, you and your partner will work together to prepare a brief Mediators' Opening Statement, which you may model on the attached "Sample Mediator's Opening Statement." The Mediators' opening statement should be <u>no longer than 5 minutes</u>. You and your partner may divide up the content of your opening statement however you see fit. You do not need to organize the mediation in the same manner provided in the "Sample Mediator's Opening Statement." You should independently decide how you plan to organize the mediation and write the opening statement after those decisions have been made.

Following your Mediators' Opening Statement, the student-attorneys from Professor Proske's class will each present a 2-3 minute opening statement on behalf of their client, with Plaintiff presenting first, then Defendant.

You and your co-mediator will have the remaining 45 minutes of class time to assist the parties in reaching a settlement of their dispute. You may bring whatever facilitative or evaluative mediation techniques to bear in your efforts to obtain a settlement.

Sample Attorney Mediation Opening Statement

My name is _____ and I represent Ms. Lu Parker. First, let me start by saying that we appreciate T-Shirts for Fun's efforts to be here today. We are hopeful that we can resolve our dispute today and find a solution that works for everyone.

As you know, Ms. Parker has worked for the last 15 years on building her career and developing her reputation as a journalist. She has won numerous awards, including an Emmy for her journalism, co-hosted national shows, interviewed A-list celebrities, high-ranking politicians, and well-known authors, and reported live from the Democratic Headquarters in Los Angeles when Barrack Obama was elected President. Because of the recent events, however, Ms. Parker's hard-earned reputation has been damaged.

The t-shirt, of which I have brought with me, implies that the Mayor influenced Ms. Parker's reporting. Ms. Parker does have a great sense of humor and if she had been approached, she and TFF may have been able to jointly create a t-shirt that parody's her relationship with the Mayor. But, no one asked her and instead a hurtful and false image was created and distributed without her permission.

There are two main issues in this case. The first is the issue of consent. Ms. Parker did not consent to have TFF use her photograph. If there was not consent, the law provides that her right of publicity was violated. Admittedly, there are exceptions to the consent requirement. We admit that the issue is in the public interest – the public does have an interest in Ms. Parker and the Mayor, as they are public figures and their relationship made national headlines. We are not disputing that issue. What we are disputing, however, is how the photograph was used. As the law provides, if the use provides commentary on a matter in the public interest, then consent is not needed. But, here, where the use was not commentary, then consent is required. The photograph was used as a way for TFF to make money and not to provide commentary on a matter in the public interest. TFF is in the business of selling t-shirts and to make money, not to provide commentary, like a newspaper or broadcast.

The second is the issue of falsity. The t-shirt creates a false implication about Ms. Parker and her ethics. The t-shirt implies that the Mayor controlled Ms. Parker's reporting. Ms. Parker denies this and her television station supports her – they deny that there has ever been a problem with her reporting or her ethics. It is not clear to us whether TFF intended to create a false implication, but Ms. Parker feels the result does just that.

At the end of the day, Ms. Parker just wants this matter resolved. She just wants the t-shirts out of production and distribution and to have her reputation restored. To get this to happen, she is willing to consider forgoing any profits TFF received as a result of the t-shirt sales, which she likely would be entitled to under the law.

Sample Mediator's Opening Statement

Good morning. My name is _____. I'll be your mediator today and if you would why don't each of you identify yourselves and tell me whom you represent, whether the plaintiff or the defendant.

I am the mediator who has been appointed to your case by the Superior Court. Although I understand that this is court-ordered mediation, I hope and trust that you are participating in the mediation process with an open mind and in good faith to explore the possibilities of a resolution of your dispute. The mediation process is a proven, successful process and I would hope that you would participate in this frame of mind.

Let me say, also, at the outset, that I have no connection with this case. I know nothing about it other than the materials submitted by the parties. I have not met either one of you before and I do not have any connection with nor know any of the parties involved in this case and thus I have no opinion or preconceived ideas about the nature of your dispute or how it ought to be resolved.

Also, let me explain to you the mediation process, in case there is any question. I am not a judge or a decision-maker; rather my job is to facilitate communication between the two parties with the hopes that it will enable the parties to reach a settlement. My job will be to probe and ask questions and attempt to get each of the parties to reevaluate their positions and reevaluate their opponent's positions with the view toward possibly reaching a resolution of this dispute.

The mediation process is confidential, and I will do everything in my power to ensure that it remains confidential. Confidentiality with respect to mediation means that what we say here cannot be introduced in court and neither of you may call me as a witness in a court proceeding. It does not mean that we will not talk openly with one another in the mediation. In our private sessions, if you say something you do not want the other side to hear, please let me know that you would like it to be kept private.

Now let me describe to you briefly the procedure we are going to be following. When I get through making my remarks, I will be calling on each of you, first, the plaintiff and then the defendant, to make an opening statement. I will call on the plaintiff first, because the plaintiff is the one who initiated the law suit and it is customary for the claimant to go first. Do you, Mr. Jones, have any objection to that? Okay, fine, thank you.

An opening statement, I should tell you, is simply to state what your client's thoughts are, what the history of this dispute is, what relief or resolution you think is appropriate and anything you wish to add to shed light on the situation of your client that may be relevant. After each of you makes an opening statement, we will then remain together in what I call a joint session, and I will attempt to ask some questions to be sure I have all the information I need.

At some point in our discussion, we will probably break into what is called a "caucus," where I will ask one of you to leave. After caucusing with one of the parties, I will send that party out and ask to caucus with the other party. I think it is very important that you understand during those caucuses, while we are meeting privately, I may meet longer with one party than another. It has nothing to do with anything other than I may have more questions to ask one side. It has nothing to do with favoring one side or the other. Next, I want to mention that we may have several caucuses and we may have several joint sessions. As you know, we have set aside a period of three hours to complete this mediation. If at any time anybody feels a break is needed, we will do so.

Our goal today is to seek to get a complete resolution of this dispute. I again commend you for your commitment to this process and agreement to participate. Does anybody have any questions at this time?

Alright, then, before we begin the opening statements, let me just clarify that each of you does have authority from your respective clients to settle this case. You have come to the mediating process with authority to settle. Is that correct? Okay, thank you. _____, would you like to proceed then with your opening statement on behalf of the plaintiff?

Adapted from :   http://www.internetmediator.com/medres/pg1017.cfm

SAMPLE SETTLEMENT AGREEMENT AND RELEASE

Preamble

THIS SETTLEMENT AGREEMENT AND RELEASE ("Settlement Agreement") dated March 27, 2013 is entered into between Rian Wolfe ("Plaintiff"), and Horatio Caine ("Defendant") in connection with the lawsuit entitled Wolfe v. Caine (PS-148-29-4 RW) which is presently pending in Riverside County Superior Court.

Recitals

RECITALS [recite broad factual bases for the dispute and statements of what each party seeks through the litigation.]

A. _____
   _____

B. _____
   _____

C. The parties desire to enter into this Settlement Agreement in order to obtain a full settlement and discharge of all claims which are, or might become, the subject of the Complaint, upon the terms and conditions set forth herein.

The parties agree as follows:

1. Release and Discharge

In consideration of Defendant's agreement to _____ called for herein, the Plaintiff completely releases and forever discharges the Defendant, of and from any and all past, present or future claims, demands, obligations, actions, causes of action, rights, damages, costs, loss of services, expenses and compensation which the Plaintiff now has, or which may hereafter accrue or otherwise be acquired by Plaintiff, on account of, or in any way growing out of their dispute.

2. Consideration

In consideration of the release set forth above,

3. Attorneys' Fees

4. Representations and Warranties of Plaintiff

   a. Capacity to Execute Agreement

5. Representations and Warranties of Defendant

   a. Capacity to Execute Agreement

6. Covenants and Conditions of Plaintiff [Does the settlement require Plaintiff to perform any specific acts, such as prepare and file a Request for Dismissal of the action?]

7. Covenants and Conditions of Defendant [Does the settlement require Defendant to perform any specific acts, such as pay money to the Plaintiff?]

8. Dispute Resolution [What method of resolution will you choose if the parties don't do what they promise to do in this agreement?]

9. Remedies for Breach [liquidated damages? Injunctive relief?]

10. This Settlement Agreement contains the entire agreement between the Plaintiff and the Defendant with regard to the matters set forth herein.

11. Successors in Interest

    This Settlement Agreement shall be binding upon and inure to the benefit of the executors, administrators, personal representatives, heirs, successors and assigns of   Plaintiff and Defendant.

12. Representation by Counsel

    In entering into this Settlement Agreement, the parties represent that they have relied upon the advice of counsel, and that the terms of this Settlement Agreement have been completely read and explained by their counsel, and that those terms are fully understood and voluntarily accepted by them.

13. Governing Law

This Settlement Agreement shall be construed and interpreted in accordance with the laws of the State of California.

14. Additional Acts

The parties agree to cooperate fully and execute any and all supplementary documents and to take all additional actions which may be necessary or appropriate to give full force and effect to the basic terms and intent of this Settlement Agreement.

To evidence the parties' agreement to this Agreement's provisions, they have executed and delivered this Agreement on the date set forth in the Preamble.

_____

Plaintiff

_____

Defendant

In-Class Exercise (Court-Ordered Mediation):

The following exercise can be done right before the students write an appellate brief. It is a court-ordered mediation. The exercise below uses one of our appellate brief problems. The basic instructions and questions posed can be used with any factual and legal problem.

The Thirteenth Circuit has a mediation program. All appeals must be assessed for eligibility for the mediation program. If the case is determined to be appropriate for mediation, the parties must discuss the case with a court-appointed neutral mediator. The role of the mediator is to facilitate a mutual agreement by the parties, if possible.

It has been determined that your case will be referred to mediation. Each student in the class will play a role in the mediation. You will be assigned one of the following roles: 1) the mediator, 2) the appellants' counsel, 3) the appellee's counsel, 4) the appellant Bettina Arroyo, or 5) the appellee Mitch Lanham.

The goal for each group is to explore the possibility of negotiated settlement with the help of a neutral mediator. The mediator will need to decide the following: 1) whether to meet with the parties together or in separate sessions, 2) whether to adopt a facilitative, evaluative, or transformative approach, 3) whether to encourage a settlement that may impact constitutional principles or public policies.

The advocates will need to decide the following: 1) whether to allow your clients to talk to each other or the mediator without you present, 2) whether to encourage a settlement, and 3) whether to take a conciliatory or aggressive position in the negotiation.

The parties will need to decide the following: 1) whether to take a conciliatory or aggressive approach in the negotiation and 2) whether to consider settlement.

Before the end of class, each student in every group should draft an assessment of the mediation. Please reflect on the mediation approach used, how it worked, whether you think this case can be settled through further mediation, and why you have reached this conclusion.

Mediation Assessment

Group #: _____

Describe the mediation approach used:

Did the mediation result in a resolution of the case? If so, what was the resolution? If not, what were the obstacles that could not be cleared?

Do you think this case could be settled through further mediation? Why or Why not?

<u>Alternative Exercise</u>: For a class where going through the entire process of mediation is too time-consuming or ambitious, consider using a mediation opening statement as a short oral presentation exercise. When our students write a mediation brief, we frequently add an oral component to the assignment by requiring the presentation of a mediation opening statement. The following exercise can be done in small groups or one student at a time.

Arbitration exercises tend to take even longer than mediation exercises, although a mediation opening statement exercise can be transformed into an arbitration opening statement exercise by a slight shift of focus and tone. In international arbitration, very often the opening statements are given while sitting around a conference table. Students can practice delivering arbitration opening statements in small break out groups. Below are some slides that can be used in a presentation on arbitration.

CHAPTER 20

NEGOTIATION AND SETTLEMENT

■ ■ ■

By Adrienne Brungess

The purpose of this chapter is to introduce students to basic principles of negotiating as a lawyer. It provides students an overview of the negotiation process, starting at the preparation stage and concluding at the negotiation table, highlighting the importance of cross-cultural awareness. Students tend to enjoy negotiation materials and simulations as it provides them an opportunity to act like lawyers.

There is some flexibility as to when this material should be assigned. Ideally, skills like negotiations can be introduced in a 1L course and then revisited in later courses. It can also be implemented in a more advanced persuasive research and writing course. Negotiation exercises can be done quickly or with more significant preparation.

For example, 1L students can be instructed to assume that after the work they completed on an objective memo, the parties' attorneys set a conference to discuss the possibility of settlement. The students can role-play and simulate a negotiation with opposing counsel and try to reach a resolution. This can also be done in a "fish bowl" where certain students participate in the negotiation and others observe and have opportunities to assist the participants.

In a 2L or persuasive writing semester, students could negotiate the issue of a pre-trial motion or an issue on appeal. Mediation can be added at this stage also.

Example slides illustrating the negotiation process are included below.

PRACTICE EXERCISE – CHAPTER 20, PAGE 11

The "Cross the Line" exercise has a few possible outcomes. The best outcome for both players is for each to cross to the other's side and each would be awarded $1000. The rules do not indicate that only one player can win. Most students fail to recognize this and few will negotiate this result.

More frequently, students will agree to split the $1000 is some fashion. One might agree to cross in exchange for more than 50% of the prize. Students may also be more creative and, for example, one might agree to exchange the prize money for the title of victor in the game.

In class, this exercise takes very little time to complete. It is a good idea to "de-brief" after and have students share what kind of agreements they reached. It provides a good example of how to create value and expand the pie rather than focusing on division only.

Example Slides

NEGOTIATIONS OVERVIEW

Foundations of Effective Negotiating

Preparation
- Identify both parties' interests
- Set clear and reasonable goals
- Analyze rights and powers of the parties
- Assess alternative solutions
  - Establish a clear reservation point based on analysis of BATNAs/WATNAs
- Research
  - Locate relevant legal authority
  - Locate other objective sources
- Plan Concessions

Setting Goals

When setting goals:
- Make them specific
- Make them justifiable
- Make the reasonably optimistic

Assessing Alternatives

- An alternative refers to how you will satisfy your interest if you cannot reach a deal with your negotiation counterpart.
- This is your BATNA.
  - The better your BATNA, the more power you have in the negotiation.
- Explore and invent as many alternatives as possible; evaluate them to determine the best and worst.
- Knowing your BATNA helps you to set your reservation point.
  - Reservation point represents the minimally acceptable agreement, i.e., your bottom line.

Researching

- Locate legitimizing sources that support your positions in the negotiation.
  - That might include legal authority
  - Look also for other objective criteria
    - Examples: market value, precedent, professional opinions, costs, etc.

Planning Concessions

- Consider concessions you might make or expect to reach agreement

- Acknowledge concessions made

- Make opening offers that leave room for concessions

- Be prepared to explain the reasons for concessions

- Reciprocate concessions

At the Negotiation Table

Goals of Opening Stage

1. Establish rapport with your counterpart
2. Assess your counterpart's credibility and trustworthiness
3. Determine the issues to be negotiated

At the Negotiation Table, cont.

First exchange **information**, then exchange **value**
- Information exchange is where parties should communicate their interests
  - Gather missing information, cautiously share information, concerns, and needs
  - You will make wiser offers when you have more complete information
  - Your offer will have greater credibility having been made after an investment of time and discussion

At the Negotiation Table, cont.

- Value exchange is where parties should make offers, bargain, claim value, create value and make concessions

At the Negotiation Table, cont.

- When confronted with a position, <u>ask why</u> or <u>how</u> that position works for them

- If your proposal or offer is rejected, ask <u>why not</u>, or what aspects of the proposal are unacceptable

At the Negotiation Table, cont.

- Answer questions directly and as simply as you can.

- Do not evade or ignore questions.

- Focus on common ground.

At the Negotiation Table, cont.

- Be patient
  - Don't give up at the first sign of impasse or disagreement.
  - Impasses and disagreements are part of the negotiation process.

At the Negotiation Table, cont.

- The end of the negotiation is often when one or all participants begin to feel time pressure to make an agreement.

- In this stage major concessions are often made and true concerns and needs emerge.

At the Negotiation Table, cont.

- A party is vulnerable when he/she feels that time is running out to make an agreement:

  - Stay focused on your goal

  - Know your reservation (walk-away) point

Final Decision and Closure

- Obtain appropriate level of commitment (verbal promise, informal writing, contract)

- Write the contract yourself, if possible

- Read the contract, especially the final draft

CHAPTER 21

CONTRACT DRAFTING

■ ■ ■

By Jeffrey Proske

This chapter is designed to provide students with a survey of the range of considerations that come in to play in drafting contracts, from the bare-bones statutory framework underlying the formation of contracts, to standards of professionalism in transactional practice, to practical considerations about the basic components of any contract with examples of well-crafted provisions and explanations of their legal significance. Sample exercises have been included below to assist students in achieving specific learning outcomes related to the material in the chapter.

The contract drafting chapter can be a stand-alone component of the course, or it can be assigned in conjunction with a persuasive writing exercise as an introduction to drafting settlement agreements. It may also be useful in connection with a mediation or other ADR exercise to expose students to the reality that settlement agreements, just like any other agreement, are contracts that need to embody the basic elements of an enforceable contract.

The due diligence exercise below is a fun exercise designed to help students identify a range of potential risks inherent in a proposed fictitious transaction and consider the possible downside consequences of those risks to the client.

The exercise can take anywhere from 30 minutes to an hour depending on how in depth the risk analysis gets. Have the students review the Assigning Partner's Memorandum individually or in small groups, identify as many issues as they can related to Pollyanna Pennywise's project, and note what the impact of that risk on Pollyanna's plan could be. The students may not recognize all of the issues presented in the facts, but they will likely recognize many of them.

A sample list of potential issues follows the Assigning Partner's Memorandum below.

Pollyanna Pennywise Due Diligence Exercise [Approximately 30 minutes]

MEMORANDUM

TO: Summer Associate

FROM: Beau "Gus" Billings, Assigning Partner

RE: Notes from meeting with Pollyanna Pennywise of May 23, 20__

DATE: May 26, 20__

Pollyanna Pennywise is an insurance adjuster from San Frangeles, California. She wants to buy some land and build a country cottage on it, and has asked this firm to review the Purchase Agreement prepared by the seller and advise her.

On May 21, 201_ Ms. Pennywise took a drive in the countryside outside of San Frangeles when she discovered a meadow with a "For Sale By Owner" sign with a phone number on it poking up through some flowers next to the gate to the property, "**Rancho Floribunda**."

While touring the property, Ms. Pennywise discovered a grove of oaks abutting a river that runs through the property. She also mentioned that she heard the distinctive sounds of frogs on the river bank and songbirds in the trees, which caused her to decide that that was the spot where should would build her cottage. She noted that there was an outhouse structure on the property near the site. She also saw a group of nature lovers in kayaks rowing down the river.

Ms. Pennywise telephoned the seller, **Glib Flipper**, that afternoon and learned that he had just inherited the property from his great aunt, **Gloria Floribunda**, who, we are informed, was a famous botanist and conservationist. Mr. Flipper told Ms. Pennywise he was selling the Rancho because he was graduating from high school and needed the cash to pay for college. Ms. Pennywise told him she wanted to build her dream cottage on it with a large organic garden to grow greens to sell at the farmers market in town. Mr. Flipper agreed to sell Ms. Pennywise the entirety of Rancho Floribunda for $25,000, and Ms. Pennywise accepted.

Please make a list of any issues you think we may need to address in the purchase agreement based on the meeting notes above, and note how the issue might impact Ms. Pennywise project.

List of possible issues:

Due Diligence Red Flags

1.   The wildflowers on the property should have gotten your antennae up. Those references, together with the fact that Great Aunt Gloria was a noted conservationist and botanist would alert us to the possibility that Rancho Floribunda might very well be a habitat of endangered plant species, and might be the subject of various protections and land use restrictions under state and federal laws.

2.   The "for sale by owner" sign. Not having a licensed broker on the listing who could bear some responsibility and liability for failing to make appropriate disclosures and to ensure that the transaction closes effectively with everybody getting what they want should make us more cautious. Of course, not having a broker could simply mean the seller, like Polly, is unwilling to part with any more cash than necessary, but we take heed nonetheless.

3.   The reference in the story to a "grove of oaks" would have raised a warning to the wary that the oaks, like the wildflowers, might also be protected by law.

4.   The fact that the property has a river flowing through it with kayakers using it would potentially serve as notice of a host of riparian rights and prior use issues.

5.   What about the lullaby of the frogs and the birds in the boughs? The presence of either of these would also have raised a red flag. There is a vast array of species of birds, frogs, toads and other animals that are explicitly protected under California and federal law which would make modification of their habitat illegal or impossibly expensive.

6.   What about Polly's primary goal – to build her dream cottage near the oaks next to the river? Without checking county records, how would we even know if the zoning for Rancho Floribunda would permit her to build her cottage? Additionally, Rancho Floribunda is located in California, which has a unique set of seismic and weather   conditions that come into play in building a home. So, it would behoove us to check the zoning records to tell us whether or not the proposed site of Polly's cottage lies in a hazardous flood, fire or earthquake zone.

7.   The presence of an outhouse on the property suggests the possibility of a hazardous waste issue or even an underground storage

tank issue, which might have state and federal environmental liability implications. Polly would be foolish to proceed with her purchase if she didn't first obtain an environmental study to find out what contaminations if any there might be on the property.

8. Glib's statement to Polly that he just inherited the property from his great aunt should cause you to raise an eyebrow. The word "inheritance" usually has the word "probate" somewhere close by. A probate case involving Rancho Floribunda could impact Glib's ability to convey clear title to the property, and we would want to know for sure one way or another.

9. What about Glib's statements that he is in high school and is selling the ranch to get funds to pay for college? What are we to make of that? The fact that Glib is in high school tells us that he may not be old enough to enter into a contract.

10. Does the fact that Polly wants to plant an organic garden to grow greens to sell at the farmers market in town make you squint? Well it should. Polly needs to know if Rancho Floribunda can even be used as an organic garden. The zoning for the property may not permit agricultural uses for one thing. What's more, the organic greens Polly wants to grow and sell might be invasive species that impact native plants and animals which could result in great liability to Polly.

Chapter 21(E) Sample Exercise: Developing a Timeline for the Transaction

The concept of transactions having a lifespan with a beginning, middle and end, and plotting where on that lifespan certain actions must take place is crucial to contract drafting. This simple exercise is a fun and easy way to have students identify the basic elements of the beginning, middle and end of a contract and to note on that timeline when certain actions must be taken by one or both of the parties. The exercise should take about 30 minutes. Have students work either individually or in groups to develop a timeline noting the specific actions required at certain points on the timeline. By identifying with specificity the actual dates when actions need to be taken and amounts of money that need to be paid and received, students make the connection between the concepts on the page and their implementation in the real world.

Memorandum

To: Summer Associate

From: Assigning Partner

Date: May 15, 2013

Re: Employment Agreement Between Alpha Systems, LLC and Dorothy Mae Trix

---

Our new client, Dorothy Mae Trix, has asked us to draft an employment agreement for her with Alpha Systems, LLC in connection with her proposed employment as a Senior Manager. Ms. Trix has outlined the terms of her employment for us. The principal terms are listed below:

1. Her start date will be June 1st, 2013 and her employment will continue for two years.

2. Her salary will be $50,000 annually, payable in equal monthly installments on the last business day of the month.

3. Her benefits, including health insurance and 401K matching fund plan will commence 30 days after her start date and will continue for 60 days after the termination date of her contract.

4. Both Ms. Trix and Alpha have the right to terminate the contract upon the delivery of 2 weeks prior written notice.

5. Alpha has the right to terminate Ms. Trix contract at any time for cause.

Please create a timeline demonstrating the start date, the end date [assuming neither party terminates prior to the end date] and the dates between those two points when the parties have promised to perform some action and list the specific action the parties have promised on that date. Where you can determine specific dates and payment amounts, please list those too. Where a party has a right to receive the benefit of the other party's act, please note that too.

Sample Timeline with termination:

June 1, 2013	Start Date:
	Ms. Trix must report to work
	Alpha Systems, LLC must have work space ready for Ms. Trix
June 30, 2013	Monthly salary payment of $4,166.66 due today
	Ms. Trix must receive payment
	Alpha Systems, LLC must deliver payment
July 1, 2013	Benefits commence
	Ms. Trix must be notified of commencement of benefits
	Alpha Systems, LLC is required to take steps to ensure benefits are in place
July 30, 2013	Monthly salary payment of $4,166.66 due today
August 31, 2013	Monthly salary payment of $4,166.66 due today [pay dates for the months between August 2013 and May, 2015 can be inserted to fully depict the required payments under the contract.]
May 31, 2015	Contract Termination Date
July 31, 2015	Termination of benefits

Chapter 21(F) Sample Exercise: Building a Settlement Agreement

The "Building a Settlement Agreement" exercise can be assigned in conjunction with a persuasive writing exercise as an introduction to drafting settlement agreements. It is a useful exercise to assist the students in connecting the materials in the chapter regarding the components of contract with the resolution of a dispute that they have some familiarity with already. The students should read the Contract Drafting Chapter prior to doing this exercise so they have a basic understanding of the purpose underlying the contract components in the settlement agreement. The Sample Settlement Agreement below provides the basic components of an enforceable settlement agreement, but provides blanks where the students will be required to consider how best to draft specific components to achieve the client's goals, and then draft them. The exercise takes about an hour with students working in teams of two with each member of the team representing the client they have written their persuasive brief for. Time should be allowed after each team has completed their draft to discuss the provisions each team has arrived at.

SETTLEMENT AGREEMENT AND RELEASE

Preamble

THIS SETTLEMENT AGREEMENT AND RELEASE ("Settlement Agreement") dated _____ is entered into between _____ ("Plaintiff-Appellant"), and _____ ("Defendant-Appellee") in connection with the lawsuit entitled _____ (Case Name and Number) which is presently pending in _____ court.

Recitals

[recite broad factual bases for the dispute and statements of what each party seeks through the litigation in this section]

A._____
_____

B._____
_____

C. The parties desire to enter into this Settlement Agreement in order to obtain a full settlement and discharge of all claims which are or might become the subject of the Complaint, upon the terms and conditions set forth herein.

The parties agree as follows:

1. Release and Discharge

In exchange for Defendant-Appellee's agreement to _____ called for herein, the Plaintiff-Appellant completely releases and forever discharges the Defendant-Appellee, of and from any and all past, present or future claims, demands, obligations, actions, causes of action, rights, damages, costs, loss of services, expenses and compensation which the Plaintiff-Appellant now has, or which may hereafter accrue or otherwise be acquired by Plaintiff-Appellant, on account of, or in any way growing out of their dispute.

2. Settlement Payment

In exchange for the release set forth above, Defendant-Appellee shall pay Plaintiff-Appellant a Settlement Payment as follows:

    a. Payment Amount

    _____

    b. Payment Method

    _____

3. Attorneys' Fees.

4. Representations and Warranties of Plaintiff-Appellant

    a. Capacity to Execute Agreement

    _____
    _____.

    b.

    _____.

5. Representations and Warranties of Defendant-Appellee

    a. Capacity to Execute Agreement

    _____

    _____

    b.

    _____

    _____

6. Covenants of Plaintiff-Appellant

_____

_____

7. Covenants of Defendant-Appellee

_____

_____

8. Conditions to Plaintiff-Appellants' Performance

_____

_____

9. Conditions to Defendant-Appellee's Performance

_____

_____

10. Dispute Resolution

_____

_____

11. Remedies for Breach

_____

_____

12. Integration

This Settlement Agreement contains the entire agreement between the Plaintiff-Appellee and the Defendant-Appellant with regard to the matters set forth herein.

13. Successors in Interest

This Settlement Agreement shall be binding upon and inure to the benefit of the executors, administrators, personal representatives, heirs, successors and assigns of each.

14. Representation of Comprehension of Document

In entering into this Settlement Agreement, the parties represent that they have relied upon the advice of counsel, and that the terms of this Settlement Agreement have been completely read and explained by their counsel, and that those terms are fully understood and voluntarily accepted by them.

15. Governing Law

This Settlement Agreement shall be construed and interpreted in accordance with the laws of the State of _____.

16. Additional Acts

The parties agree to cooperate fully and execute any and all supplementary documents and to take all additional actions which may be necessary or appropriate to give full force and effect to the basic terms and intent of this Settlement Agreement.

To evidence the parties' agreement to this Agreement's provisions, they have executed and delivered this Agreement on the date set forth in the Preamble.

_____

Plaintiff-Appellant

_____

Defendant-Appellee

CHAPTER 22

RESEARCH STRATEGIES

■ ■ ■

By Maureen Moran

The purpose of this chapter is not to teach any specific methods of legal research; rather, it is to help students form strategies for approaching any legal research project. Students should come away from this chapter with a better understanding of how to plan a research project and how to incorporate different search terms and different sources into a plan. This chapter could be assigned after students have learned how to issue-spot, and are familiar with the basic sources of primary law. Other chapters that may be helpful for students to read prior to this one are Chapter 2, Domestic and Foreign Legal Systems; Chapter 3, Transnational Legal Practice and Cultural Awareness; Chapter 4, Legal Reasoning and Analysis Toolkit; and Chapter 5, The Process of Legal Writing.

The following exercises are designed to test students' knowledge of research sources and research strategies; most answers will be found within this chapter, though a supplemental research text will give more detail. You may change the jurisdiction or sources as you see fit.

SAMPLE RESEARCH EXERCISES

Facts for all exercises:

Your client, Susan, is a wealthy young woman who lives in Sacramento, California. Susan, who is the heiress to a kitty litter fortune, keeps a number of exotic animals on her property, including a young leopard named Baby, which she keeps in her house and takes for walks around Midtown on a jeweled leash. The family business keeps Susan well-supplied with enough kitty litter to ensure that Baby's litter box, which is quite large, is kept clean. Baby, while generally fairly serene in temperament, has a few habits which have resulted in Susan's inability to keep household employees. Baby is still a young leopard, and is quite playful. One of Baby's favorite games is to stalk the housekeeper through the house and pounce on her while she is busy cleaning. While Baby has never bitten or mauled a housekeeper, several housekeepers have quit Susan's employ, and now that word is getting around about Baby's games, Susan has had trouble hiring a new housekeeper. And given how large Baby's litter box is, Susan really needs a housekeeper. Another game that

Baby likes to play is to steal objects and bury them in inconvenient places. Since Susan likes to take Baby out and let her off leash, Baby has a lot of opportunities to steal objects outside of Susan's house. Often, these objects cannot be recovered, and Susan pays a lot of money to settle the claims of angry homeowners whose laundry, mailboxes, Ming vases and other objects have been carried off by Baby and cannot be recovered because Baby will not reveal the hiding place.

A few months ago, Susan brought Baby to a fundraiser at the Cropper Museum of Natural History in honor of David, a paleontologist who had spent fourteen years assembling a brontosaurus skeleton for the museum. The very last bone needed to complete the skeleton, an intercostal clavicle bone, had taken David many years and many trips to the Rift Valley to locate and obtain. The intercostal clavicle bone was to be unveiled during the fundraiser to great acclaim, and David was to have made a speech in support of the efforts of the donors to the Cropper Museum, who funded his trips to the Rift Valley and the purchase of the final bone. However, things did not go as planned. During the fundraiser, Susan had let Baby off the leash because she could not manage a leopard, a cocktail, and canapés at the same time. When the time came for David to unveil the intercostal clavicle bone and put it into place, the bone was missing. So, for that matter, was Baby. After a search, Baby was located in the Egyptian Wing of the museum, curled up asleep in a sarcophagus, but the bone could not be found. David is furious. So is the Board of Docents of the Cropper Museum. Each has threatened suit. Susan would like to know if she can be held responsible for the missing bone when no one actually saw Baby take the bone.

RESEARCH ASSIGNMENT 1: RESEARCH STRATEGY:

1. <u>Generate Search Terms</u>

Using the fact pattern above and the "5W's and H" approach outlined in your reading, brainstorm some possible search terms you may want to use.

Identify the following:

a) Who are the possible parties?

b) What is the nature of the harm alleged?

c) Is this a civil or criminal matter?

d) What kind of relief will be sought?

e) What is the jurisdiction?

f) When did the events take place?

g) How did this happen?

h) What proof is there of Susan's responsibility?

2. <u>Alternate search terms and synonyms</u>

For each search term that you list above, list an alternate term or synonym you could try to get more results.

3. <u>Broadening and narrowing your search</u>

a) Describe how you can broaden your search query to get more results.

b) Describe how you can narrow your search query to get fewer results.

4. <u>Boolean syntax</u>

Use the following Boolean terms to answer this question:
- w/s = within the same sentence
- w/n = within n words (where "n" is a number)
- w/p = within the same paragraph
- ! = root expander to find variations on a term past a certain point
- Or = this term or that term must appear in the results
- And = both this term and that term must appear in the results
- "quotation marks" = will find the exact phrase enclosed within the quotation marks

For each of the following search queries, translate the Boolean syntax into English:

a) Exotic w/3 animal! w/p liabil! or liable

b) Theft w/s pet and owner! /s responsib! or liab!

c) Leopard or panther or "big cat" w/p owner and liab! w/s theft or stolen or steal!

d) Dinosaur or brontosaurus w/5 bone! and theft and museum

e) Negligen! and animal! and owner w/s liab! w/3 harm

5. <u>Choosing Your Sources</u>

a) List at least four types of sources you intend to consult to research your client's case.

b) Which type of source should you start with in most legal research situations?

c) Which of these sources are primary authority ("the law")?

6. <u>Expanding Your Search</u>

a) Describe how you can expand your search by using Secondary Sources.

b) Describe how you can expand your search by using Citators.

c) Describe how you can expand your search by using Finding Aids.

7. <u>Closing the Loop</u>

a) Describe how you will use a citator to update your research.

b) Describe how you will use a citator to find additional sources or search terms you may have missed in your original search.

c) How will you know when your research is finished?

RESEARCH ASSIGNMENT 2: SECONDARY SOURCES:

1. What are two ways to find what you're looking for in a <u>print</u> secondary source?

2. When should secondary sources be used in your research process?

3. What are the benefits of using a secondary source – what can it provide you?

4. For American Law Reports, what are the entries called and what tools are available for locating them?

5. If you had a federal law question, what secondary source would you go to first?

6. If you had a California state law question, what secondary source would you go to first?

7. Describe how you would find a law review article on a topic you are researching.

For the following three questions, we will be using the fact pattern from Research Assignment 1.

8. <u>Print Research:</u> Please only use print legal encyclopedias and treatises to answer the following questions:

A. Draft 1-2 paragraphs advising your client regarding whether she can be held liable for the loss of the dinosaur bone if it can be shown that her leopard took it. Please answer this question using California law. You may use any print legal encyclopedia or treatise to answer this question.

B. Provide the citation to the secondary source(s) you used to answer this question including the specific page number(s).

9. <u>Online Research:</u> Please only use online C.J.S., A.L.R., Witkin, Cal. Jur., or Am. Jur. research materials to answer the following questions:

A. Draft 1-2 paragraphs advising your client regarding whether your client can be civilly liable for the loss of or damage to the dinosaur bone if she had no prior notice of the leopard's propensity for stealing items? Please answer this question using California law and provide the citation to the secondary source you used to answer this question including the specific section number(s).

B. Draft 1-2 paragraphs advising your client regarding whether your client could be strictly liable should Baby bite a housekeeper, even if Baby has not shown any propensity towards viciousness in the past? Please answer this question using California law and provide the citation to the secondary source you used to answer this question including the specific section number(s).

10. <u>Comparative Paragraph:</u> After you have completed Questions 7 and 8, please draft a comparative paragraph regarding secondary source research materials. A comparative paragraph describes your research experiences with print sources and online sources. Please use the following questions as your guide:

- Which secondary source research materials did you like better in print? Why?
- Which secondary source research materials did you like better online? Why?
- When using secondary sources in the future, where do you think you will most likely start, print or online? Why?

RESEARCH ASSIGNMENT 3: STATE AND FEDERAL STATUTES:

1. (2 points) How are federal codes organized?
2. (2 points) How are California codes organized?
3. (2 points) What is the difference between the U.S.C. and the U.S.C.A.?
4. (2 points) What is the difference between the Deerings and West's Annotated California Codes?
5. (2 points) If you know the name of a federal statute, how would you locate it?
6. (2 points) If you know the citation of a California statute, how would you locate it?
7. (2 points) Can you use a citator (Shepard's, KeyCite, or BCite) for statutes?
8. (2 points) What type of materials are included in the annotations of state and federal codes?
9. <u>Print Research</u> (14 points): Please only use print state statute research materials to answer the following questions:

FACTS: Your client, a middle-aged Caucasian female, recently was terminated from her job as an administrative assistant. The employer did not provide any reason for her termination, despite your client's repeated requests for an explanation. Your client would like to file a complaint against her employer on the grounds that she was terminated without good cause.

A. Draft 1-2 paragraphs advising your client regarding whether an employer is required to have good cause to terminate and whether she could have a claim against her employer? Please answer this question using California statutory law (and annotations).

B. Provide the citation to the source you used to answer this question. Include the publisher and any section or subsection numbers.

10. <u>Online</u> Research (28 points): Please only use online federal statute research materials to answer the following questions:

   A.   Westlaw

FACTS: Your client accidentally set an American flag on fire at a Fourth of July parade. Several law enforcement officers witnessed the event and took down his name, address, and telephone number. Your client is worried that he may be subject to a fine or other penalty for desecrating or destruction of the American flag.

1. Draft 1-2 paragraphs advising your client regarding whether he will likely be subject to a fine or other penalty for desecrating or destruction of the American flag? Please answer this question using federal statutory law (and annotations).

2. Provide the citation to the source you used to answer this question. Include the publisher and any section or subsection numbers.

B. Lexis

FACTS: Your client, Susan, owns a mischievous pet leopard, Baby. She recently discovered that Baby, which she thought was an African species of leopard, is really a Javan leopard and an endangered species. Susan's leopard broker had told her that Baby was from a breeder in Ivory Coast. After all the trouble that Baby caused Susan at the Cropper Museum, Susan would like to sell Baby. Now she's concerned there may be restrictions on her ability to sell the leopard.

1. Draft 1-2 paragraphs advising your client regarding whether there are any restrictions on her ability to sell her leopard. Please answer this question using federal statutory law (and annotations).

2. Provide the citation to the source you used to answer this question. Please include all sections and subsections.

11. Comparative Paragraph (14 points): After you have completed Questions 9 and 10, please draft a comparative paragraph regarding statutory research materials. A comparative paragraph describes your research experiences with print sources and online sources. Please use the following questions as your guide:

- Which statutory research materials did you like better in print? Why?
- Which statutory research materials did you like better online? Why?
- When using statutes in the future, where do you think you will most likely start, print or online? Why?

RESEARCH ASSIGNMENT 4: CASES, DIGESTS, AND CITATORS:

True or False

1. T or F   Digests may summarize cases from only one jurisdiction or cases from multiple jurisdictions.
2. T or F   A summary of a case in a West digest corresponds exactly to a headnote at the beginning of the case published in a West reporter.
3. T or F   Digests contain summaries of cases organized by subject.
4. T or F   Digests are considered primary authority.
5. T or F   A headnote is an editorial enhancement.
6. T or F   A headnote is written by the court and is an authoritative part of the court's opinion.
7. T or F   A headnote is a paragraph summarizing a point within a case.
8. T or F   A headnote appears at the beginning of case.
9. T or F   Case reporters may contain cases from only one jurisdiction or cases from multiple jurisdictions.
10. T or F   Case reporters may be official (published under government authority) or unofficial (published by a commercial publisher).
11. T or F   Case reporters are organized by subject.
12. T or F   Case reporters are published in chronological order.
13. T or F   In Shepard's or KeyCite, you should always read cases with a red icon.

14. T or F   Shepard's or KeyCite only are an updating tool to see if the law is still good authority.

Multiple Choice

15. In reporter or case published on Westlaw or Lexis, where does the official opinion of the court begin?

    a. After the citation

    b. After the summary or synopsis

    c. After the headnotes

    d. After the judges name

16. Which of the following steps are part of the print digest research process?

    a. Updating your research

    b. Locating relevant topics and key numbers in the digest

    c. Locating the correct digest set

    d. Reading case summaries

    e. All of the above

17. On either Shepard's or KeyCite, search results can be sorted or limited by which of the following?

    a. Jurisdiction

    b. Type of Authority

    c. Date

    d. Headnotes

    e. Key Words

    f. All of the above

18. **Print Research:** Please only use print digests to answer the following questions:

    FACTS: Your client would like to sue McKing's fast food restaurant. Last month, your client was eating lunch at McKing's. She ordered a hamburger, French fries, and a soda. After eating several French fries, she bit into another one. When she bit into it, she noticed it seemed different. When she looked down at the French fry she was eating, she realized it was a partially fried rat tail. She immediately vomited and left McKing's. Your client now claims she will never eat at McKing's again, or fast food, and probably will never be able to eat French fries again, which had been her favorite food.

A. Draft 1-2 paragraphs discussing cause of action(s) your client should bring against McKing's.

B. Identify one case and its citation that best addresses this research issue. You may choose any jurisdiction.

19. **Online Research:** Please only use online citators to answer the following questions (if you do not have access to Lexis, please answer both using Westlaw):

Please use the case you found in response to Question 18 to answer the following questions.

    A.   Westlaw (KeyCite)

    1) Evaluate whether the case is still "good law." Explain your answer.

    2) Identify one secondary source that provides a good discussion of the case you are evaluating.

    3) Identify one case that you would rely upon for your research issue that you found from KeyCiting your case. Explain your answer. (NOTE: when selecting your case, be sure to evaluate level of court, the citator treatment of the new case, factual similarities or differences, amount of reasoning, etc.)

CHAPTER 23

FOREIGN AND INTERNATIONAL LEGAL RESEARCH

■ ■ ■

By Maureen Moran

The purpose of this chapter is to provide a broad overview on legal research in foreign and international law sources. This chapter could be assigned after students have become proficient at researching domestic U.S. law and are familiar with research strategies as discussed in Chapter 22. Creating a writing assignment in which a treaty may be implicated is a good way to introduce students to treaty research and to incorporate some transnational practice. Other chapters that may be helpful for students to read prior to this one are Chapter 2, Domestic and Foreign Legal Systems; Chapter 3, Transnational Legal Practice and Cultural Awareness; Chapter 4, Legal Reasoning and Analysis Toolkit; Chapter 5, The Process of Legal Writing; and Chapter 24, Citation.

The following are some suggested research exercises for treaties and for European Union law using online resources. Please note that no specific directions have been given for Westlaw and Lexis because the international materials databases on those platforms is changing rapidly and any directions may be inaccurate by the date of publication. Your law librarians or Westlaw and Lexis representatives can help you formulate searches for those sources.

SAMPLE RESEARCH EXERCISES

U.S. TREATY IN-CLASS RESEARCH EXERCISE:

Question Set 1: Treaties in Force (Bilateral Agreements)

1. Log onto Google (or other internet search engine);
2. Type in "Treaties in Force;"
3. Locate the U.S. Department of State web page with "Treaties in Force;"

4. Read the materials on the U.S. Department of State Treaties in Force web site;

5. Click "view or download Treaties in Force 2012;"

6. Under "Section 1 – Bilateral Treaties and Other Agreements" find Spain;

7. Locate a treaty between the US and Spain on the issue of "customs;"
   - To do this, either scroll through the text of Section 1 – Bilateral Treaties and Other Agreements; use the "Ctrl F" function to "find" a word (this is not a great search tool); use the "+" function to move through the index;

8. Describe the treaty:

9. Identify the citation of a relevant treaty:

10. Now go to HeinOnline [this may be accessed through your library's database page]:
    - Once on HeinOnline, select "Treaties and Agreements Library;"
    - Then select "Treaties and International Act Series" and find your treaty(using the TIAS citation you listed above).

Question Set 2: Treaties in Force (Multilateral Agreements)

1. Log onto Google (or other internet search engine);

2. Type in "Treaties in Force;"

3. Locate the U.S. Department of State web page with "Treaties in Force;"

4. Read the materials on the U.S. Department of State Treaties in Force web site;

5. Click "view or download Treaties in Force 2012;"

6. Under "Section 2 – Multilateral Treaties and Other Agreements", locate a treaty (or treaties) on the issue of "Marine Pollution:"
   - To do this, either scroll through the text of Section 2 – Multilateral Treaties and Other Agreements; use the "Ctrl F" function to "find" a word (this is not a great search tool); use the "+" function to move through the index;

7. Locate the treaty specifically on "oil pollution casualties;"

8. Describe the treaty:

9. Identify the citation for the treaty:

10. Where was it created and on what date was it entered into force?

11. How many "Notes" are there? What are the "Notes?"

12. Is there a "Note" for the United States? If so, what number is it and what does it say?

13. Click on the Depository or Status link provided under the title of the Treaty. Once connected to that site, work through it to pull up a copy of the treaty. (HINT: remember that treaties can also be called conventions or agreements).

EUROPEAN UNION LAW EXERCISES:
A. EUR-LEX

EUR-Lex is the official legal database of the European Union. The site is at **eur-lex.europa.eu**. The EU posts all of its decisions, rules, regulations, opinions, treaties, etc., on EUR-Lex for free. That said, you get what you pay for, and what you get is a very limited user interface.

1. Treaties

The text of European Union treaties is available on EUR-Lex as searchable PDFs. These can be somewhat large files, but they are the text of the treaties as they appear in the Official Journal, either as they appeared originally or in an unofficial consolidated format. One very useful item in the treaty menu is the conversion table; since the 2010 Lisbon Treaty renumbered and amended the existing treaties, this table can help you determine which article can be found where, or can help you determine what changes were made to the existing treaties.

2. Official Journal

The Official Journal is available here as well, though you need to know the date of the issue you're looking for.

3. Legislation and Case Law

If you'd like to search for legislation or case law, the best option is to do a simple search. As an example, perform a search related to the protection of geographical designations of origin for cheese, such as Parmigiano-Reggiano. The simple search screen provides a few options, such as limiting the search to legislation first. Once that option is selected, the user can limit the type of legislation and further refine the search by search words, date, author, classification number or keyword, which is a controlled vocabulary search. For this example, select search words.

The first display is a screen that gives very limited fields for searching, and a series of hints about search syntax. One of the limitations here is that if you want to search for two terms together, you need to put one in the first box and one in the second, which means a user could not use a term such as "geographical designation of origin."

As an alternative, students could use "geographic* WITH cheese." Just above the search button appears the option of searching titles only (the default) or title plus full text.

Searching titles only gives a small number of results. The results listed have a number of references to other laws and decisions, but do not hyperlink any of them. If students want to retrieve some of these, they will have to write down the citations and plug them into the database, or use cut and paste.

The same search terms (geographic* WITH cheese) returns over 100 results.

The same search in the case law returns about three results for titles only, and over 40 for full-text.

One thing to keep in mind when searching EU law online is that while there are many documents in English, the English used is British English. So students who wish to search for harmonization measures should be sure to spell harmonization with an "s," or they won't get any results.

B. WESTLAW AND LEXIS

There are other ways students can search for EU law. Westlaw and Lexis both have EU databases, which consist of the materials available on EUR-Lex for free. The main advantage in using Westlaw or Lexis is the ability to construct much more complex search queries and to use additional terms to edit or focus the search and get better results. Neither service is free, however, and in many cases, a student's future employer will not subscribe to EU databases on Westlaw or Lexis.

Chapter 24

The Citation Requirement

■ ■ ■

By Stephanie J. Thompson

The purpose of this chapter is to emphasize to students not only why citations are needed but also how citations can be a persuasive writing technique. This chapter should be assigned before the citation rules are taught. Students need to have the correct frame of mind when learning citation, which is what this chapter provides.

The discussion of the purpose of citation should focus on the following:

- The need for proper citation
- The frequency of citation
- The consequences of improper or incomplete citations
- The persuasive impact of citations

The emphasis should also be on learning how to use a citation manual generally, not to memorize a particular citation manual. This is why the chapter presents a variety of citation manuals from a variety of jurisdictions. This demonstrates to the students the importance of the skill of using citation manuals generally. While most students will use The Bluebook in practice, they may eventually use a different citation manual. As such, they need to learn general concepts of citation and learn to be flexible when working with citations. If you have a regional citation manual, it may be a good idea to teach both The Bluebook and your regional citation manual. In my class, I teach The Bluebook in the fall semester and the California Style Manual in the spring semester. I have found that my students do well with both citation manuals because they are more focused on the purpose of citation rather than memorizing all of the nuanced rules and requirements for one citation manual.

This chapter is not designed to teach students how to write citations. We assume that professors will teach a specific citation manual and use various citation exercises (either self-created, online, or a citation workbook) to teach how citations are written. Some of the most commonly used sources to teach citation include: Interactive Citation Workbook

(Lexis) for both ALWD and Bluebook, the ALWD Companion: A Citation Practice Book, CALI exercises (Westlaw), CiteStation (TWEN via Westlaw), and exercise on Bluebook Training: http://www.bluebooktraining.com/index.html.

Additionally, below is a list of some other useful sources and online guides you may want to consult when teaching citation:

- Introduction to Basic Legal Citation by Peter W. Martin. It includes explanations, comparisons with ALWD, and examples from both citation manuals. It is available at http://www/law.cornell.edu/citation/full_toc.htm \
- Suffolk University Law School Bluebook Guide: http://www.law.suffolk.edu/library/research/bluebook/
- Georgetown Library Bluebook Guide: http://www.law.georgetown.edu/library/research/bluebook/
- Legal Bluebook: http://www.legalbluebook.com/Public/BlueTips.aspx.

Finally, there are online tutorials and videos available on various law school websites, Westlaw, Lexis, and YouTube that can be found by doing a simple Google search for "legal citation videos."

Chapter 25

The Last Critical Task: The "White-Glove Inspection"

■ ■ ■

By Edward H. Telfeyan

This chapter can be used in a variety of ways. As intended by its placement as the last chapter in this text, it can be used to emphasize the necessary concluding work that must be done on any legal document. In using it in this way, three goals of most legal writing courses can be achieved. First, students will gain an understanding of the importance of complete proof-reading. Concomitantly, they should also come to understand what complete proof-reading entails. Second, they will gain an appreciation for the requisites and impact of good legal writing. And third, they will begin to comprehend the definition of professionalism as it relates to their writing, i.e., error-free final drafts.

The chapter can also be presented in stages as the various substantive components of a legal writing course are covered. Thus, for example, the section on organization could be given as an assignment when the first complex memos or briefs are being written. The section on citations could be assigned when that aspect of the course is being covered. And the section on grammar and punctuation could be assigned at the beginning of the course or at any time during the course when the students appear to be in need of some remedial work on the basics of good writing.

The chapter can also be used if the course syllabus includes an introduction to professional responsibility and ethics if those topics are meant to include the kind of attention to detail in legal writing that the chapter emphasizes.

The chapter can also suffice as a basic text for the mechanics of good legal writing. In this regard it would best serve its purpose if it were supplemented with specific exercises to emphasize the various points covered in a full white-glove inspection. One such exercise is the Grammar Bee,* the essence of which is to make a contest (akin to the grade school spelling bees) out of basic rules of grammar, punctuation and preferred writing styles.

*Author's note: I created the Grammar Bee after my first year as an instructor of legal writing at McGeorge. I then presented it at a Legal Writing Institute conference as a way to get students to focus on basic writing skills. Many legal writing faculty members at law schools across the country now use it in one form or another, and I am most pleased to offer it again here.

The Grammar Bee can be conducted over the course of a full semester or in one or more dedicated classes. Here is a sample of the kind of questions that can be posed to student contestants:

1. Pick the correct alternative:

   A) Scientists now agree that the sun moves in it's own orbit.

   B) Scientists now agree that the sun moves in its own orbit.

   C) Scientist now agree that the sun moves in its' own orbit.

   "B" is correct because "its" is the possessive form of "it."

   "A" contains the contraction for the words "it is," which is the only time an apostrophe properly appears in the word.

   "C" is incorrect because "its'" is not a word.

2. Which of the following sentences is punctuated correctly?

   A) The professor, a crusty old coot, never referred to his students by their names.

   B) The professor, who was, a crusty old coot, never referred to his students by their names.

   C) The professor who never referred to his students by their names, was a crusty old coot.

   "A" correctly sets off the parenthetical phrase with commas.

   "B" incorrectly places a comma after the verb "was."

   "C" is missing a comma before "who."

3. Select the correctly punctuated sentence:

   A) I can't remember why, I used to think I was special.

   B) I used to think I was special, but I can't remember why.

   C) If I ever thought I was special I can't remember why I was.

   "B" correctly places a comma before the conjunction joining the independent clauses.

   "A" incorrectly places a comma in the middle the sentence. It does not contain two independent clauses joined by a conjunction and is, therefore, not a compound sentence.

   "C" does not contain a comma after the introductory independent clause. The preferred form is to place one before the beginning of the second introductory clause.

4. Select the correctly punctuated sentence:

   A) The conclusion therefore is that this attorney was incompetent.

   B) The conclusion, therefore, is that this attorney was incompetent.

   C) The conclusion, therefore is that this attorney was incompetent.

   "B" correctly sets off "therefore" with commas.

   "A" fails to segregate "therefore" with commas.

   "C" is missing a second comma after "therefore."

5. Which alternative is correct?

   A) Dogs like Mr. Simpson's can be dangerous, especially when it bites without warning.

   B) A dog can be dangerous, if, like Mr. Simpson's, it bites without warning.

   C) A dog like the one Mr. Simpson owns, can be dangerous, especially when they bite without warning.

"B" contains the correct pronoun, "it," to relate to the noun, "dog," to which it refers.

"A" contains the incorrect singular pronoun, "it," to relate to the plural noun, "dogs," to which it refers.

"C" contains the incorrect plural pronoun, "they," to relate to the singular noun, "dog" to which it refers.

6. Which sentence is grammatically correct?

   A) If the plaintiff is successful, he will prevail on the basis of his counsel's arguments.

   B) If they're points are considered, the representatives for the plaintiff would be likely to prevail.

   C) If the plaintiff's points are stated accurately, it would lead to only one conclusion.

"A" is correct (assuming the plaintiff is a male). The apostrophe is placed correctly in "counsel's," (assuming the plaintiff has only one attorney).

"B" uses "they're" incorrectly. That word is a contraction for "they are." The correct word in that sentence would be "their," referring to the plaintiff's representatives.

"C" contains the incorrect pronoun ("it") when referring to the subject ("points") of the first clause in the sentence.

7. Which sentence best states the writer's intended meaning?

   A) When one considers all of the factors at play, it can only lead to one conclusion.

   B) When all of the factors are considered, there is only one logical conclusion.

   C) When considering all of the factors, only one conclusion is possible.

"C" properly avoids uncertain/indefinite references, and correctly focuses on the action of the sentence (the conclusion that is reached by considering all of the factors).

"A" and "B" are less desirable ways to compose the sentence, because they both fail to focus on the action (reaching a conclusion). The key is to avoid sentences that include indefinite uses of words like "it" and "there."

8. Choose the best sentence:

A) This agreement is necessary for the reason that the parties no longer wish to be engaged in the ongoing dispute that the agreement resolves.

B) This agreement properly expresses the party's agreement.

C) This agreement is appropriate because the dispute is over.

"C" states the writer's point directly.

"A" contains the compound construction, "for the reason that" and is otherwise excessively verbose.

"B" uses the apostrophe incorrectly. As written, it refers to only one party. Any agreement would, perforce, require at least two. The correct word, therefore, would be "parties'."

9. Choose the sentence with the correct punctuation:

A) The doctrine of res judicata includes: merger, bar, and collateral estoppel.

B) The doctrine of res judicata includes: merger; bar; and collateral estoppel.

C) The doctrine of res judicata includes merger, bar, and collateral estoppel.

"C" correctly omits any punctuation after the word "includes."

"A" and "B" both improperly place a colon after "includes," and B also improperly separates the three concepts in the series with semi-colons. A colon is used to introduce a series only when the phrase that precedes it can stand alone as an independent clause (one that contains a subject, verb and object) and semi-colons are used to separate items in a series only if the series is complicated or contains internal commas).

10. Select the accurately-worded sentence:

A) Powell and Miller/Starr are excellent treaties for our research problem.

B) One of the difficulties in researching the law of easements is the indefinite nature of this type of interest in land.

C) In analyzing our research problem, we must focus on the applicable statues from both the California Legislature and Congress.

"B" uses and spells all the words in it correctly.

"A" improperly uses "treaties" for "treatises."

"C" improperly uses "statues" for "statutes."

11. Select the sentence that best expresses the thought the writer intended to convey:

A) In legal academia, disagreements regarding almost every issue in the law are common.

B) The lack of uniformity of perceptibility is apparent to anyone who reads any number of treatises.

C) Legal scholars are almost never in complete unification on any issue in the law.

"A" uses appropriate words to express the thought the writer intended to convey.

"B" uses the wrong form ("perceptibility") of what is probably the wrong word for the sentence. ("Opinion" is probably what the writer means.)

"C" uses the wrong form ("unification") of what may be the wrong word for the sentence. ("Accord" or "agreement" is probably closer to what the writer means.)

12. Select the sentence that is the most "reader-friendly":

A) The fact that she died, especially under the circumstances that pertained, left many feeling overwhelmed with grief.

B) Her death caused widespread grief.

C) Grief was felt by many when her death was reported.

"B" conveys the necessary information in a minimum number of words.

"A" is loaded with surplus wording ("The fact that she died" instead of "her death," "under the circumstances that pertained" instead of "as it occurred" and "left many feeling overwhelmed with grief" instead of "caused widespread, overwhelming grief").

"C" states the point in the less desirable passive voice ("Grief was felt by many") instead of the preferable active voice ("Many felt grief").

13. Choose the best alternative:

A) In jury trials, the trial judge may not express an opinion on the defendant's guilt or innocence, nor may he or she respond to a question from a juror in such a way as to suggest any such opinion.

B) In jury trials, judges must refrain from giving any indication of an opinion regarding the defendant's guilt or innocence.

C) Judges have to be careful not to reveal their own opinions in jury trials.

"B" is neither too long (containing too many words and thoughts) nor is it too short (leaving out words that would clarify the import of the sentence).

"A" is too long (both as to actual number of words and thoughts contained).

"C" omits critical qualifying information, thereby making the sentence less meaningful than it should be.

14. Which sentence is punctuated correctly?

A) Judges must decide whether to exclude testimony, and whether to permit expanded cross-examination.

B) Judges must make numerous decisions in every trial, including whether they should exclude testimony and permit expanded cross-examination.

C) Judges must decide whether to exclude testimony and they must also rule on objections to expanded cross-examination.

"B" correctly places a comma before the subordinate clause in this complex sentence.

"A" incorrectly places a comma in the middle of this simple declaratory sentence.

"C" improperly omits a comma (before "and") in this compound sentence.

15. Which sentence has the best structure?

A) To satisfy the timeliness requirement, a response must be filed with the hearing officer within twenty days after the petition is served.

B) A response, in order to be timely, must be filed with the hearing officer within twenty days after the petition is served.

C) To satisfy the timeliness requirement, a response must be filed within twenty days after the petition is served with the hearing officer.

"A" correctly avoids a gap between the subject, verb and object of the sentence. ("Gaps" between these three elements of a sentence make the meaning of sentences more difficult to absorb quickly.)

"B" places a qualifying phrase between the subject and the verb in the sentence.

"C" places a qualifying phrase between the verb and the object in the sentence.

16. Which sentence is constructed in the preferred manner?

A) A lawyer may disclose (if disclosure is necessary to prevent a crime that will result in physical harm to another) a client's confidential information.

B) A lawyer may disclose a client's confidential information, if disclosure is necessary to prevent a crime that will result in physical harm to another.

C) If disclosure is necessary to prevent a crime that will result in physical harm to another, a lawyer may disclose a client's confidential information.

"B" correctly places the lengthy condition after the main clause. (But note that short conditions or exceptions, without a comma following them, can be placed before the main clause.)

"A" creates a difficult gap (parentheticals always break the chain of thought) between the verb and the object in the sentence.

"C" incorrectly places the lengthy condition before the main clause.

17. Which sentence best states the writer's point?

   A) Having been found insane, Judge Jones ordered the defendant confined in a mental institution.

   B) Judge Jones confined the defendant, who had been found insane, in a mental institution.

   C) Judge Jones ordered the defendant confined to a mental institution, because he had been found insane.

"B" avoids the ambiguity regarding who is insane by placing the modifying clause immediately after the person it describes (the defendant).

"A" seems to suggest, by placing the modifying clause immediately in front of Judge Jones, that it is the judge who is insane.

Because of the placement of the modifying clause at some distance from both of the individuals referred to in the sentence, "B" raises questions as to just who is insane.

18. Choose the correct form for the sentence:

   A) The defendant shouted an obscenity when he heard her testimony; and immediately thereafter the judge held him in contempt.

   B) The defendant shouted an obscenity when he heard her testimony, immediately thereafter the judge held him in contempt.

   C) The defendant shouted an obscenity when he heard her testimony, and immediately thereafter the judge held him in contempt.

"C" properly separates the second clause from the first by placing a comma before the conjunction.

"A" incorrectly separates the two clauses with a semi-colon. Semi-colons are used to separate independent clauses when there is no conjunction used to join them.

"B" fails to join the two independent clauses with a conjunction, thereby creating a run-on sentence (or a "comma splice," as this type of incorrectly constructed sentence is often called).

19. Choose the correctly punctuated sentence:

A) The witness had no personal knowledge of the event; therefore, her testimony was excluded.

B) The witness had no personal knowledge of the event: therefore, her testimony was excluded.

C) The witness had no personal knowledge of the event; therefore her testimony was excluded.

"A" properly places a semi-colon before the transitional word between the independent clauses and also properly places a comma after it.

"B" improperly places a colon before the transitional word.

"C" fails to place a comma after the transitional word.

20. Choose the correctly punctuated sentence:

Assume the actual quote from the opinion is:

The trial court properly found a clear preponderance of the evidence.

A) The court affirmed the judgment by finding "a clear preponderance of the evidence".

B) The court affirmed the judgment by finding "a clear preponderance of the evidence.".

C) The court affirmed the judgment by finding "a clear preponderance of the evidence."

"C" properly places the closing quotation mark after the period.

"A" improperly places the closing quotation mark before the period.

"B" improperly places a second period after the closing quotation mark.

21. Choose the correctly punctuated sentence:

Assume the defendant's actual statement was, "I don't care."

A) Should the defendant have been held in contempt of court when he said, "I don't care?"

B) Should the defendant have been held in contempt of court when he said, "I don't care"?

C) The defendant should have been held in contempt of court when he said he "don't care."

"B" correctly places the question mark after the closing quotation mark. Regarding the placement of closing punctuation marks inside or outside of closing quotation marks, the American rule is that periods and commas precede the closing quotation mark and everything else goes outside, unless the punctuation is part of the original quote.

"A" improperly places the question mark inside the closing quotation mark.

"C" creates a grammatical error in the way in which the quote is used, even though the quoted material itself may be accurate. This simple example points up a cardinal rule regarding the use of quoted material: Always ensure that you construct any sentence that includes a quote so that the sentence is still grammatically correct. The fact that the quote is stated accurately does not excuse bad grammar. (Hint: use ellipses or only portions of the quote to ensure grammatical accuracy.)

22. Choose the preferable alternative:

A) Several agencies draft regulations in the field of laboratory experiments. These often deal with animal rights.

B) Several agencies draft regulations to protect the rights of laboratory animals.

C) Several agencies draft laboratory animal rights protection regulations.

"B" correctly separates the numerous nouns with words that break up the chain and does so without creating ambiguity.

"A" contains an ambiguous reference. (Does "these" refer to the agencies, the regulations or the laboratory experiments?)

"C" contains a lengthy "noun chain"; a long list of nouns meant to identify something will almost always be the source of a mental hiccup for the reader.

23. Select the best sentence:

A) One must never avoid the exercise of reasonable care, even when another party does not.

B) The lack of reasonable care is never proper, even when it is not being exercised by another party.

C) One must always exercise reasonable care, even when another party is not.

"C" properly avoids excessive negatives.

"A" and "B" contain negatives in the second phrases that relate almost incomprehensibly to the double negatives in the first.

24. Choose the best sentence:

A) The accident was a rather catastrophic event in light of the injuries suffered.

B) The witness became quite incensed when he understood the attorney's meaning.

C) The plaintiff was enraged when she heard the defendant's testimony.

"C" states the plaintiff's attitude directly and forcefully without modifiers that dilute the impact of the statement.

"A" uses a softening modifier ("rather") for the action word ("catastrophic").

"B" qualifies the action word ("incensed") with an ambiguous modifier ("quite").

25. Choose the preferred alternative for a formal, written contract:

A) The clause dealing with dismissal, included hereinabove in Section IIA of this agreement, is hereby incorporated by reference and is deemed to be included in this provision.

B) The dismissal clause from Section IIA is also applicable to this provision.

C) The foregoing clause dealing with dismissal in Section IIA herein is included in this provision.

"B" accomplishes the goal of including the particular clause in the new provision without the use of unnecessary "lawyerisms."

"A" and "C" are loaded with excessive words and phrases that only lawyers consider beautiful or desirable.

26. Choose the best sentence:

A) The testimony given by the defendant went to the point in his case with reference to his state of mind at the time of his action.

B) The defendant's testimony concerned his state of mind when he acted.

C) The defendant's testimony was offered in connection with his state of mind when he acted.

"B" avoids excessive "glue" words and states the point directly. ("Glue" words are connectors in sentences; they often add nothing of value to the sentence.)

"A" contains an abundance of unnecessary "glue" words ("went to the point," "with reference to").

"C" also contains unnecessary "glue" words ("in connection with") and adds an unnecessary action verb ("was offered").

27. Choose the preferable construction:

A) The fact that the defendant was young may have contributed to the verdict.

B) The youthfulness of the defendant may have contributed to the verdict.

C) The defendant's youthfulness may have contributed to the verdict.

"C" states the point as clearly and concisely as possible.

"A" contains a completely unnecessary idiom ("the fact that"). Such phrases are sometimes referred to as "word wasting idioms" because they usually add nothing of substance to the sentence.

"B" uses a prepositional phrase ("of the defendant") in lieu of a simple possessive ("defendant's usefulness"). While both sentences are grammatically correct, this one contains two extra words that add nothing to the sentence.

28. Choose the grammatically correct sentence:

A) The issue regarding the defendants' contradictory statements are whether either of them can be believed.

B) Contradictory statements, such as those uttered by the defendant, makes credibility an issue.

C) When the defendant contradicted himself, especially after his attorney gave him an opportunity to correct his testimony, his credibility became an issue.

"C" contains no grammatical errors.

"A" fails to conform subject to verb. (If the subject is "issue" the verb should be "is"; if the verb is "are" the subject should be "issues.")

"B" contains the same defect. (If the subject is "statements" the verb should be "make"; if the verb is "makes" the subject should be "statement.")

29. Identify three errors in the following sentence.

He could of done better with the jury if he'd prepared a summation that appealed to its' emotions rather than their intellects which weren't always so great anyway.

1 - "... could of ..." should be "... could have ..." ("of" is not a verb);

2 - "its'" should be "its" ("its'" is not a word);

3 - "their" should be "its members'" (the noun, "jury," is singular, so the later reference must be modified to identify correctly whose intellects are being impugned.)

30. Assume that each of the following sentences appeared in a legal memo. Indicate whether each is written in an acceptable form. For any that are not, indicate what changes should be made.

A) In this memo, I will seek to establish how provocation has been defined by the courts pursuant to the Illinois Dog Bite Statute.

B) The court held that mere presence alone is not sufficient to establish provocation.

C) Without addressing the question of lawful presence, the boys were found by the court to have provoked the dog, even though they held for the plaintiff on other grounds.

"A" is undesirable as to form and probably unnecessary as to content. Regarding the form, it reads like an introductory line from a term paper. In a legal memo, brevity and succinctness are valued above personal statements of purpose and intent. Regarding the content, the issue will have already been stated and the fact that the courts have interpreted the element will be apparent from the substantive explanations provided in the memo.

"B" uses the correct tenses in both instances (past for reference to what the court did; present as to the actual statement of the rule), and is perfectly fine in every other respect.

"C" is a mess. Among its many problems are these: it misplaces the subject, so as to suggest that the boys, not the court, did not address the question of lawful presence; it uses the passive rather than the active voice in describing what the boys did; and, it uses the wrong pronoun (they) to refer to the court (which is a singular noun).

* * * * *

A word about the "piles on the reader's desk": Some professors may want to point out that not all attorneys maintain such piles and that, in fact, the idea is really only a metaphor for the way many attorneys view the large amount of reading material they receive daily. The purpose of the metaphor is to alert students to the importance of establishing their bona fides as competent legal writers with every document they prepare so that the reputation they develop in their writing is consistent with a highly professional approach to all the work they do as practicing attorneys.

The term "white-glove inspection" is intended to suggest the rigors of military precision and discipline. Some professors may find this reference to military training off-putting or be otherwise uncomfortable with it. If so, they may wish to soften the specific reference by making clear to students, as the text of the chapter does, that the term is only meant to clarify what the best attorneys do with legal documents they draft before the documents leave their offices. In this respect the term is a good substitute for "polishing" or "proof-reading," which are too often interpreted by students to require nothing more than a light once-over of a working draft before it is sent to its intended reader.